"We need people we can abuse, exploit and then turn loose."

—*Dean Ann Marcus, NYU, on how to hire adjunct*
professors in the School of Education*

*From a captured e-mail used for evidence in the case of Joel Westheimer.

STEAL THIS UNIVERSITY

THE RISE OF THE CORPORATE UNIVERSITY AND THE ACADEMIC LABOR MOVEMENT

Edited by Benjamin Johnson,
Patrick Kavanagh, and Kevin Mattson

ROUTLEDGE
New York & London

Published in 2003 by
Routledge
29 West 35th Street
New York, NY 10001
www.routledge-ny.com

Published in Great Britain by
Routledge
11 New Fetter Lane
London EC4P 4EE
www.routledge.co.uk

Routledge is an imprint of the Taylor & Francis Group.
Printed in the United States of America on acid-free paper.

10 9 8 7 6 5 4 3 2 1

Library of Congress Cataloging-in-Publication Data

Steal this university : the rise of the corporate university and an
academic labor movement / edited by Benjamin Johnson, Patrick Kavanagh,
and Kevin Mattson.
    p. cm.
Includes bibliographical references and index.
  ISBN 0-415-93483-4 — ISBN 0-415-93484-2 (pbk.)
  1. Universities and colleges—Employees—Labor
unions—Organizing—United States. 2. College teachers' unions—United
States. 3. Education, Higher—Economic aspects—United States. 4.
Universities and colleges—Employees—United States—Social conditions.
I. Johnson, Benjamin, 1972- II. Kavanagh, Patrick, 1972- III. Mattson,
Kevin, 1966-
  LB2335.865.U6 S43 2003
  331.88'11'378120973—dc21

                                                        2002009326

Contents

Not Your Parents' University or Labor Movement Any Longer

Myths and stereotypes die hard. So it is with academia—a world that seems so populated by stereotypes and myths as if to be literally unreal. The images are easy to conjure up: pipe-smoking, absentminded, tweedy professors giving rambling lectures that echo within ivy-covered buildings secluded from the rest of the world. For much of the public, the university is disembodied, abstract thought divorced from the lives of normal people trying to make a living. The "community of scholars" is insular, protected, safe from all else. The walls around it are both literal and metaphorical. University leaders—seemingly stuck in the genteel values of the past—look down upon the world of mammon and disdain efficiency in favor of older, classical values. Students pursue questions soon forgotten as they assume the responsibilities and demands of jobs in what so many call the "real world."

The culture wars of the 1990s added to the pool of academic stereotypes. Listen to conservative cultural critics and you imagine the modern university a haven for left-wing wackos, snobbishly out of touch with the beliefs of most Americans. Academics are the type that the right-wing populist George Wallace complained about during the late 1960s—"pointy headed intellectuals who can't park their bikes straight." It's just that now these pointy heads are searching out the politically incorrect thoughts of their students. Or they blather on about deconstruction, feminism, or Marxism in a language that few care to understand. The humanists may have been displaced by politicos, but still academic conversations stay behind ivy-covered walls. They have nothing to do with the realities of American society, we are told. Academics care only about the realms of culture and language—those abstract realms that they themselves inhabit.

1

Certainly these stereotypes exist in reality; there really *are* absent-minded professors and politically correct ones to boot. But to focus on them would be to overlook the enormous sea changes that have taken place in academia over the past twenty years. We now live in a time when the walls between the "real world" and academia have fallen down. Professors are no longer comfortable or tweedy (in the deeper sense of that term); they increasingly take the form of underpaid graduate students or part-time adjuncts rushing from one university to the next. The professoriate is not a "community of scholars" that governs itself; rather its work is reviewed by administrators who chant "accountability" while throwing merit pay rewards at those lucky enough to have full-time jobs. University leaders don't sneer at the profit seekers at their gates; rather they welcome them with open arms, cutting deals and pioneering high-tech schemes that put courses online, packaged cheaply for worldwide consumption. Welcome to academia, twenty-first-century style.

Of course, some might argue that the business imperative has always invaded the hallowed halls of academia. Toward the end of the nineteenth century, social critic Thorstein Veblen noted that those who gave their dollars to the universities—the Gilded Age wealthy who sought out new forms of conspicuous consumption—did so in order to build up their reputations. They wanted their names on buildings, their reputations bolstered by being connected to genteel institutions of higher learning. If some professor espoused radical politics, the pressure might be turned on, and said professor would hit the pavement. Trustees called the shots, no doubt, making clear that wealth spoke clearly and audibly in the hallowed halls of academia even a century ago.

Today, business leaders have gone one step further. They want to assert not just influence but much more control over the educational processes themselves, and understanding this transition is crucial. Our *au courant* jet-setting business types concern themselves not just with conspicuous consumption but with direct management of education on their own terms: They don't want ivory-covered buildings with their names on them but rather training camps for their workforce. They probably don't even care all that much if nutty left-wing profs shoot their mouths off. They've got more important things on their minds, namely what the new managerial theorists call "just in time" knowledge. Corporate leaders want their employees to gain knowledge *now*, immediately, not on the plodding terms set by the ivory tower of yesteryear but the terms set by corporations, providing only enough knowledge for their employees to get their jobs done, not to ask fundamental questions about the society in which they live. If need be, corporations will do the educating themselves (but, for obvious reasons, still prefer others to float the costs). In his *Free Agent Nation*, a manifesto for today's new economy, Daniel Pink glorifies the radiant promises of distance learning—the selling of courses online by for-profit educational institutions. "More free agent teachers and more free agent students," he writes, "will create tremendous liquidity in the learning market—with the Internet serving as the matchmaker and market maker for this marketplace of learning."[1] The use of the term "market" three times in a single sentence tells us something about the demands that the new economy is putting on higher education. The message is clear: So long, ivy-covered walls, tweedy professors, and genteel university presidents—hello to markets, profits, and computers.

If you want to get a better sense of this, just read about John Sperling, CEO of the Apollo Group, the parent company of the University of Phoenix. He's no Rockefeller who hands out money to the University of Chicago and then sits back and waits for the prestige to rise; this is a man who wants to call the shots—down to ensuring that his temporary teachers make next to nothing and have no say in course content as they conduct job training that is shamefacedly called higher education. Sperling is not someone who hopes to lift up his name by attaching it to an institution of genteel culture; this is a man who would probably like to dynamite the universities that still exist physically (those like Rockefeller's University of Chicago) and replace them with for-profit entities. Sperling symbolizes the revolutionary power of market thinking in terms of the world of higher education.

This love affair between the market and higher education has helped prompt some within academia to rethink their status as laborers and their relation to labor unions. Once again, noticing historical changes that have taken place is crucial. Sure, there have been professional associations and faculty unions since the early twentieth century, but they've often been old boy networks, looking out for the academic freedom of a select few. Historically, organizations like the American Association of University Professors (AAUP) stepped into occasional political disputes, sanctioning schools for threatening the professoriate's civil liberties in time of war, for instance. Today, academic unions might still be concerned with academic freedom, but the terms have changed. The threat is no longer an occasional war or political crisis, but the ever present pressures of corporatization. Now unions are fighting for academic freedom, plus some much more basic needs—pay that can put food on the table, health-care benefits. You will read in this collection how graduate students organized themselves into unions precisely because they stopped thinking of themselves as teaching apprentices taking their first step into a community of scholars. Rather, they think of themselves as employees—recognizing the economic imperatives that recent academic reforms have made brutally clear. The world of tweedy profs and culture wars seems to have faded.

This book explores this sea change in academia—the rise of the corporate university and an academic labor movement. For readers interested in learning more about academia—that is, readers not part of this world—this book can highlight significant changes; it can tell you something about the reality of contemporary academic life, breaking through the myths that have dominated so much current debate. For those concerned with the future of progressive politics, this book offers a new look at how some within academia are thinking about this future (and it may surprise some to find an emphasis on Old Left concerns with socioeconomic inequalities, not just cultural problems). For those working within academia, we are certain that this book will strike a chord but that it may also challenge you to see things differently. For those who have faced the brunt of these changes—especially graduate students doing the bulk of teaching at many institutions or those adjuncts paid next to nothing for their travails (and travels)—we hope this book inspires you to think about ways to improve your situation. But be warned: We are not cheerleaders. We don't just tell how the good guys always win. Since they don't, we talk about academic labor's defeats as well as its victories. We make clear that organizing within the corporate university is an uphill battle.

To appeal to this wide range of readers, we have organized this anthology as follows. We open with a section on the changing world of academia, stressing the importation of corporate practices into the university. We then move onto a section documenting how these changes affect those who work here and close with descriptions of labor conflicts that have erupted. Section 1 tries to make clear just how much the ethic of profit has invaded the university. It opens with Ana Marie Cox's essay about the rise of for-profit universities that increasingly turn education processes into commodities bought and sold on the market. Cox's essay is a prime example of an older style of journalism that seems waning today—namely, muckraking. She digs up the ways in which for-profit education leaders have wielded influence in Washington to get what they want and how, in the process, they have degraded our conception of higher education. After introducing the reader to the literal meaning of the *corporate* university, we then reprint an essay that has become something of a classic among academic labor activists—David Noble's "Digital Diploma Mills," which discusses the perils of distance learning. Noble shows that by putting courses online, administrators can easily commodify teaching and manage teaching (the way the

University of Phoenix has). The next two essays extend from Noble's critique of the de-skilling of the professoriate and the evisceration of faculty control over their own labor. Denise Tanguay dissects the rise of merit pay systems, showing how they increase managerial control over faculty members. Benjamin Johnson then makes clear just how far the "part timing" of America's teaching force has gone. As he suggests, the full-time tweedy professor is now truly a thing of the past, replaced by a pool of underpaid contingent laborers with little, if any, benefits and no job security.

The essays in section 1 use historical and sociological approaches to understand changes wrought in academia. But this is only a part of the story. Historical changes affect real, living people, as social historians have been telling us for years.[2] So it is with the restructuring of academia. This is, of course, partially obvious. When full-time jobs are replaced by part-time jobs, for instance, some people cannot find work. But much more happens. There's the scramble to make ends meet, doing what can be done to put food on the table, as Alexis Moore documents so painstakingly. The lives of adjunct professors are structured around the need to accept the terms of those doling out bit jobs. This is no victory for "free agents" as Daniel Pink would have it; it is a hard life of traveling from one teaching gig to the next, patching together a meager salary and expending a great deal of personal energy and gas doing so. When this happens, one's consciousness changes. In academia today, a new generation of young scholars are not just finding it harder to locate decent work, they are changing the way they think about themselves. It might once have been easy for professors to see themselves as different from the rest of America's working population, as white collar and privileged, as the sort who work with their heads rather than their hands. But for someone like Kevin Mattson, this distinction makes little sense today. The changing circumstances of work in the modern academy are such that academics see themselves increasingly as workers. This change in consciousness—felt, lived, experienced in everyday life—goes a long way in explaining the energy and anger that sustain the new academic labor movement.

This anger has generated conflicts among those who work within academia. Perhaps most explicitly, it has destroyed the ideal of teaching apprentices learning from their mentors. Nothing makes this clearer than the story Corey Robin tells. As he points out in his essay on the drive among Yale graduate students to get a union, the terms of full-time teaching can implicate people in unfair systems that prompt their worst behavior. Robin shows how full-time faculty often turned on the very same people they were supposed to be mentoring, even writing letters of recommendation for prospective employers that chastised their students. A worse fate can await those who have the courage to side with their graduate students. Witness the story of Joel Westheimer. Testifying on behalf of graduate students organizing at New York University (NYU), Westheimer found himself fired—denied tenure by the very same people who just months before his testifying were singing his praises.

Westheimer's story makes for a nice transition into section 3, which tries to show how people caught within this new academic system can in fact do something about it. Westheimer's story shows the stakes of these struggles, as do the opening essays in section 3. Lisa Jessup documents the long and hard struggle to win rights for NYU's graduate students—the struggle Westheimer was supporting. She makes clear that university leaders have clued into what's happening and have garnered hired guns willing to crush union drives, precisely the sort of highly paid organizations that helped quash a struggle at the University of Minnesota. Telling this story, Michael Brown and his colleagues explain just how difficult organizing can be, even in the seemingly free and open world of academia in a state with a strong presence of organized labor.

The union drives at NYU and Minnesota sought to organize graduate student teaching assistants at individual institutions. Many academic labor activists are starting to move beyond this approach in order to find wider forums in which to make their case. Cary Nelson argues that disciplinary associations need to become places where full-time professors can articulate the need to confront the problems of academic underemployment. Of course, this relies upon struggle, debate, contention, and, ultimately, negotiation and making what were once simply "networking" and professional associations into voices of criticism. But what Nelson's argument makes clear is the widening perspective of academic labor activists, as does the struggle documented by Barbara Gottfried and Gary Zabel in their discussion of the Coalition of Contingent Academic Labor (COCAL). These activists try to expand beyond isolated drives on different campuses (and even among different types of employees) within the Boston area. In other words, they are trying to put the word "movement" back into the labor movement by building broad popular support for what might otherwise become localized struggles. Because a more just system at one university doesn't entail justice at another, a network and coalition approach is utterly necessary. We end this section with a discussion of the California Faculty Association, a union representing a broad coalition of employees in the nation's largest state university system. Susan Meisenhelder makes clear that the union has not only struggled to better the conditions of its members but has also tried to change the terms of debate about the future of higher education in this country.

And that is the purpose of this book: to make a new entry into the debate about the future of higher education in America and what role the academic labor movement has in shaping this debate. Any critical reader of these essays will notice that the authors carry on a debate among themselves. We have collected a diverse set of writers; all of them speak from experience with the conditions they describe rather than as "experts" in some theory of education or administration. Some, like Cox, are journalists who have covered the world of academia for a variety of magazines; others are full-time or part-time academics trying to get along in this often strange world; and some are organizers working within unions and professional associations to win a voice for those who have been screwed over by the system. Beyond this diversity, our authors come to differing conclusions about the problems addressed. For instance, Ana Marie Cox argues for professors to stop clinging to tenure as a solution—one of the most well-known and controversial higher education practices—so as to embrace more fully collective bargaining. But Benjamin Johnson sees tenure as defensible and as part of a larger attempt to defend not just academic freedom but job security. Though they may disagree, they both want to *look beyond* tenure for new ways to confront the problems at hand.

Another tension is with the ways in which authors characterize how far corporatization has gone—that is, how much room is left for struggle. At times, David Noble suggests that de-skilling has almost fully transformed the university, yet he documents how faculty have successfully fought it. Ana Marie Cox argues that the for-profit spirit has captured numerous institutions and has spread far beyond what it was five years ago, but she too believes that something can be done about it. If you look at the cold hard numbers that Benjamin Johnson presents—60 percent of the teaching is now done by contingent teachers—the struggle to improve academic labor conditions would seem hopeless. Still, while presenting gloomy prognoses, the authors resist talking about academia as if it were some "one-dimensional society," to use Herbert Marcuse's term. In fact, most of them recover a vision of education that stresses democratic processes and critical self-insight. Though this vision may have been suppressed, none of us thinks it useless to resuscitate it in protest against what's happening today. Just how much can be done with it, of course, is still open to debate.

There are other tensions throughout this book, but there's no need to spell them out here. A diversity of viewpoints is a central indicator that a social movement has reached a certain level of maturity. That seems to be the case with the academic labor movement. Disagreement and debate need to be aired, if only to show that the movement is healthy and vibrant. So long as those debates help a wider public think more critically about the future of higher education, then the movement has obtained the first step in a long-term strategy.

If the academic labor movement has something to teach us about the future of higher education, we also believe it needs to learn from and teach the wider labor movement. After all, the academic labor movement emerged at an opportune moment in organized labor's history. Since the 1970s, labor unions have been losing members and influence. What labor historians call "business unionism" provided services for those organized in certain industries (automobile manufacturing, steel production, mining, etc.), but those industries have become less and less important to the overall economy as service sector work has replaced America's industrial base. One result of all this is that unions became stereotyped as things of the past, relics of an industrial era gone by. Steelworkers may have needed unions, but fast-food fry chefs and computer programmers don't—or so the reasoning went.

The academic labor movement shows this up for what it is: ideological reasoning. Sure, unions haven't scored too many victories in the service sector. But this is not the same thing as saying that employees are banishing unions from the public consciousness (social researchers constantly point out that when polled, many Americans openly embrace unionization). The terrain has shifted, as "flexibility" and "contingency" have made things harder. But gradually the union movement is starting to think more creatively about these changes in order to find new ways to inject some equality back into the picture. Some activists are returning to older models of craft unionism—such things as "hiring halls and employment bureaus," as one author describes them. Instead of focusing on individual firms through which contingent employees are moving in and out faster and faster, labor activists are trying to create a "unionism emphasizing cross-firm structures and occupational identity."[3] This new direction—one that can truly grapple with increased contingency—is seen evocatively in the COCAL example discussed in section 3. Academic labor activists are pioneering some new ways of organizing, and they are showing that *white-collar* employees—and those with advanced degrees at that—do not see unions as dinosaurs or things of the past. For these reasons, academic labor activists have a lot to learn from the labor movement, both in historical and contemporary terms—including a sense that unions can emerge where you least expect them.

In identifying with white-collar unionization, the editors of this anthology (if not necessarily all its writers) identify with a broader tradition of activism among middle-class citizens. Historically, it's been fairly easy for social critics to assume that the middle class is stupid, self-interested, complacent, and conformist. This tendency has created some provocative social criticism, but it has also allowed us to forget that the middle classes often face some of the worst aspects of socioeconomic change. For instance, deskilling, loss of control over one's work life, job insecurity—these are things that all workers in America face today, white collar and otherwise. As this anthology makes clear, white-collar employees face them in distinct ways that can prod us to think more critically about their ramifications. Additionally, the problems of the professoriate are linked to the problems of doctors struggling against the bottom-line mentality of HMOs and the problems of writers struggling to negotiate a world in which the Internet has transformed traditional meanings of intellectual property rights. Though white-collar employees feel the brunt of these changes in peculiar ways, this is no excuse for them to separate themselves from the plight of other workers. Indeed, if a Ph.D. can no longer save you from mistreatment and abuse, then it is time for the idea of middle-class exceptionalism to be tossed into the dustbin of historical clichés. The academic labor movement makes this clear.

Very often, middle-class activists focus on problems far away from home. Some might argue this is a legacy of the student movement against the Vietnam War, a movement that centered on universities. Middle-class student activists today are very worried about the plight of those within the Third World. Who could deny the importance of struggles against Third World poverty or child labor? Nonetheless, sometimes protesting conditions halfway across the world becomes abstract; worse yet, sometimes it leads middle-class people to forget the injustices that exist right in front of their noses. Confronting practices closer to home is often harder than protesting problems across the globe. At the same time, the struggles to improve the global relations of universities—how they act as consumers of goods—is clearly connected to how they treat their own employees.

As this final note makes clear, this is a book about the strange world of academia and how it has shaped the lives of those who work within it. It is a book by and about a movement trying to shape the future of this peculiar world. Recognizing the peculiarity of this world is crucial, but it can also become limiting. After all, we believe that the university holds an enormous promise—the promise of facilitating the processes of democratic education, critical thinking, self-examination, and debate. A good education ensures that citizens will have the skills necessary to govern themselves, to participate in making their world a better one. If we don't protect higher education from becoming job training in the narrowest sense of that term, if we don't ensure that citizens have access to full-time quality teaching, if we don't carve out spheres of life safe from the pressures of profit and money, we cheat our democracy of its future. As we believe this anthology makes clear, nothing less than the link between democracy and education is at stake in the struggle between the academic labor movement and the corporate university.

The Rise of the Corporate University

The 1960s stand as the last decade when big questions were raised about the modern university. Students who were starting to congeal into the New Left protested the university's collusion with government and defense corporations as the Vietnam War raged on. Intellectuals like Paul Goodman defended the free-speech movement (FSM) at the University of California-Berkeley, arguing for a renewal of the medieval conception of the university as a "community of scholars" capable of governing itself and resisting outside forces. As a key leader of and spokesperson for the FSM, Mario Savio famously strode onto the top of a policeman's car to give a ringing protest speech against the "multiversity." As Savio saw it, the vision of the university most fervently advocated by Clark Kerr, the president of California's entire university system, represented "the greatest problem of our nation—depersonalized, unresponsive bureaucracy." Its enormous size, its conformity, its tendency to churn out students like products on a factory line—all these features of the modern university symbolized how America was "becoming ever more the utopia of sterilized, automated contentment."[1]

Savio's speech captured the sensibility behind so much of the New Left's earlier protest against the university. The complaint centered on conformity and boredom, attempting to renew an existential vision of politics as resistance and rebellion. The business world that awaited students after leaving the university was dull and complacent. As Savio explained, "The university is well-structured, well tooled, to turn out people with all the sharp edges worn off."[2] Students were learning the routines of the "organization man"—the term William Whyte had used during the 1950s to describe corporate employees who worked for the large, faceless, bureaucratic corporations that came to dominate the American economy. Kerr himself, as one historian points out, was a "man of liberal, mildly social democratic views" who had wanted to make the university serve society.[3] He was no reactionary but rather a prominent labor economist and a liberal. Nonetheless, as New Left activists saw it, he had made his pact with the large bureaucratic structures in the American economy. Savio, in attacking Kerr, helped codify for the baby boom generation the problem of the "multiversity" and the nature of corporate work—bureaucratic, boring, stifling, dull.

Much has changed since that time, not the least the nature of corporate life. The organization man is now a thing of the past. Business isn't interested in stability or long-term careers.[4] Flexibility, mobility, empowerment, dynamic change—these are the terms that management theorists speak of today. It is with good reason that Daniel Pink opens his book, *Free Agent Nation*, with a section titled "Bye, Bye, Organization Guy." At the high end of the corporate world, people speak of consultancies; at the low end, of temping. What both have in common is an end to stability. The man in the gray flannel suit training it home at 5 P.M. every day has been replaced by the superhip consultant chatting on her cell phone while stuck in traffic at 8 P.M. The world of the baby boomers has disappeared, replaced by the world of Generation X—perhaps better termed the "contingent labor generation."

Universities have changed with this world. They no longer collude with big business; they have become increasingly *identical* to business. The wall between the two has grown thin. Universities have always been a party to job training—from the turn-of-the century demand for managerial professionals to the desire for safe "organization men" in Savio's time and the Internet wizards of our own time. But now corporations want to run the show themselves, or at least have more direct say in the matter. As Ana Marie Cox explains in chapter 1, many want "just-in-time knowledge"—that is, the skills necessary for the job at hand, rather than basic underlying skills. Take the example of Digipen Institute of Technology. Licensed by the state of Washington to grant a baccalaureate of science in "Real Time Interactive Simulation," this new higher education institution is run by Nintendo Corporation. A journalist points out, "Students take no humanities or social science courses whatsoever."[5] That's because those things are superfluous for the needs of the Nintendo Corporation. What's necessary is what's good for the bottom line—that is, education for the immediate tasks at hand.

What is new about today's university is not only that it serves the corporation—for it always has done that—but that it *emulates* it. This is the most essential feature of the new university that the authors discuss here. Universities now see the potential for profit; they import managerial techniques from corporations; they use new technologies by which administrators assume more control over professors' labor; they "temp" their workforce. Perhaps the only thing that the university hasn't done that the corporation has is move all over the globe. After all, many universities are rooted in a specific city or town. Needless to say, via new computer technologies, they have scrambled across the globe in search of new students, all the while driven by the search for more profits.

What the authors in this section make clear is just how deeply these developments have already reshaped the contemporary university. The first stories heard about Phoenix University made it sound quirky and odd: a university without any campus that traded on the stock market. What Ana Marie Cox shows here is just how advanced the for-profit sector in higher education has become, as witnessed in massive growth and a mimic pattern among nonprofit universities. David Noble points out just how quickly numerous universities have taken up the questionable practice of distance education. Denise Tanguay shows that even at universities with faculty unions, merit pay and other corporate work schemes have skyrocketed. And Benjamin Johnson shows that most attempts to measure the amount of teaching done by underpaid graduate students, adjuncts, and postdocs have vastly underestimated the extent and effects of such teaching.

What shapes these authors' understanding of the problems they discuss is firsthand experience—Cox from her years as a journalist, Noble in his struggles against distance learning at numerous universities, Tanguay in her work for the American Association of University Professors (AAUP), and Johnson in his work to organize Yale graduate students. Though they are dispassionate—in the best sense of that term—they are also committed to working on the issues they document and discuss.

Like the New Left before them, the authors here also want to initiate a debate about the broader purposes of higher education. They aren't content simply to document the rise of corporate practices but want to ask a bigger question: What exactly is the purpose of education? Underlying their essays is a major assumption about education in today's society: It should be democratic in the deepest and richest sense of that term. In this day and age, that makes them conservative to large extent (which might sound slightly odd, since all of them support unionization). For instance, they all imply that education should be wedded to a classical view of citizenship—that is, the cultivation of a well-rounded individual not only capable of the private pursuit of well-being but also capable of "culture" (thinking critically and appreciating works of imagination) and such skills of democracy as debating and contributing to public decision making. None of them cites him, but there seems almost a harkening back to Thomas Jefferson's ideal of democratic education. What worries these authors is that by adopting corporate practices and looking only at the short term, we will shed the democratic promise of education: to educate citizens for the responsibilities of self-government.

By showing how the democratic ideal of education is threatened, these authors make clear the need for spheres of life that are not subservient to market pressures. Education must be allowed to flourish without the bottom line entering into each and every decision. The relationship between students and teachers—the give-and-take of dialogue and learning—cannot be commodified without losing something. By making this clear, the authors in this section push the debate about the future of higher education a step forward.

CHAPTER 1

None of Your Business

The Rise of the University of Phoenix and For-Profit Education—and Why It Will Fail Us All

Ana Marie Cox

Most discussions of for-profit higher education rely on the simple shock value of presenting education as a business to get readers' attention. Calling students "customers," not bothering with the humanities, skipping the physical accoutrements that make college the ivy-walled American dream—these are the characteristics editorial writers and reporters focus on when they want to throw harsh light onto the dark specter of higher education as a growth industry. Lost in that showman's spotlight, however, is an even scarier fact: the specter is getting closer. In the past twenty years, more than 500 new for-profit colleges and universities have opened their doors—at the four-year level, for-profits have increased their numbers from 18 to 192.[1] A quarter of the $750 billion spent each year on higher education stems from private, proprietary investment.[2] Analysts predict this segment will grow by about 20 percent a year, until it finally displaces nonprofit education—or what for-profit educators call the "last remaining government monopoly in the world."[3] Today, forty for-profit education ventures trade publicly, up from one decade ago. We've moved beyond the moment when the idea of selling stock in a university was a laughable exception to the rule.

No other company epitomizes this exponential growth like the University of Phoenix and its parent company, the Apollo Group. Perhaps one of the most dramatic success stories of the '90s "long boom," and certainly one of the only success stories not interrupted by the dot.bomb implosion,

15

Phoenix recently outpaced New York University to become the largest private university in the country. From its start in 1975 as a small, single-campus operation offering only a degree in business, Phoenix now grants bachelor's, master's, and even doctorates in such high-demand fields as nursing, teaching, and managing of information systems. It has grown to enroll more than one hundred thousand students on 116 campuses and "learning centers" in twenty-two states and around the world; an additional thirty-seven thousand students participate in its online component, touted as a highly efficient "computerized educational delivery system."[4] John Sperling, the founder of the University of Phoenix, told the *Financial Times* that his school was "the Cadillac of higher education."[5] At the same time, Peter Sperling, son of John, told the *Independent*, "McDonald's has not aspired to be Maxim's, but you know you're going to get a good, healthy meal."[6] One could quibble with the aptness of the specific analogies, but the general metaphor is dead-on: Phoenix has done more than almost any other education enterprise to shift the meaning of college from that of a process one goes through to a product one buys.

In *Higher Ed, Inc.*, former DeVry Institute administrator Steve Ruch lays out the recipe for the success of his own leading institution as well as Phoenix and most other for-profits:

> Imagine a regionally accredited university with a tightly focused mission of preparing students for the world of work. Imagine that this institution offers undergraduate and graduate degree programs only in fields for which there is high marketplace demand. In fields for which there is little or no market demand, by either students or employers, degree programs are not offered. Imagine also that this university runs year-round, fully utilizing its facilities during the day, evening, and weekends throughout the whole year. The full-time faculty do not have tenure, and 90 percent of them are fully deployed to teach. The energy of this institution . . . is focused primarily on the success and satisfaction of its students.[7]

One might also imagine that this institution doesn't have a library, insurance plans, dormitories, student groups, or liberal arts majors as is the case with most for-profits. To this efficient mix, Phoenix adds some specific innovations. The company owns no property whatsoever (its classes—scheduled mostly in the evening—are often held in the empty rooms of nearby traditional schools). Phoenix avoids the traditional high default rate on student loans that has traditionally plagued many proprietary institutions by enrolling only working students 23 or older, most of whose employers generally subsidize the tuition. Phoenix ensures employers' continued support by allowing companies to tailor these students' curricula to their needs. And in order to optimize its access to government money, Phoenix has until recently identified online students as residential students in applications for federal student aid. The school has also structured schedules so that up to half of any given course's class time may proceed without an instructor present.

These last two techniques aren't legal (Phoenix was fined more than $6 million by the Department of Education in 1999 and ordered to return the aid it received through false reports), but all of them have been very lucrative.[8] The Apollo Group's gross annual earnings have almost doubled in just the past three years, climbing from $384 million in 1998 to $769 million in 2001.[9] Even in the current, rather dim economic environment, industry insiders have pegged Phoenix and the Apollo Group as the "fastest-growing, high-quality companies in the sector."[10] This kind of momentum demonstrates that we can no longer wonder "what if" for-profits steal students from traditional schools. The question today is "What now?"

Phoenix Ascending

John Sperling is a former professor at the University of California at San Jose and a graduate of Reed College (a leading liberal arts college) and Cambridge University. Sperling's academic background, full of the kind of stuffiness and name-brand cachet associated with traditional educators, does not suggest the man he has become. The man who would go to the helm of the largest university in the country without a tenure system, much less any form of collective bargaining, was once a union organizer, president of his local American Federation of Teachers (AFT) branch and a member of its national board. Sperling has written hymns of praise about his graduate student days at the University of the California at Berkeley, where "we honed our academic skills by expounding and arguing theory, fact, and fiction—it was a moveable intellectual feast."[11] At the same time, he has created an approach to education centered exclusively on the development of "employability," tailoring his courses to the demands of companies who pay for their workforce's schooling. And the man who developed the prototype of Phoenix using hundreds of thousands of dollars in federal research grants is now one of the most vocal proponents for holding nonprofit colleges "accountable" for meeting specific "educational outcomes" and accuses traditional institutions of wasting taxpayer dollars.

Since founding the University of Phoenix, Sperling has put much of his considerable personal fortune (which now stands at more than $1 billion) toward pet projects that range from the mildly amusing to the outright heretical. For years, Sperling has been the primary investor in Seafire International, a company he founded to develop saltwater agriculture. In the late 1990s, Sperling teamed up with fellow multimillionaire George Soros in a campaign to legalize marijuana, a project that continues to this day. An interest in "life extension" prompted the formation of the Kronos Group, a New Age medical center dedicated to "Clinical Age Management." Sperling's most infamous investment outside Phoenix, however, is his single-handed support of Genetics Savings and Clone, a company that will allow individuals to "bank" their own (or anyone else's) genetic material for later use, and Texas A&M University's pet-cloning project. Sperling told *Fortune* that his cloning support stemmed originally from his interest in preserving his dog, Missy.[12]

In his autobiography, Sperling explains away such reversals and escapades: he's not a hypocrite; he's a rebel. As Thomas Frank has pointed out, businessmen of the past few decades have used such disassembling as a powerful weapon in their battle for public approval: "The real object of the 'revolutionary' management theory . . . [is] not efficiency or excellence or even empowerment, but a far more abstract goal: the political and social legitimacy of the corporation."[13] Talk of rebellion by billionaires requires the belief that business for profit is some underground affair, and not the default way of life for most of the world. If anything, Sperling's role in turning the production of knowledge into the production of profit is less that of a lone rebel in hostile territory than that of a general leading a conquering army toward the last enclave of stubborn holdouts against the new regime.

And just as the enthusiasts of the "long boom" investment charade used the language of dissent to disguise—or rehabilitate—greed and self-promotion, Sperling's rebel stance conceals a more conventional explanation for his roundabout journey from traditional scholar and union activist to corporate CEO. Upon examination, Sperling's seemingly inexplicable shift from AFT officer to union buster stems more from petty revenge than from freethinking: He admits that being "voted out of the presidency of a faculty union . . . cured me of my socialist sentiments in favor of nonprofits."[14] Sperling's rejection of the liberal arts and his decision to root out of his enterprise anything remotely resembling his glorious Berkeley days could be a rebellion against traditional academe, but it also happens to be the very foundation of Phoenix's massive growth. The institution's relentless focus on employability makes Phoenix classes appealing to the corporations that subsidize their employees' classes and streamlines Phoenix's operation. If you don't teach liberal arts, you don't need a library. If you don't care about the learning that takes place outside of classrooms, you don't need student unions or student publications. Forty years after finishing his "moveable feast," Sperling is happy to serve fast food: "This is a corporation, not a social entity," Sperling told one interviewer. "Coming here is not a rite of passage. We are not trying to develop their value systems or go in for that 'expand their minds' bullshit."[15]

His hammering on "accountability" after Phoenix's infant years of suckling at the federal teat is more rhetoric than reality. Though supporters of for-profits often point to their "market-enforced" efficiency, few for-profit institutions could afford to exist without Title IV monies. In 1999–2000, proprietary institutions made up a whopping 35.4 percent of all institutions participating in the Federal Pell Grant Program, and received about $945 million in Pell monies.[16] Phoenix and other proprietary schools have spent millions in the past few years in lobbying both Congress and legislatures to keep those floodgates open, primarily by manipulating the accreditation procedures that determine an institution's eligibility for federal loan programs. Phoenix is particularly motivated to loosen loan regulations: the Education Department audit of the $339 million in loans and $9 million in Pell Grants distributed by Phoenix in the mid-'90s found that the school did not provide enough instructional time to qualify for much of the money it had received in federal loans and grants. In addition, the university illegally included cost of living when calculating need for students in correspondence courses. In total, the department estimated that the university disbursed about $54 million more than what students were entitled to receive. (In its response, Phoenix officials asserted that their practices were "good for [the university's] students, for American business, for America's educational system, and for the global economy.")[17]

Historically, proprietary institutions have met with resistance from what they call "the higher education establishment" regarding accreditation. Thus, Phoenix focuses its energy (and finances) on political influence as well as economic growth, with no apologies from Sperling: "Yes, we use money to get their attention—our American system of campaign finance gives us no other alternative."[18] Thanks to this, Sperling claims, the Apollo Group and Phoenix are "better known on the Hill than all but the state universities and the nationally-known private institutions."[19] According to the Center for Responsive Politics, in the 2000 election cycle alone the Apollo Group made campaign contributions of more than $178,000 (a top contributor, just behind the University of California, Harvard, Stanford, and Princeton). In addition, the

Career Colleges Association (a largely for-profit higher education political action committee) donated more than $123,000, and other for-profit higher education political action committee (PACs) forked over around $190,000. Another comparison: Combined, the Apollo Group and Career College Association PACs last year contributed more than twice as much ($161,000) as the largest nonprofit donor, the American Association of University Women, which gave its entire $66,000 to the marginally less deregulation-happy Democrats.[20] Compared with the multimillion-dollar bundles brought in by defense contractors and drug companies, the for-profit education sector is wading in the kiddie pool of political payoff, but it's getting a bargain.

In March, the Senate confirmed Sally Stroup, the Apollo Group's top lobbyist and a former congressional advisor on federal loan programs, as the chief higher education policymaker in the Department of Education. Stroup advised the chair of the Post-Secondary Education Committee from 1993 to 2001 and was instrumental in helping to draft the 1998 reauthorization of the Higher Education Act. The 1998 reauthorization reversed many of the harsher restrictions on for-profit schools (making it easier for them to appeal penalization on loan defaults), eliminated some of the more grueling aspects of the accreditation process (making surprise visits optional, and no longer requiring inspectors to visit every branch of a campus), redefined "institutions of higher education" to include for-profit schools rather than defining them as a separate category, and created a special proprietary schools liaison with the Education Department, a privilege previously reserved for historically black universities and community colleges.[21]

Secretary of Education Ronald Paige made a less high-profile but more influential appointment in 2001 when he gave Laura Palmer Noone, the president of the University of Phoenix, a place on the National Advisory Committee on Institutional Quality and Integrity. This committee makes recommendations to the secretary regarding changes in regional and national accreditation policies and standards, including those regulations that determine an institution's eligibility for Title IV programs. The Higher Education Act is due for its next review and reauthorization in 2003.

Given his success in manipulating the system to his advantage, Sperling's rebel stance is in fact the squarest behavior imaginable, fitting quite comfortably into the paneled club-room atmosphere of big business. Still, as amusing as his contradictions are, John Sperling would be of no interest at all if his tactics and bloviations had no effect or if Phoenix were just a roadside oddity. But it's not. The success of Phoenix has transformed the maverick oddball into an influential model. Nonprofits are increasingly looking to for-profits for clues as to how to run their own institutions.

The Creeping For-Profit Ethos:
From Phoenix to the World

Clearly, nonprofits aren't trying to become profitable, but administrators at traditional institutions have now turned to the corporate model as a solution to the age-old and tax-status-independent problems of budgets and cash flow. Things have changed since the University of Chicago dropped its football team or an administration approached wealthy alumni for a generous donation. The difference is twofold: when it comes to making cuts, athletics are less likely to be on the chopping block than departments and programs. In 1998, for example, the Board of Higher Education in Massachusetts suggested "establishing a program productivity review that requires campuses to eliminate, or provide a compelling reason for retaining, academic programs that have fewer than a minimum threshold of graduates per year for a period of three years." As the authors of the report explained, "This will reduce expenditures."[22] The group also "urged a reduction in 'public service' projects that have little to do with students or teaching"—a sweeping definition that could mean anything from limiting student volunteer efforts to reducing community studies not financed by outside donors.[23] (It should be noted that these sorts of programs are intended to develop young people's civic sensibilities over their predilection toward self-interest.) And when it comes to bringing more revenue in, administrators are willing to sell more than just the name of a gymnasium—they'll trade a college's resources and reputation. In 1997, the University of Wisconsin began a joint, for-profit venture with the software firm Lotus to sell Wisconsin degrees worldwide.[24] The always inventive Massachusetts Board of Higher Education touted its "collaborations with business and industry," noting that "[a]ll campuses have developed alliances with local and regional business and industry to provide employee training and development opportunities, as well as research support."[25] A harbinger of this coziness emerged in the late 1980s, when the University of Rochester caved to the demands of a major donor, Eastman Kodak Co., to rescind its acceptance of a graduate student employed by Fuji Photo Film, Inc., a major competitor of Kodak.[26]

Other specific instances of nonprofits appropriating for-profit techniques abound. Take, for instance, Ohio State University's "selective investment" program, in which departments compete for million-dollar "prizes" by way of *U.S. News and World Report* rankings.[27] More commonly, schools simply demand that teachers offer "blockbuster" or "heavy draw" courses like those related to professional sports or other "entertaining" subjects. Such moves resemble the financial discipline that governs Phoenix's policy of developing courses only for which there is high demand. Numerous universities have started using their control over course content to license and then sell courseware to for-profit online entities. This sort of arrangement is a familiar pattern at Phoenix, where tightly structured, centrally developed lesson plans allow Phoenix's administration to dictate how a professor spends time, right down to fifteen-minute intervals, and where copyrights keep hostage what knowledge those plans may hold. What's more, streamlined courses are easier to shop out to low-paid adjunct professors.

There are dozens of more familiar ways that nonprofits have come to resemble for-profits, including the hiring of private companies to manage such capital-intensive areas as cafeteria service, campus housing, and college bookstores. At least the University of Phoenix has specific, logical reasons for pursuing such schemes: They centralize course development to take advantage of mass production. They direct funds to popular programs because no one goes to Phoenix to learn linguistics or art history, anyway. And collaborating with corporations makes sense because corporations are, for all intents and purposes, their real customers. Why have nonprofits picked up these habits? Why, for instance, did the Colorado higher education system decide in 1999 that "instead of the university deciding what ought to be taught, professors and chancellors will listen to what the chief executive officers say," and require "every college in the state" to compile "a list of technology courses it offers"? These will be "given to company executives, who will tell the educators where they fall short."[28] Why has Tulane University president Scott S. Cowen spent the last few years hammering away at shared governance, lamenting that it "stand[s] in the way of quick, effective decision-making"?[29]

To be sure, part of the motivation to be more like for-profits is simply about the bottom line: adjuncts are cheaper, and centralized courses—and not having to pay professors to develop them—are cheaper, too. The sad news is that many students seem to want it that way. Indeed, research such as the annual freshman survey conducted by the Higher Education Research Institute at the University of California at Los Angeles provides sobering evidence that whether or not students actually attend for-profit institutions, they seem to share the same values. In response to the 2001 survey, students ranked their "life goals": more than 75 percent said "being very well-off financially" was "very important." Toward the bottom of the list: "influencing the political structure" (16 percent) and "writing original works" (13 percent).[30] Everywhere young people turn in today's culture, they get the message that money is the true measure of a life. Russell Jacoby, in *Dogmatic Wisdom*, cites a classic example: Students who apply for credit cards with "humanities" listed as their area of interest are turned down; when they reapply with "finance" as their interest, they get the card.[31] What they do with the card suggests that it is not the making of money that concerns them, but the spending of it: UCLA's survey revealed that 21.4 percent had overspent their budgets and 16.7 percent had what they termed "excessive credit card debt"—this at a time when the *average* credit debt of American college students is $2,748.[32]

"Financially rewarding" or "career oriented" do not sound like hallmarks of a good education to a traditional academic's ear. But today's students operate from the profit motive, and it makes sense for their schools to do so as well. DeVry's Ruch explains, "The more traditional, abstract notion of learning for its own sake and the idea of cultivating knowledge that appears to lack utilitarian value does not resonate with a growing number of today's students and their families."[33] Never mind that few college freshmen are equipped to decide what may or may not lack utilitarian value; for-profits simply give students what the students think they need. As Sperling has said, "Academia simply doesn't understand this. They call it McEducation. What we do is every bit as much education as the Greek system that served as the model for the modern university. Greek educators prepared people for life. We prepare people for a life of work."[34]

And in the terrible symmetry of the market, the loop is completed: what the students want, well, for-profits will do almost anything to maintain the illusion that that's what they're providing. We all know how well the consumer approach has maintained high-quality standards in, say, financial markets. In a sense, for-profit institutions like the University of Phoenix are the Enrons of higher education: built on a bubble of good feeling, sustained by a siphoning off of public goods and monies. It is possible to move too quickly in response to demand, and therefore teach badly but "efficiently." Proprietary institutions call this "pleasing the customer" and, next to the flipped-collar nonchalance of the for-profit rebel, it's the most common explanation put forward by their fans for the success of places like Phoenix. Catering to the practical needs of students undoubtedly appeals to the working adults that make up the overwhelming majority of Phoenix students, and it's unlikely that it actively harms their education: You can learn as well at 8 P.M. as at 9 A.M. The assumed sensibilities of the sacred customer justify the more ideological decisions of for-profits as well.

As DeVry's Ruch sees it, he is simply empowering students: "It is ultimately the students who set the standard for what is appropriate and acceptable in terms of freedom of expression." Why? "This philosophy is grounded in the standard customer-service orientation of any successful for-profit venture."[35] Phoenix in particular takes pride in dismissing professors who score poorly on student evaluations. As Phoenix administrators see it, pleasing students should determine the "*eligibility* [emphasis added] of faculty members to provide instruction."[36] For-profits rush new courses to market, eliminate old ones, employ part-time professionals as teachers, and accept credit for "life experiences," including divorce—all for the sake of the customer.[37]

The "Costs" of For-Profit Education

These policies probably do please customers. Whether or not they add up to an education worth the investment is another matter. (Professors, for example, often report that their own sense of pedagogic mission gets steadily diluted as crowd-pleasing curricula create subordinate pressures to "get in the sandbox" with their eager-to-be-entertained charges, padding syllabi with movies, rock criticism, and various dogmatic interpretations of pop-cult transgression.) To define academic success as what the student is happy with risks not so much a low-quality education (though that is a possibility) but rather a narrow education, one focused on the here and now, "applicable skills," and conventional wisdom. But treating the student as a consumer *necessarily* turns education into a product—something consumable with benefits that are immediate and gratifying: a soda, a movie, a pornographic website. Defenders of the for-profit faith say that giving students what they want ensures a good education, but what they actually mean is that students "get what they came for, and the institution is assured continued growth, ongoing market demand, and profitability."[38]

Imagine running a government this way. It would lack revenues because citizen-consumers will have demanded an end to all taxation. (A not-too-distant possibility, really.) This kind of thinking is reminiscent of the student council candidate whose platform consisted of "longer lunch periods" and "a better prom." And just as a longer lunch period won't get students any closer to understanding algebra, so offering high-demand degrees doesn't get students closer to actually understanding and participating in their world. One of the hardest lessons to learn is knowledge isn't necessarily what you want to know—in the sense that, well, we'd be happier not knowing about Rwandan genocide or the Dresden firebombing or the Nixon administration. Education as a product means, essentially, teaching only what students want to hear, whether that's how to program in C++ or that everything is just fine, don't worry your pretty little head, nothing needs to change. A degree in Microsoft network administration may get you a job, but when we talk of the "utility" of an education, it must mean something beyond that: it must mean gaining hard-won understanding; it must mean the ability to question the world around you. It must mean hearing things you don't agree with and knowing things that upset you.

Yet nonprofits have already accepted at least the language of customer satisfaction. In addition to the rampant grade inflation that is a hallmark of for- and nonprofits alike, nonprofits pay attention to the desires of students when they trumpet graduate salaries and point to students' "return on educational investment."[39] Once fluent in this dialect, it can only become easier for traditional schools to accept for-profits' logic of education-as-commodity and to fully embrace the techniques they've taken tentative steps toward. Freemarketers would welcome this and all the "enforced efficiency" that would follow, but in this race to the bottom, existing for-profits will always win. Yes, they do have a head start—but they're also cheating.

Why Not-For-Profits Will Fail,
or the Underbelly of Market Logic

Of course, they're cheating the customer—both in a moral and a fiduciary sense that might alarm even today's business-savvy student. For-profits' proponents often point to their respect for their student/consumers as a benefit that nonprofits are not in a position to offer. Professors at traditional schools, they say, "fear . . . the loss of traditional authority, as well as the growing demand for greater accountability in their work as teachers" that would come with a customer focus. All this talk of customer service, however, is belied by one simple fact: The customer is being ripped off.

On the for-profit side, administrators say their students choose the stripped-down, sped-up, frill-free education they offer because students don't want to pay for the cafeterias, dorm rooms, and sports teams that drive up the cost of tuition at other schools. But those students aren't saving their own money; they're allowing proprietary schools to charge them for amenities the schools aren't providing. Traditional education is expensive, and in part that's because of the frills, student groups and insurance coverage and the like, but students at traditional schools are rarely charged for those frills. As educational economist Gordon C. Winston has shown, a combination of scholarships, grants, and simple discounting allows the average nonprofit to subsidize students to the tune of about $8,800 a year. That is, an education that costs (on average) $12,500 to produce is being sold to students for $3,700. Breaking the nonprofit group into private and public institutions doesn't dilute the subsidy much, though the end price to the student differs.[40]

Phoenix, on the other hand, offers no such discount—neither do most other for-profits—because charging at least as much as the education costs to produce is what makes them who they are: Price − cost = profit. Traditional institutions operate at a loss: public universities sell a $10,150 education for $1,230; private schools sell a $15,310 education for $6,640.[41] By contrast, the University of Phoenix generates a net return of $101 per student annually.[42] And when one considers that the cost of a Phoenix education—$8,000—is about the same as tuition at a private institution with comparable programs, it all becomes clear: Students get much less than they pay for, and that's not even considering the quality of education they get.[43]

Overcharging like this works because of the intimate relationships proprietary schools (especially Phoenix) enjoy with their clients, the employers of their students. These partnerships are so intertwined that the institutions basically become the exclusive providers of job training. In fact, Phoenix has created several business partnerships in which employees can take classes at a corporate training center and then apply those toward a University of Phoenix degree. Some nonprofit institutions have made similar deals, but not with the enthusiasm of Phoenix, which will accept corporate training as credit for up to 15 percent of a student's degree.[44] John Sears, Apollo's vice president, argues that such a deal is a natural fit for employers concerned with getting the quickest education possible for their students. In such a situation, he told one reporter, "Which model makes more sense: the traditional four-year university, which is essentially a model of inefficiency? Or a virtual education machine like the University of Phoenix, which brings a total quality management discipline to academic cost control?"[45]

Such cooperation with employers raises some obvious concerns. For one: Is job training really education? The president and chief executive officer of the Apollo Group, Jorge Klor de Alva, says simply that "the lines between education and training are blurring." But it would seem that one distinction remains clear: Mere training—especially training that's designed so that you can, as de Alva says, "take what you learn and apply it to work immediately"—is poor preparation for the inevitable moment when the technology improves, methods change, and your training becomes out of date.[46]

By providing just-in-time education that's designed to exact specification of what employers need *right now*, Phoenix has put the finishing touches on its model of education-as-consumer-product. Phoenix has built planned obsolescence into knowledge, and made an education as disposable as paper plates and Ikea furniture. This works brilliantly as a business plan. What are you going to do when your training becomes out of date? Well, go out and buy some more, of course. If you don't, your employer can simply buy a new worker, with more cutting-edge content.

This market logic also works to discipline students as they pursue their training—all to the detriment of free speech and thought. Already, Sperling justifies the absence of liberal arts courses at Phoenix by saying the employers who subsidize students "won't support Greeks and Romans."[47] There are surely other subjects that employers would rather keep their staff from studying: Would ExxonMobil want its people studying the effect of greenhouse gases? Would IBM want a programmer to learn about his company's ties to the Nazis?

Considering these rather problematic possibilities, it's unlikely that nonprofits will take the exact same steps as for-profits, but it's worth exploring what might happen if they did. Could a nonprofit become as cost-effective as the University of Phoenix, wiping out residential features, libraries, and such? It seems impossible at a large state school, but what about a small private commuter college? Or a community college? These two types of institutions are Phoenix's real competitors and are schools that stand to lose the most students when Phoenix or a company like it moves into town. They also have the fewest campus amenities to begin with. But should they go the cost-cutting route, they'd be faced with a problem that proprietary schools always escape: once you cut student services, who provides them? This is the secret of for-profit education. While Phoenix relies upon the federal government much more than its leaders would ever admit, it also gets a free ride on the backs of nonprofit institutions.

A huge chunk of the University of Phoenix's savings, for instance, comes out of its insistence that a "virtual library"—a collection of nine thousand or so electronic journals—is a reasonable substitute for the real thing. The head of Phoenix's "learning research center" has said that books are "far less critical than they were 30 years ago when I was in college."[48] Of course, books are just as central as they've ever been, but they're also about as expensive. Last year, Harvard spent $22 million on its library of 14 million volumes; at the low end, tiny McMaster Divinity College spent $854,000 on its 1.8 million volume library. The average university research library contains 3.6 million volumes and costs about $1.9 million a year.[49] When the University of Phoenix negotiated its way into New Jersey— where strict accreditation standards had stalled it—the school overcame the state's provision that all institutions of higher education have a library of at least fifty thousand volumes by purchasing access to New Jersey City University's 245,000 volume library in exchange for five computers and shared access to a suite of business databases—a deal worth about $25,000 to the public university.[50]

Places such as Phoenix can get away with eliminating libraries in most cases because their students can use public ones, sometimes the libraries of the very institutions that have lost students to for-profits. Jacqueline Raphel and Shelia Tobias have reported that "Phoenix frequently piggybacks on the 'competition.'" According to Raphel and Tobias, students from Phoenix's Santa Teresa campus in New Mexico, located immediately across the border from the University of Texas at El Paso, use the public school's library resources to such an extent that "reference librarians sometimes have to ask the Phoenix students to step aside so that the UTEP students' needs can be accommodated."[51]

This leeching off public resources extends the for-profit labor model, as well. Phoenix's practice of hiring only part-time professors who are actively working in the field they teach allows it to take advantage of human capital investment made elsewhere: at the universities that support full-time teachers who train the next generation of scholars. This generous transfer-credit policy allows it to do the same with students—essentially inflating its graduation and enrollment statistics without actually having to educate every student. Traditional schools remain caught in an unyielding conundrum: There has to be a first place where people learn—where, for example, students can get the M.A. that's the only requirement to teach at Phoenix. A traditional college literally can't afford to save money the way Phoenix does.

What the Future Holds

This longer range view shows that pursuing corporate models could be the end of higher education as we know it rather than, as some insist, the next step forward. However, even the oldest universities sometimes don't look much past tomorrow, and at its present pace, the for-profit approach seems destined to triumph. It may not be that the University of Phoenix is, as Sperling has said, in commissar-like fashion, "moving inexorably eastward," but the sleight-of-hand policy changes that inch nonprofits ever-closer to a corporate form may mean that most traditional schools become for-profit in everything but tax status.

The myth of social mobility notwithstanding, American higher education has always been poised to split in two: on the one hand, expensive, elite private schools for those who can afford them (and the handful of gentrifying "public ivies" like Michigan and Berkeley); on the other, resource-strapped, poorly funded public institutions for everyone else. The rise of the for-profit has merely exacerbated this divide, precisely because in the for-profit future, only the richest private universities may thrive. The social capital afforded by an Ivy League diploma is worth protecting (why dilute the brand with branch campuses of Yale™?), and selling at a premium. The humanities will become (some might argue they'll simply continue to be) an affluent affectation, like $600 Prada bike messenger bags.

The less well off schools will be forced to compete against the elites, and will either run themselves into the ground doing so, or will adopt all the for-profit tactics that they can, perhaps even chucking libraries, dorms, departments (what's the percentage in a classics department?). Another strategy would take them to for-profit status by half measures: they'll charge more for "low-demand" courses, offer discounts to students who give up their library privileges, create an airline-esque class system in which "first class" students get more comfortable chairs and better computers in exchange for a premium tuition. And then who knows? If an institution acts like a corporation, it becomes a corporation.

Those who wish to see higher education maintain its relative freedom and accessibility can't rely on the incongruity of education being treated as a consumer product to make their case, or use traditional institutions' moral superiority to attract students. With continuing education becoming something of a political jackpot (like helping children or the elderly, who could possibly be against continuing education?), for-profit lobbyists are positioned to push their clients as the ideal providers of continuing education, and therefore the likely recipients of whatever federal or state aid is available. And with state aid will come more acceptance of proprietary institutions. Greater acceptance, in turn, will accelerate the continued erosion of regional and national accreditation standards.

As mentioned above, for-profit lobbyists are already busy negotiating changes to the regional and national accreditation systems, making it easier for them to compete with traditional schools. Lobbyists go state by state to check the power of state legislatures over regional accrediting bodies. Regional accrediting standards are often flexible, but state laws can toughen—or weaken—them. That is, especially if unions and organizations like the American Association of University Professors exert pressure on them.

Even against counterpressure, the for-profit logic is bulldozing ahead. One proposal would guarantee accreditation to any school that is able to prove that a certain percentage of its graduates had obtained jobs. Clearly, proprietary schools, with their close corporate relationships, would be the institutions to benefit from this. Another change would allow for-profits to hire less-qualified and thus cheaper instructors. Traditional institutions must have a minimum number of professors with Ph.D.'s in order to grant degrees in any particular field. For-profit lobbyists would like to reduce this minimum number for their clients.

For-profits would also love to dip their fingers into the pot of state loans and grants that until now local legislatures have been reluctant to give them. Proprietary administrators argue, as the executive vice president of ITT Technical Institutes has said, "If we're good enough to pass state standards, to meet the bar where states raised it, then our students should have fair standing to access taxpayer dollars to finance their education."[52] Critics point out that this would essentially amount to corporate welfare. As with federal grants and loans, the students who receive such scholarships would simply be the conduits for the money going from taxpayers to institutional profits.

There are changes that are more seriously afoot at the national level, where the Education Department creates guidelines for all regional accreditation and sets up the requirement for federal loan eligibility. For-profits would like to eliminate a federal loan eligibility requirement that students receive at least twelve hours of in-class instruction a week to be considered full time. They also want to abolish a federal law that prohibits colleges from providing bonuses or other incentive payments to admissions officers or financial-aid administrators for enrolling students. According to the *Chronicle of Higher Education*, lobbyists for for-profits say "the law does not allow employees to be financially rewarded for exceptional performance." That is sort of the point, though, as the regulation was created in response to recruiters from diploma mills, who earned such bonuses by enrolling clearly unqualified students out of unemployment centers. The students, who generally flunked out, were simply a means by which proprietary schools received federal loans.

But the most important of the for-profit initiatives is the push to revise Education Department rules stipulating that at least 10 percent of a for-profit's income must come from sources other than federal aid. Once this restriction is lifted, the proprietary schools are in a position to siphon off a much larger portion of the aid available to all schools—another blow to the viability of resource-poor colleges. Phoenix and its cohorts are in essence pushing for the deregulation of higher education, and it could have the same disastrous results that followed the deregulation of savings and loans, telecom businesses, and airlines.

The best response, then, is to push to maintain and strengthen higher education regulation at the local, state, and federal levels. Ideally, one could put an end to federal and state student aid for students at for-profits, perhaps legislate a definition of what a college degree is, including a minimum number of credits in various disciplines. One could argue that such a policy is akin to the national standardized tests that are being proposed at the K–12 level.

Still, imagine how outraged the happily consumerist students who responded to the UCLA survey would be if they were suddenly held accountable for their educations. Then again, realism enters the picture: these young people don't vote. (The UCLA study also found this class to have the least interest in politics in years.)[53] Imagine, as well, the response of capitalist-friendly courts to a restraint-of-trade challenge that for-profits would inevitably bring in response to any harsh regulations actually enacted. So what looks on paper to be the most promising path to curbing for-profits' growth is also the steepest one. In any event, legislation will not stanch what is essentially a seismic cultural shift. To counter the predominance of for-profit education, nonprofit schools need to assert the autonomy of their mission— while also introducing important changes in their own institutional culture.

Traditional universities could stop competing with for-profits by trying to be like them and instead look at why proprietary schools appeal to students. Understanding this appeal doesn't mandate mimicking the for-profit mantra of pursuing customer satisfaction at every level. Schools could compete with the practical advantages of for-profits: year-round campuses, schedules convenient to nontraditional students (who are, statistically speaking, actually very traditional). There are ways to moderately accelerate programs without losing their spirit.

More radically, faculty at traditional schools could make a preemptive strike at tenure. Already decreasing at an alarming rate, the number of tenured positions is heading toward zero—not because tenure as an institution is being abolished, but because it's eroding. Universities replace tenure-track jobs with full-time adjuncts, and tenured professors continue to see academic freedom as a reward rather than as a right. For faculties to take the initiative and actively seek a replacement for tenure through collective bargaining would benefit professors at traditional schools by strengthening their power to maintain the standards of liberal education. A contract that protected academic freedom could also extend that right to adjuncts, librarians, teaching assistants, and faculty at for-profit schools, for whom tenure has rarely existed. The power of an entire academic community would be something to reckon with. The bond that would be formed between teachers at for-profits and nonprofits could strengthen both their positions at their respective institutions, and break down the stereotypes (of being elitist and condescending, of being poorly educated and unqualified) that currently keep them apart.

Still, a realist might ask, what about the students who just want jobs? What about the students' parents, who think academics exist in ivory towers and come down only to indoctrinate their children into communism, feminism, and same-sex romance? What about the policymakers who look at universities and see nothing but the red ink flowing out of them? These are obstacles that can be addressed only by deep cultural shifts. We need changes in our political culture that articulate wider civic needs over short-term benefits. For instance, what about a wider discussion about universal military service—the sort that would draft all young people, no matter their income or connections, and that would induce a much more realistic debate about the use of armed forces abroad? What about requiring, as some of the original advocates for AmeriCorps proposed, mandatory community service as a means of educating young people for the responsibilities of active citizenship? We need to have political discussions in this country that challenge us to become something more than just self-interested individuals. In this case, we need a higher education policy that emphasizes the need for well-rounded, thoughtful citizens.

CHAPTER 2

Digital Diploma Mills

David Noble

In 1997, the UCLA administration launched its historic "Instructional Enhancement Initiative" requiring computer websites for all of its arts and sciences courses by the start of the fall term, the first time that a major university made mandatory the use of computer telecommunications technology in the delivery of higher education. In partnership with several private corporations (including the Times Mirror Company, parent of the *Los Angeles Times*), moreover, UCLA spawned its own for-profit company, headed by a former UCLA vice chancellor, to peddle online education (the Home Education Network).

That same year, the full-time faculty of York University, Canada's third largest, ended an historic two-month strike after securing for the first time anywhere formal contractual protection against precisely the kind of administrative action being taken by UCLA. The unprecedented faculty job action, the longest university strike in English Canadian history, was taken partly in response to unilateral administrative initiatives in the implementation of instructional technology, the most egregious example of which was an official solicitation to private corporations inviting each to permanently place its logo on a university online course in return for a $10,000 contribution to courseware development. As at UCLA, the York University administration spawned its own subsidiary (Cultech), directed by the vice president for research and several deans and dedicated, in collaboration with a consortium of private sector firms, to the commercial development and exploitation of online education.

At both UCLA and York, the presumably cyberhappy students have given clear indication that they were not exactly enthusiastic about the prospect of a high-tech academic future. Students at UCLA recommended against the initiative, and those at York lent their support to striking faculty and launched their own independent investigation of the commercial, pedagogical, and ethical implications of online educational technology. Thus, at the very outset of this new age of higher education, the lines have already been drawn in the struggle that will ultimately determine its shape. On the one side are university administrators and their myriad commercial partners, on the other are those who constitute the core relation of education: students and teachers. (The chief slogan of the York faculty during the strike was "the classroom vs. the boardroom.") It is no accident, then, that the high-tech transformation of higher education is being initiated and implemented from the top down, either without any student and faculty involvement in the decision making or despite it. At UCLA the administration launched its initiative during the summer when many faculty were away and there was little possibility of faculty oversight or governance; faculty were thus left out of the loop and kept in the dark about the new web requirement until the last moment. And UCLA administrators also went ahead with its initiative, which is funded by a new compulsory student fee, despite the formal student recommendation against it. Similarly the initiatives of the York administration in the deployment of computer technology in education were taken without faculty oversight and deliberation much less student involvement.

What is driving this headlong rush to implement new technology with so little regard for deliberation of the pedagogical and economic costs and at the risk of student and faculty alienation and opposition? A short answer might be the fear of getting left behind, the incessant pressures of "progress." But there is more to it. For the universities are not simply undergoing a technological transformation. Beneath that change, and camouflaged by it, lies another: the commercialization of higher education. For here as elsewhere technology is but a vehicle and a disarming disguise.

The major change to befall the universities over the last two decades has been the identification of the campus as a significant site of capital accumulation, a change in social perception which has resulted in the systematic conversion of intellectual activity into intellectual capital and, hence, intellectual property. There have been two general phases of this transformation. The first, which began more than twenty years ago and is still under way, entailed the commoditization of the research function of the university, transforming scientific and engineering knowledge into commercially viable proprietary products that could be owned and bought and sold in the market. The second, which we are now witnessing, entails the commoditization of the educational function of the university, transforming courses into courseware, the activity of instruction itself into commercially viable proprietary products that can be owned and bought and sold in the market. In the first phase the universities became the site of production and sale of patents and exclusive licenses. In the second, they are becoming the site of production of—as well as the chief market for—copyrighted videos, courseware, CD-ROMs, and websites.

The first phase began in the mid-1970s when, in the wake of the oil crisis and intensifying international competition, corporate and political leaders of the major industrialized countries of the world recognized that they were losing their monopoly over the world's heavy industries and that, in the future, their supremacy would depend upon their monopoly over the knowledge that had become the lifeblood of the new so-called knowledge-based industries (space, electronics, computers, materials, telecommunications, and bioengineering). This focus upon "intellectual capital" turned their attention to the universities as its chief source, implicating the universities as never before in the economic machinery. In the view of capital, the universities had become too important to be left to the universities. Within a decade there was a proliferation of industrial partnerships and new proprietary arrangements, as industrialists and their campus counterparts invented ways to socialize the risks and costs of creating this knowledge while privatizing the benefits.

This unprecedented collaboration gave rise to an elaborate web of interlocking directorates between corporate and academic boardrooms and the foundation of joint lobbying efforts epitomized by the work of the Business–Higher Education Forum. The chief accomplishment of the combined effort, in addition to a relaxation of antitrust regulations and greater tax incentives for corporate funding of university research, was the 1980 reform of the patent law, which for the first time gave the universities automatic ownership of patents resulting from federal government grants. Laboratory knowledge now became patents, that is, intellectual capital and intellectual property. As patent-holding companies, the universities set about at once to codify their intellectual property policies, develop the infrastructure for the conduct of commercially viable research, cultivate their corporate ties, and create the mechanisms for marketing their new commodity, exclusive licenses to their patents. The result of this first phase of university commoditization was a wholesale reallocation of university resources toward its research function at the expense of its education function. Class sizes swelled, teaching staffs and instructional resources were reduced, salaries were frozen, and curricular offerings were cut to the bone. At the same time, tuition soared to subsidize the creation and maintenance of the commercial infrastructure (and correspondingly bloated administration), which has never really paid off. In the end students were paying more for their education and getting less, and the campuses were in crisis.

The second phase of the commercialization of academia, the commoditization of instruction, is touted as the solution to the crisis engendered by the first. Ignoring the true sources of the financial debacle—an expensive and low-yielding commercial infrastructure and greatly expanded administrative costs—the champions of computer-based instruction focus their attention rather upon increasing the efficiencies of already overextended teachers. And they ignore as well the fact that their high-tech remedies are bound only to compound the problem, increasing further, rather than reducing, the costs of higher education. (Experience to date demonstrates clearly that computer-based teaching, with its limitless demands upon instructor time and vastly expanded overhead requirements—equipment, upgrades, maintenance, and technical and administrative support staff—costs more, not less, than traditional education, whatever the reductions in payments to actual professors, hence the need for outside funding and student technology fees.) Little wonder, then, that teachers and students are reluctant to embrace this new panacea. Their hesitation reflects not fear but wisdom.

But this second transformation of higher education is not the work of teachers or students, the presumed beneficiaries of improved education, because it is not really about education at all. That's just the name of the market. The foremost promoters of this transformation are rather the vendors of the network hardware, software, and "content"—Apple, IBM, Bell, the cable companies, Microsoft, and the edutainment and publishing companies Disney, Simon and Schuster, Prentice-Hall et al.—which view education as a market for their wares, a market estimated by the Lehman Brothers investment firm potentially to be worth several hundred billion dollars. "Investment opportunity in the education industry has never been better," one of Lehman's reports proclaimed, indicating that this will be "the focus industry" for lucrative investment in the future, replacing the health-care industry. (The report also forecasts that the education market will eventually become dominated by EMOs—education maintenance organizations—just as HMOs have come to dominate the health-care market.) It is important to emphasize that, for all the democratic rhetoric about extending educational access to those unable to get to the campus, the campus remains the real market for these products, where students outnumber their distance learning counterparts six to one.

In addition to the vendors, corporate training advocates view online education as yet another way of bringing their problem-solving, information-processing, "just-in-time" educated employees up to profit-making speed. Beyond their ambitious in-house training programs, which have incorporated computer-based instructional methods pioneered by the military, they envision the transformation of the delivery of higher education as a means of supplying their properly prepared personnel at public expense.

The third major promoters of this transformation are the university administrators, who see it as a way of giving their institutions a fashionably forward-looking image. More important, they view computer-based instruction as a means of reducing their direct labor and plant maintenance costs—fewer teachers and classrooms—while at the same time undermining the autonomy and independence of faculty. They are also hoping to get a piece of the commercial action for their institutions or themselves, as vendors in their own right of software and content. University administrators are supported in this enterprise by a number of private foundations, trade associations, and academic-corporate consortia that promote the use of the new technologies with increasing intensity. Among these are the Sloan, Mellon, Pew, and Culpeper Foundations, the American Council on Education, and, above all, Educom, a consortium representing the management of six hundred colleges and universities and a hundred private corporations.

Last but not least, behind this effort are the ubiquitous techno-zealots who simply view computers as the panacea for everything, because they like to play with them. With the avid encouragement of their private sector and university patrons, they forge ahead, without support for their pedagogical claims about the alleged enhancement of education, without any real evidence of productivity improvement, and without any effective demand from either students or teachers.

In addition to York and UCLA, universities throughout North America are rapidly being overtaken by this second phase of commercialization. There are the stand-alone virtual institutions like University of Phoenix (see chapter 1), the wired private institutions like the New School for Social Research, the campuses of state universities like the University of Maryland and the new Gulf Coast campus of the University of Florida (which boasts no tenure). On the state level, Arizona and California have initiated their own statewide virtual university projects, while a consortia of western "Smart States" have launched their own ambitious effort to wire all of their campuses into an online education network. In Canada, a national effort has been undertaken, spearheaded by the Telelearning Research Network centered at Simon Fraser University in Vancouver, to bring most of the nation's higher education institutions into a "Virtual U" network.

The overriding commercial intent and market orientation behind these initiatives is explicit, as is illustrated by the most ambitious U.S. effort to date, the Western Governors' Virtual University Project, whose stated goals are to "expand the marketplace for instructional materials, courseware, and programs utilizing advanced technology," "expand the marketplace for demonstrated competence," and "identify and remove barriers to the free functioning of these markets, particularly barriers posed by statutes, policies, and administrative rules and regulations."

"In the future," Utah governor Mike Leavitt proclaimed, "an institution of higher education will become a little like a local television station." Start-up funds for the project come from the private sector, specifically from Educational Management Group of the world's largest education publisher, Simon and Schuster, and the proprietary impulse behind the company's largesse is made clear by Simon and Schuster CEO Jonathan Newcomb: "The use of interactive technology is causing a fundamental shift away from the physical classroom toward anytime, anywhere learning—the model for post secondary education in the twenty-first century." This transformation is being made possible by "advances in digital technology, coupled with the protection of copyright in cyberspace."

Similarly, the national effort to develop the "Virtual U" customized educational software platform in Canada is directed by an industrial consortium which includes Kodak, IBM, Microsoft, McGraw-Hill, Prentice-Hall, Rogers Cablesystems, Unitel, Novasys, Nortel, Bell Canada, and MPR Teltech, a research subsidiary of GTE. The commercial thrust behind the project is explicit. Predicting a potential $50 billion Canadian market, the project proposal emphasizes the adoption of "an intellectual property policy that will encourage researchers and industry to commercialize their innovations" and anticipates the development of "a number of commercially marketable hardware and software products and services," including "courseware and other learning products." The two directors of the project, Simon Fraser University professors, have formed their own company to peddle these products in collaboration with the university. At the same time, the nearby University of British Columbia has recently spun off the private WEB-CT company to peddle its own educational website software, WEB-CT, the software designed by one of its computer science professors and now being used by UCLA. In recent months, WEB-CT has entered into production and distribution relationships with Silicon Graphics and Prentice-Hall and is fast becoming a major player in the American as well as

Canadian higher education market. WEB-CT licensees now include, in addition to UCLA and California State University, the Universities of Georgia, Minnesota, Illinois, North Carolina, and Indiana, as well as such private institutions as Syracuse, Brandeis, and Duquesne.

The Discontents of the Diploma Mill: The Proletarianization of the Faculty

With the commoditization of instruction, teachers as labor are drawn into a production process designed for the efficient creation of instructional commodities, and hence become subject to all the pressures that have befallen production workers in other industries undergoing rapid technological transformation from above. In this context faculty have much more in common with the historic plight of other skilled workers than they care to acknowledge. Like these others, their activity is being restructured, via technology (and capital), in order to reduce their autonomy, independence, and control over their work and to place workplace knowledge and control as much as possible into the hands of the administration. As in other industries, the technology is being deployed by management primarily to discipline, deskill, and displace labor.

Once faculty and courses go online, administrators gain direct control over faculty performance and course content more than ever before, and the potential for administrative scrutiny, supervision, regimentation, discipline, and even censorship increase dramatically. At the same time, the use of the technology entails an inevitable extension of working time and an intensification of work as faculty struggle at all hours of the day and night to stay on top of the technology and respond, via chat rooms, virtual office hours, and e-mail, to both students and administrators to whom they have now become instantly and continuously accessible. The technology also allows for much more careful administrative monitoring of faculty availability, activities, and responsiveness.

Once faculty put their course material online, moreover, the knowledge and course design skill embodied in that material is taken out of their possession, transferred to the machinery and placed in the hands of the administration. The administration is now in a position to hire less skilled, and hence cheaper, workers to deliver the technologically prepackaged course. It also allows the administration, which claims ownership of this commodity, to peddle the course elsewhere without the original designer's involvement or even knowledge, much less financial interest. The buyers of this packaged commodity, meanwhile, other academic institutions, are able thereby to contract out the work of their own employees and thus reduce their reliance upon their in-house teaching staff.

Most important, once the faculty convert their courses to courseware, their services are in the long run no longer required. They become redundant, and when they leave, their work remains behind. In Kurt Vonnegut's classic novel *Player Piano* the ace machinist Rudy Hertz is flattered by the automation engineers who tell him his genius will be immortalized. They buy him a beer. They capture his skills on tape. Then they fire him. Today faculty are falling for the same tired line, that their brilliance will be broadcast online to millions. Perhaps, but without their further participation. Some skeptical faculty insist that what they do cannot possibly be automated, and they are right. But it will be automated anyway, whatever the loss in educational quality. Because education, again, is not what all this is about; it's about making money. In short, the new technology of education, like the automation of other industries, robs faculty of their knowledge and skills, their control over their working lives, the product of their labor, and, ultimately, their means of livelihood.

None of this is speculation. Some UCLA faculty, at administration request, dutifully or grudgingly (it doesn't really matter which) placed their course work—ranging from syllabi and assignments to the entire body of course lectures and notes—at the disposal of their administration, to be used online, without asking who will own it, much less how it will eventually be used and with what consequences. At York University, untenured faculty have been required to put their courses on video, CD-ROM, or the Internet or lose their jobs. They have then been hired to teach their own now automated course at a fraction of their former compensation. The New School in New York now routinely hires outside contractors from around the country, mostly unemployed Ph.D.s, to design online courses. The designers are not hired as employees but are simply paid a modest flat fee and are required to surrender to the university all rights to their courses. The New School then offers the courses without having to employ anyone. And this is just the beginning.

Educom, the academic-corporate consortium, has recently established its Learning Infrastructure Initiative, which includes a detailed study of what professors do, breaking the faculty job down in classic Tayloristic fashion into discrete tasks, and determining what parts can be automated or outsourced. Educom believes that course design, lectures, and even evaluation can all be standardized, mechanized, and consigned to outside commercial vendors. "Today you're looking at a highly personal human-mediated environment," Educom president Robert Heterich observed. "The potential to remove the human mediation in some areas and replace it with automation—smart, computer-based, network-based systems—is tremendous. It's gotta happen."

Toward this end, university administrators are coercing or enticing faculty into compliance, placing the greatest pressures on the most vulnerable—untenured and part-time faculty, and entry-level and prospective employees. They are using the academic incentive and promotion structure to reward cooperation and discourage dissent. At the same time they are mounting a propaganda campaign to portray faculty as incompetent, hidebound, recalcitrant, inefficient, ineffective, and expensive—in short, in need of improvement or replacement through instructional technologies. Faculty are portrayed above all as obstructionist, as standing in the way of progress and forestalling the panacea of virtual education allegedly demanded by students, their parents, and the public.

Resistance May Not Be Futile

The York University faculty had heard it all. Yet still they fought vigorously and ultimately successfully to preserve quality education and protect themselves from administrative assault. During their long strike they countered such administration propaganda with the truth about what was happening to higher education and eventually won the support of students, the media, and the public. Most important, they secured a new contract containing unique and unprecedented provisions that, if effectively enforced, give faculty members direct and unambiguous control over all decisions relating to the automation of instruction, including veto power. According to the contract, all decisions regarding the use of technology as a supplement to classroom instruction or as a means of alternative delivery (including the use of video, CD-ROMs, Internet websites, computer-mediated conferences, etc.) "shall be consistent with the pedagogic and academic judgements and principles of the faculty member employee as to the appropriateness of the use of technology in the circumstances." The contract also guarantees that "a faculty member will not be required to convert a course without his or her agreement." Thus, the York faculty will be able to ensure that the new technology, if and when used, will contribute to a genuine enhancement rather than a degradation of the quality of education, while at the same time preserving their positions, their autonomy, and their academic freedom. The battle is far from won, but it is a start.

At UCLA, the widely touted Instructional Enhancement Initiative, which mandated websites for all thirty-eight hundred arts and sciences courses, has foundered in the face of faculty recalcitrance and resistance. By the end of 1997, only 30 percent of the faculty had put any of their course material online, and several dozen had actively resisted the initiative and the way it was unilaterally inspired and implemented. UCLA Extension's partnership with the Home Education Network (which changed its name in the spring to Onlinelearning.net) ran aground on similar shoals when instructors made clear that they would refuse to assign any of their rights in their course materials to either UCLA (the regents) or the company. In already up to their necks, the partners decided simply to claim the rights anyway and proceed apace, flying without wings on borrowed time.

While the strike at York awakened the faculty there to a new vigilance and militancy with regard to the computer-based commercialization of the university, it also emboldened others elsewhere to do likewise. At Acadia University, for example, which had linked up with IBM in hopes of becoming the foremost wired institution in Canada, the threat of a faculty strike forced the administration to back off from some of their unilateral demands for online instruction, and faculties at other Canadian institutions have been moving in the same direction. And even within Simon Fraser University's Department of Communications, home of the recently re-funded Canadian flagship Telelearning Research Center, serious faculty challenges to the virtual university enterprise have emerged and gone public.

In the United States as well, resistance is on the rise. Faculty and students in the California State University system, the largest public higher education institution in the country, fought vigorously and effectively against the California Educational Technology Inititiative (CETI), an unprecedented deal between CSU and a consortium of firms (Microsoft, GTE, Hughes, and Fujitsu) that would have given them a monopoly over the development of the system's telecommunications infrastructure and the marketing and delivery of CSU online courses. Students resisted being made a captive market for company products, and faculty responded to the lack of faculty consultation and threats to academic freedom and their intellectual property rights. In particular, they feared that CETI might try to dictate online course content for commercial advantage and that CSU would appropriate and commercially exploit their course materials.

So What's Really So Bad about Computers? The Commodification and Destruction of Education

This resistance highlights what has gone wrong in higher education over the past number of years—namely, the commoditization of instruction and the transformation of the university into a market for the commodities being produced. Administrative propaganda routinely alludes to an alleged student demand for the new instructional products. At UCLA officials are betting that their high-tech agenda will be "student driven," as students insist that faculty make fuller use in their courses of website technology. To date, however, there has been no such demand on the part of students, no serious study of it, and no evidence for it. Indeed, the few times students have been given a voice, they have rejected the initiatives hands down, especially when they were required to pay for it (the definition of effective demand, i.e., a market). At UCLA, students recommended against the Instructional Enhancement Initiative. At the University of British Columbia, home of the WEB-CT software being used at UCLA, students voted by a ratio of four-to-one against a similar initiative, despite a lengthy administration campaign promising them a more secure place in the high-tech future. Administrators at both institutions have tended to dismiss, ignore, or explain away these negative student decisions, but there is a message here: students want the genuine face-to-face education they paid for, not a cybercounterfeit. Nevertheless, administrators at both UCLA and UBC decided to proceed with their agendas anyway, desperate to create a market and secure some return on their investment in the information technology infrastructure. Thus, they are creating a market by fiat, compelling students (and faculty) to become users and hence consumers of the hardware, software, and content products as a condition of getting an education, whatever their interest or ability to pay. Can all students equally afford this capital-intensive education?

Another key ethical issue relates to the use of student online activities. Few students realize that their computer-based courses are often thinly veiled field trials for product and market development, that while they are studying their courses, their courses are studying them. In Canada, for example, universities have been given royalty-free licenses to Virtual U software in return for providing data on its use to the vendors. Thus, all online activity including communications between students and professors and among students is monitored, automatically logged and archived by the system for use by the vendor. Students enrolled in courses using Virtual U software are in fact formally designated "experimental subjects." Because federal money was used to develop the software and underwrite the field trials, vendors were compelled to comply with ethical guidelines on the experimental use of human subjects. Thus, all students are required to sign forms releasing ownership and control of their online activities to the vendors. The form states "as a student using Virtual U in a course, I give my permission to have the computer-generated usage data, conference transcript data, and virtual artifacts data collected by the Virtual U software . . . used for research, development, and demonstration purposes."

According to UCLA's Home Education Network president John Korbara, all of its distance learning courses are likewise monitored and archived for use by company officials. On the UCLA campus, according to Harlan Lebo of the provost's office, student use of the course websites will be routinely audited and evaluated by the administration. Marvin Goldberg, designer of the UCLA WEB-CT software acknowledges that the system allows for "lurking" and automatic storage and retrieval of all online activities. How this capability will be used and by whom is not altogether clear, especially since websites are typically being constructed by people other than the instructors. What third parties (besides students and faculty in the course) will have access to the students' communications? Who will own student online contributions? What rights, if any, do students have to privacy and proprietary control of their work? Are they given prior notification as to the ultimate status of their online activities, so that they might be in a position to give, or withhold, their informed consent? If students are taking courses that are just experiments, and hence of unproven pedagogical value, should students be paying full tuition for them? And if students are being used as guinea pigs in product trials masquerading as courses, should they be paying for these courses or be paid to take them? More to the point, should students be content with a degraded, shadow cybereducation? In Canada student organizations have begun to confront these issues head-on, and there are some signs of similar student concern emerging in the United States.

In spelling out what is wrong with the digital diploma mills of today, it is important to spell out what is meant by both "education" and "commodification," since these terms are often used with little precision. To begin with, education must be distinguished from training (which is arguably more suitable for distance delivery) because the two are so often conflated. In essence, training involves the honing of a person's mind so that that mind can be used for the purposes of someone other than that person. Training thus typically entails a radical divorce between knowledge and the self. Here knowledge is usually defined as a set of skills or a body of information designed to be put to use, to become operational, only in a context determined by someone other than the trained person; in this context the assertion of self is not only counterproductive, it is subversive to the enterprise. Education is the exact opposite of training in that it entails not the disassociation but the utter integration of knowledge and the self, in a word, self-knowledge. Here knowledge is defined by and, in turn, helps to define, the self. Knowledge and the knowledgeable person are basically inseparable.

Education is a process that necessarily entails an interpersonal (not merely interactive) relationship between people—student and teacher (and student and student) that aims at individual and collective self-knowledge. (Whenever people recall their education experiences they tend to remember above all not courses or subjects or the information imparted but people, people who changed their minds or their lives, people who made a difference in their developing sense of themselves. It is a sign of our current confusion about education that we must be reminded of this obvious fact: that the relationship between people is central to education.) Education is a process of *becoming* for all parties, based upon mutual recognition and validation and centering upon the formation and evolution of identity. The actual content of the education experience is defined by this relationship between people, and the chief determinant of quality education is the establishment and enrichment of this relationship.

Like "education," the word "commodification" (or "commoditization") is used rather loosely with regard to education, and some precision may help the discussion. A commodity is something created, grown, produced, or manufactured for exchange on the market. Of course, some things that are bought and sold on the market were not created for that purpose, such as "labor" and land—what the political economist Karl Polanyi referred to as "fictitious commodities." Most education offerings, although divided into units of credit and exchanged for tuition, are fictitious commodities in that they are not created by the educator strictly with this purpose in mind. Here we will be using the term "commodity" not in this fictitious, more expansive sense but rather in its classical, restricted sense to mean something expressly created for market exchange. The commoditization of higher education, then, refers to the deliberate transformation of the education process into commodity form for the purpose of commercial transaction.

The commodification of education requires the interruption of this fundamental education process and the disintegration and distillation of the education experience into discrete, reified, and ultimately salable things or packages of things. In the first step toward commodification, attention is shifted from the experience of the people involved in the education process to the production and inventorying of an assortment of fragmented "course materials": syllabi, lectures, lessons, exams (now referred to in the aggregate as "content"). As anyone familiar with higher education knows, these common instruments of instruction barely reflect what actually takes place in the education experience and lend an illusion of order and predictability to what is, at its best, an essentially unscripted and undetermined process. Second, these fragments are removed or "alienated" from their original context, the actual education process itself, and from their producers, the teachers, and are assembled as "courses," which take on an existence independent of and apart from those who created and gave flesh to them. This is perhaps the most critical step in commodity formation. The alienation of ownership of and control over course material (through surrender of copyright) is crucial to this step. Finally, the assembled "courses" are exchanged for a profit on the market, which determines their value, by their "owners," who may or may not have any relationship to the original creators and participants in the education process. At the expense of the original integrity of the education process, instruction has here been transformed into a set of deliverable commodities, and the end of education has become not self-knowledge but the making of money. In the wake of this transformation, teachers become commodity producers and deliverers, subject to the familiar regime of commodity production in any other industry, and students become consumers of yet more commodities. The relationship between teacher and student is thus reestablished, in an alienated mode, through the medium of the market, and the buying and selling of commodities takes on the appearance of education. But it is, in reality, only a shadow of education, an assemblage of pieces without the whole.

Again, under this new regime, painfully familiar to skilled workers in every industry since the dawn of industrial capitalism, educators confront the harsh realities of commodity production: speed-up, routinization of work, greater work discipline and managerial supervision, reduced autonomy, job insecurity, employer appropriation of the fruits of their labor, and, above all, the insistent managerial pressures to reduce labor costs in order to turn a profit. Thus, the commoditization of instruction leads invariably to the "proletarianization" or, more politely, the "deprofessionalization" of the professoriate discussed above.

But there is a paradox at the core of this transformation. Quality education is labor-intensive; it depends upon a low teacher-student ratio and significant interaction between the two parties—the one utterly unambiguous result of a century of education research. Any effort to offer quality in education must therefore presuppose a substantial and sustained investment in education labor, whatever the medium of instruction. The requirements of commodity production, however, undermine the labor-intensive foundation of quality education (and with it, quality products people will willingly pay for). Pedagogical promise and economic efficiency are thus in contradiction. Here is the achilles heel of distance education. In the past as well as the present, distance educators have always insisted that they offer a kind of intimate and individualized instruction not possible in the crowded, competitive environment of the campus. Theirs is an improved, enhanced education. To make their enterprise profitable, however, they have been compelled to reduce their instructional costs to a minimum, thereby undermining their pedagogical promise. The invariable result has been not only a degraded labor force but a degraded product as well.

In his classic 1959 study *American Degree Mills* for the American Council on Education, Robert Reid described the typical diploma mill as having the following characteristics: "no classrooms," "faculties are often untrained or nonexistent," and "the officers are unethical self-seekers whose qualifications are no better than their offerings." It is an even more apt description of the digital diploma mills now in the making. Quality higher education will not disappear entirely, but it will soon become the exclusive preserve of the privileged, available only to children of the rich and the powerful. For the rest of us a dismal new era of higher education has dawned. In ten years, we will look upon the wired remains of our once great democratic higher education system and wonder how we let it happen. That is, unless we decide now not to let it happen.

CHAPTER 3

Inefficient Efficiency
A Critique of Merit Pay
Denise Marie Tanguay

Those working within academia have heard some variant of the following complaint: "He's never there during office hours, uses old yellowed notes, hasn't done research since God was born, and hates students; and the dean can't do a thing about it! Boy, I want to be a professor—what a life!" If such behavior ever existed, it is not the reality faculty members face today. Post-tenure review, budget cutbacks, outcomes assessment, public criticism, "continuous improvement" and reengineering of review processes, legislated time on campus—all of these so-called reforms are helping to define the new corporate university. Heading the list is merit pay, a reform that has played an increasingly important role in academic life since the 1980s.

Though not all administrators support the use of merit pay, many see it as a way to placate their boards of regents or state legislators, and anecdotal evidence suggests an increase in and adoption of merit pay in institutions of higher education. The College and University Professional Association for Human Resources (CUPA-HR) showed that approximately 34 percent of colleges and universities use a merit pay system.[1] This number has been rising since the 1980s.

Recently, many faculty members have spoken out against this increased use of merit pay. Unfortunately, it is all too easy to see their protest as motivated by little more than self-interest. After all, who can really complain about a system that rewards individuals based upon performance? There is always someone who points out that most corporations use a merit-based system. Indignant students and administrators who have read the latest managerial tract often ponder why faculty members should be treated any differently from other employees. You can hear the question on the lips of the American public: Do professors really expect to have no one telling them what to do and no accountability for what they *should* be doing?

Arguments for merit pay typically center on fairness. Merit pay systems are based upon the idea of well-communicated, predetermined standards providing a higher level of reward for those performing better. Other arguments exist as well. Some supporters argue the need for institutions of higher education to use their resources judiciously and to make salary decisions that attract and retain prolific scholars (the "rock stars" of the profession), the desire to satisfy the demands of governing boards or state legislatures, and the hope of some administrators to apply corporate trends to academic institutions, making them more businesslike (and their members more "up to date"). All of these arguments are dressed up with the code word and mantra of "accountability."

While it is hard to argue with the general philosophy behind merit pay—that those performing at higher levels should receive greater rewards—the debate over merit pay in higher education has always been contentious. First, there is the question of "fit." Drawing upon the insights of organizational theorists who have studied different types of organizational cultures, many faculty and some administrators have argued that merit pay systems distort the mission of colleges and universities. Though it is clear that there is no "one best way" for all organizations to run themselves, what is known is that environment, structure, culture, policies, and systems (including reward systems) must work in tandem. For example, an employment-at-will policy, under which employees may be terminated for any reason or no reason at all, does not fit an institution that values academic freedom, pursues the development of all members, and believes in open feedback. After all, institutions of higher education are not like corporations because they do not produce clearly defined commodities or services but rather processes that are often open-ended. As organizational theorist Karl Weick points out, universities are "loosely coupled units" with a mission to deliver a social good that is "owned" by society, rather than by an individual consumer.[2] This is just the first place where the analogy between universities and corporations breaks down. Listen to the former president of Yale University A. Bartlett Giamatti in a 1987 address:

> A college or university is an institution where financial incentives to excellence are absent, where the product line is not a unit or an object

but rather a value-laden and life-long process; where the goal of the enterprise is not growth or market share but intellectual excellence; not profit or proprietary rights but the free good of knowledge; not efficiency of operation but equity of treatment; not increased productivity in economic terms but increased intensity of thinking about who we are and how we live and about the world around us. In such an institution, leadership is much more a rhetorical than a fiscal or "strategic" act. While never denigrating the day-to-day, never scorning the legitimate and difficult chores of management, never pretending that efficiency is useless or productivity irrelevant, leadership in such an institution must define institutional shape, that is, define its standards and purposes—define the coherent, sustainable, daring, shared effort of learning that will increase a given community's freedom, intellectual excellence, human dignity.[3]

Giamatti's statement makes clear that an individually based, annual merit pay or incentive plan may distort the basic mission of the university. Merit pay does this by rewarding a narrow set of goals, particularly those that are easily measurable: number of journal articles published, external dollars brought into the institution in grants, and perhaps student evaluations of the faculty member's courses (themselves quantifiable). This reduction of goals to the measurable is one of the most potentially distorting elements of such a system.

Another argument against merit pay is that the very nature of academic work makes the design and implementation of a successful merit pay system difficult if not impossible. The three activities traditionally evaluated are teaching, research, and service. It is unclear in most institutions precisely how to weight each element, however. Furthermore, though the quantity of such work may be measurable, the *quality* of outcomes is much more difficult to assess. But even still, is more better than less? Say, for instance, that a faculty member makes his career by publishing large numbers of articles capturing small refinements of an area such as game theory, while another scholar spends fifteen years or more gathering data on the long-term effects of a social phenomenon such as divorce. The number of yearly publications for the second scholar may be much lower than for the first, but the impact of the scholarship may be much larger. In addition, it is unclear how accurately the effectiveness of teaching can be judged from student evaluations (high marks here often correlate with higher grades received) or classroom visits made by peers. Nor is it easy to judge the quality of service (i.e., does simply "showing up" at meetings count, or should there be some stronger contribution?) and the quality and impact of publications (should certain journals rank higher than others?). Other issues include the wisdom of assessing the quality of long-run activities, such as research and service, on an annual basis, when in fact it may take two, three, or more years to bring an important research project to completion (or what happens when there is no discernible outcome—say a journal article—because the research, though duly done, did not turn up anything publishable?). Indeed, many critics point out that merit pay pressures have simply increased the number of repetitive, incremental, and barely substantive journal articles that fill the plethora of new, hyperspecialized journals (which are rarely read). Some journals seem little more than promotional machines. Summing up their research, three scholars argue that performance evaluation methods used in higher education are "rarely based on solid ground."[4]

Finally, strong *economic* arguments have also been made against the use of merit pay in higher education. After all, effective merit pay works only when there are fair base salaries in place—and then substantial rewards are given to high performers, highlighting just how much hard work has been truly rewarded in comparison to others. Unfortunately, cost-of-living adjustments for all faculty who perform satisfactorily are too often sacrificed to provide greater rewards for those who have been evaluated as performing in an "above-average" manner. Without a cost-of-living raise, or without a large enough merit pool to provide an award to all those performing at the satisfactory level, some faculty members will experience a decline in real income in order to support increases for those at the high end. This is quite obviously a looming issue for colleges and universities during the current economic times when all budgets are tight, and some state budgets are cutting back higher education budgets.

Merit Pay as a Catchall Solution

Merit pay has been around a long time but has come to prominence since the 1980s. This is especially true in the corporate sector. Indeed, corporations using some type of merit pay plan today are reported to be close to 100 percent. Not satisfied with the ability of merit pay to motivate high levels of employee performance, nearly 90 percent of public companies also offer short-term incentives to various groups of their employees, as reported in the Society of Human Resource Management/Arthur Andersen Strategic Compensation Survey completed in 1999.[5] These short-term incentives are tied to various factors, usually preestablished targets that are both objective and quantifiable, and that link individual goals to business goals. It might be, for example, that annually a pharmaceutical sales representative is rewarded on overall sales performance, but on a monthly basis gets a bonus for reaching sales targets to physicians who have not previously prescribed a certain drug. These short-term incentives might be given at a number of different levels, for example the individual, the work group, or team level. Seventy-four percent of public U.S. organizations provide long-term incentives as well, such as stock options.

In the world of education (both K–12 and academia) merit pay was used as early as 1908. While there was some growth in the use of merit pay in the 1930s, by the 1940s many schools had abandoned it.[6] However, it hit the scene again in the 1950s and '60s as a retention device for good teachers. As education reform became a national discussion, merit pay was increasingly applied to both K–12 teachers and faculty in colleges and universities. In October 1989, the *Chronicle of Higher Education* reported anecdotal evidence of the spread of salary increases based upon merit. The coordinator of higher education at the National Education Association (NEA) suggested that "community colleges in particular are taking a serious look at merit pay because of the influence of the reform movement in education, which emphasizes rewarding outstanding service."[7]

Though the number of actual merit pay systems in higher education still seems small in comparison to the corporate world, the higher education institutions engaged in the study or design of merit pay plans is increasing. In the College and University Personnel Association-HR 2000–2001 *National Faculty Salary Survey*, of the 319 tenure-awarding institutions responding, pay for performance was offered as a benefit at 108 (34 percent).[8] However, it is useful to note that while colleges and universities are moving toward merit pay, corporations are investing in pay plans such as competency-based pay and pay-for-skills plans, rarely used in the academic world. It is clear from the corporate use of multiple pay plans that no one incentive system guarantees either accountability or excellence. Institutions of higher education should pay attention to all corporate trends if they are going to follow any, as contemporary corporations generally understand that systems that fit their individual cultures are most effective.

The Devil Is in the Details: Some Problems and Case Studies

In spite of the *apparent* desirability of merit pay, *implementation* often produces dissatisfaction, inequity, competition, decreased performance, and resistance.[9] Ironically, those who trumpet the supposed efficiency incurred by merit pay ignore just how much time and money it takes to create elaborate evaluation processes and train managers or administrators in how to evaluate employees' work without bias and with regularity. They ignore how difficult it is to provide good feedback to those being evaluated and how much time it takes to move from evaluation to pay raises taking effect. As the cliché goes, the devil is in the details.

When faculty members are evaluated by multiple levels of administration (the department head, dean, and provost), which is the case on many campuses, then the organizational challenge is to make sure that each administrator utilizes the same criteria that have been previously communicated to the faculty. In so doing, evaluation should result in feedback to the faculty member about how the evaluation was made, and what he or she would have to do to be rated more highly in the future. Only when this system works and is monitored for integrity will faculty perceive the system to be fair, seeing what they can do to improve down the road. This may sound simple, but corporations have struggled with it for years, and entire sets of employees are often hired to ensure the integrity of the merit system by examining evaluations and rewards. This type of system must be designed with excruciating care and then implemented consistently and monitored thoroughly. Why is it so painstaking? Because the temptation of those involved in a time-consuming process is to shorten the process by making quick, and sometimes arbitrary judgments, to "get it done." These shortcuts typically create bias, and often, feedback is not present at all.

Conflict often emerges between collegiality and competition and between older systems of tenure and newer systems of merit. This is because at many institutions, merit systems are add-ons to an already established tenure system. Within the tenure system, faculty are evaluated by peers against criteria that are outlined (one hopes) in a tenure and promotion document, and clearly explicated to junior faculty. Promotion and/or tenure are given or denied based upon these peer assessments of performance. Usually, increases in salary are delivered with both tenure and promotion. These processes take tremendous time from all involved, and rightly so. It is questionable whether layering an annual system on top of this review process makes sense, and whether the impact increases collegiality. Tenure and promotion, after all, are not competitions between individuals in most institutions. There may be a tenure cap, in which case some deserving faculty may not be tenured because of a rigid, budget-driven figure. However, in general, if a faculty member earns a promotion by fulfilling the criteria, then he or she is not taking that away from anyone else; rather it is a benefit available to anyone who has done the same. But then again, with merit pay, given scarce and usually low salary pool dollars, it becomes clear quickly that what is given to one faculty member must be taken away from another. If 3 percent of the salary dollars in a department is what is available to be distributed, then for a high performer who gets 5 percent, either one other person must receive only 1 percent or two people may only get 2 percent, and so on. Anecdotal evidence abounds that collegiality suffers when merit pay systems are instituted in colleges or universities. For instance, Roger Bowen found that collegiality and collaboration suffered when merit pay for faculty was introduced at Colby College.[10] Three short case studies make all of this even more evident.

The California State University Plan

During much of 1999–2001, the California State University System was at impasse in negotiations with the California Faculty Association (CFA), which represents the roughly twenty-three thousand faculty members in the system. In this case, the faculty union had previously agreed to the implementation of a multitiered merit system for part of the compensation awards. After receiving many complaints and grievances and then commissioning a study to review the equity of the plan, the union concluded that the plan should be suspended. The administration did not agree, and a lengthy impasse began.

In an article published in the CUPA-HR journal in winter 1998, the CSU senior director of Academic Personnel Services and the CSU interim vice chancellor of Human Resources described the objectives of merit pay plans as "providing incentives for superior performance, creating a system to evaluate and reward outstanding performance, and demonstrating accountability to constituencies (e.g., taxpayers and governing boards)."[11] Distrust of public government had grown in California for quite some time now (after all, this is the state that brought us not only Ronald Reagan but the famous taxpayers' revolt), and the CSU system's chancellor was placed under pressure to demonstrate accountability. The issues regarding merit-based compensation in the CSU system, however, quickly moved from accountability of the chancellor to the California politicians, to the accountability of the CSU administration to their faculty. When the CFA demanded a moratorium on the merit pay system, it was in part because six grievances had been filed on six different campuses, all in response to the addition of new (and therefore noncontractual) criteria for making merit recommendations or awards. The contract the chancellor bargained with the CFA contained specific criteria for the merit awards, but in a decentralized system the lack of monitoring of administrative decisions allowed for the violation of the contract at individual institutions.

Debates and allegations continued over the design and implementation of the CSU merit pay plan for several years. One particularly difficult area was the issue of discrimination against women in the distribution of merit

increases. The CFA's initial analysis of salary data (the data had been provided by the CSU administration) illustrated that female faculty on several
CSU campuses had most likely been the victims of pay discrimination for at
least two years. Male faculty were found to be compensated at a rate 12.8
percent higher than female faculty. Additionally, under the CSU system of
merit increases, women received 8 percent less in merit awards than did
men. This finding was especially disturbing to the CFA because that type of
differential in rewards clearly would have the long-term effect of perpetuat-
ing and increasing a gap in salaries. Trying to get a handle on these issues,
the CFA hired a consulting group, Abacus Associates, to perform a survey
and a more complete analysis of data at the time the bargaining impasse
moved forward to fact-finding. The findings were bleak, concluding that
when nine hundred full-time CSU faculty members were selected at ran-
dom, and data on salary, years in rank, and rank were appended, full-time
men were found to make 15 percent more than the full-time women in the
sample. Even when rank and years in rank were controlled for in a multiple
regression, gender was found to have a statistically significant effect on a
faculty member's salary.

Perhaps more disturbing than the evidence of gender discrimination,
however, was how the Faculty Merit Increase program changed relationships within campuses. For example, 75 percent of those faculty responding
to the Abacus Associates survey believed that the merit program had lowered the quality of relationships with their administrations, 71 percent reported that the merit program had lowered the quality of their relationships
with peers. Just as troublesome was how the merit increase rarely related to
the quality of teaching. In whole, the merit pay plan seems to have created
more negative than positive outcomes. It is very difficult to project the long-
term consequences of the California State University system's merit pay
plan and resulting conflicts, but as of this writing, it is clear that it has damaged trust between the faculty and campus and systems administrators,
helped solidify gender inequalities, and has undervalued teaching. The effects of these dynamics could be devastating to this system and its students
over time.

Fairfield University

A second case example is the ongoing situation at Fairfield University in
Connecticut, where late in 2000 the Board of Trustees at Fairfield University
issued a request to the faculty to develop a merit pay system. As the faculty
examined the issues involved, the effort it would take, and the benefits they

and their university might gain, they recommended against a merit pay plan. This was not without a large expenditure of faculty time and thought. The faculty spent weeks working through the issues involved in merit pay, inviting an external consultant to discuss the elements of a good design and implementation as well as problems with merit pay at an open faculty meeting.

Though eventually the trustees backed down from their initial request, it took the better part of a year for the faculty to convince them of the inappropriateness of such a system for their school. During discussions, the trustees were asked what they hoped to gain by mandating such a compensation system. Their only response was given on June 7, 2001, that other good schools had merit plans and that "adoption of a merit pay system for faculty compensation is vital to the long-range development and growth of the University." By the same board resolution, a committee was formed to examine the question of decision making and governance. This committee was formed and met four times before the board and administration unilaterally dissolved it.

Later, in a response to a request from faculty for the board's goals for a merit pay plan, they responded that they want to "attract and retain an increasingly excellent faculty, and to implement a compensation structure that links, in some way, compensation to faculty and academic goals." The faculty, however, were puzzled in that they had no evidence of any problem either hiring or retaining good faculty, and that the second board goal appeared to be a means to an end, rather than a goal at all.

On December 6, 2001, a second board resolution was passed that ended the system that provided across-the-board salary increases by ranks. The board directed the academic vice president to consult with the faculty, but to present to the board a new compensation system that included individual performance evaluations as part of the mechanism for distributing individual faculty merit increases. Though the board's resolution recognizes the need for a collaborative process, it is still insisting upon what it wants—a merit system of some type. On the other hand, it has refused to spell out what this could achieve for the university that is not being achieved now.[12]

The same resolution also directed the academic vice president to work with the deans and faculty to make appropriate equity adjustments for those faculty who need them. One immediate result of this altercation has been a fracturing of the faculty into various groups. With a deadline of March 2002 for an interim report, and a full plan required by June 2002 for board action, a rational and collaborative process has been impossible to achieve. Instead, the five deans have worked somewhat independently, sometimes with faculty as in the case of the College of Business, and sometimes without them, as in the case of the College of Liberal Arts. While all of these plans were not complete by the June board meeting, all were approved by the board at least in terms of general direction. One question of concern to faculty is that since January 1, 2002, their performance will be reviewed for a merit increase; however, as of late summer 2002, many faculty members still did not know the evaluation criteria to be used.

It seems that the board and faculty are now pitted against one another. The board's reticence to engage in the development of a carefully thought out statement of purpose for the compensation changes it is requesting, in addition to its lack of responsiveness in general to the faculty concerns over the "fit" of merit pay to their institution, has created a difficult relationship between faculty and the administration. Even if a resolution is found in the near future, the damage done to faculty and administration relations is quite clear. So is the fractiousness created within the university as a whole.

Rutgers University

The faculty of Rutgers University have a union (a local branch of the American Association of University Professors [AAUP]) and a number of years of experience with their merit pay plan, the Faculty Academic Service Increment Program (FASIP). Prior to the 1995–1999 collective bargaining contract, the FASIP accounted for a fairly small percentage of the overall compensation package, in addition to across-the-board salary increases and automatic annual increments (or steps). After difficult negotiations that resulted in the use of state fact-finding procedures (a public-sector process that appoints a person to hear both sides of an issue and "report out the facts"), the settlement resulted in a contract that eliminated the automatic increments entirely and that split the available salary money evenly between across-the-board salary increases and the merit program. During the negotiations for the current contract, 1999–2003, the AAUP and the university administration agreed to maintain the 50-50 split; however, there is significantly less money available for the FASIP increases as compared to the previous contract's awards. Seemingly, merit pay looks in this case, as it does elsewhere, like cost-cutting. Within the last few years, a number of questions have been raised about the program in terms of the effects on faculty, and as of the date of this writing, a study is under way to examine the attitudes of the faculty toward the FASIP and the effects it has had on pay. Preliminary polling of faculty about the pay plan shows a predominantly negative view of the elements of the FASIP awards system.

At Rutgers, faculty merit pay is affected by peers, chairs, deans, and provosts. In a system of nearly twenty-three hundred faculty, the idea that the campus provosts will have the time to review all applications for merit pay is difficult to imagine. Additionally, a provost on such a large campus has little to no contact with many faculty members and thus cannot assess their performances very well. The lack of proximity hurts the trust in evaluations and modifications to awards that are generated at that level of the administration. By grafting the corporate world's practice of merit pay onto the academic world's desire for administrative control, the university seems to have gotten the worst of both worlds. The Rutgers AAUP consistently has expressed concern over the fairness of awards, and is currently involved in research to examine the issue of possible disciplinary, gender, and racial bias in the FASIP awards, as well as other issues. One additional concern that is troubling is the effect at Rutgers on non-tenure-track faculty salaries. With the limited resources available, members of this group of faculty were often overlooked in their departments and at subsequent steps in the evaluation sequence, with the dollars saved being allotted to more senior, tenured faculty. With non-tenure-track faculty doing the majority of undergraduate teaching at Rutgers, teaching clearly has been, once again, underevaluated.

As the Rutgers AAUP council of chapters prepares for negotiations once again, the issues with FASIP are accumulating. Trust in awards modified by provost and deans, potential discrimination, the time-consuming nature of the evaluation process, the reported distribution by some departments of essentially across-the-board "merit increases," and a substantially negative faculty attitude toward the program are the primary issues. Grievances regarding the implementation of the program are in process, and frustration is fairly evident on the part of faculty leaders toward a program that does not appear to be resulting in gains for the institution.

Conclusions

Though the demand for merit pay systems by board members, administrators, and legislators may sound sensible and put faculty leaders/dissenters into a difficult position of arguing the indefensible, there is very little evidence that the system can be implemented within most colleges or universities with fairness and positive outcomes for the institution. The claims that merit pay and other "market mechanisms" will create efficiency seem little more than common sense, but in fact these systems create more, not fewer, tiers of bureaucracy by adding layers of ineffective evaluation procedures. Most important, market-based techniques *do not work* in institutions whose reason for being is to provide high-quality social goods, rather than return a profit to their shareholders. Efficiency is not the end-all and be-all of every sphere of life. In terms of education, what matters more are such things as academic freedom, trust, collegiality, and concern for the processes of critical inquiry. Merit pay, as implemented in many institutions, does nothing to enhance these values.

Does the *possibility* of implementing a merit pay system that works actually exist? Yes, of course. To design and implement such a system, however, means that the institution must define clearly the purpose of such a program, use a participatory process to develop the system itself, use a peer system of evaluation that fits the culture, and then encourage the development of a process that will be regarded as fair with which to settle pay grievances that arrive (which would seem to suggest the need for some sort of collective representation). In any institution, this means that real resources of money and time must be provided. As I have shown here, the prospects of this happening are not high, precisely because of the likelihood of cutting corners. We need to ask some serious questions if we truly want to create a system that is just and rewards merit at the same time.

CHAPTER 4

The Drain-O of Higher Education
Casual Labor and University Teaching
Benjamin Johnson

If there is a common element in all of the best-known threats to higher education—the uncritical import of business models of administration, the erosion of faculty governance, the inordinate difficulty that new Ph.D.s have in securing decent academic employment, the rise of wholly corporate universities—then it is surely the replacement of well-paid tenure-track jobs with short-term and part-time positions. When universities turn to the business world for guidance, the first advice they get is to cut labor costs. Faculty who find themselves losing effective control over key academic decisions to administrators can see both a cause and effect in the small army of adjuncts that complemented and eventually overtook their own teaching. Institutions like the University of Phoenix most clearly differ from traditional universities in their complete lack of a regular faculty. We may not know exactly what the academy will look like in another generation, but if these trends continue we can be certain that it will be full of part-time and contingent teachers.

The use of part-time hires, including graduate student teachers and postdocs, has grown and grown for the last several decades. As a result, a majority of those who now teach in the nation's colleges and universities are paid poorly, have little or no job security, few or no retirement or health benefits, only the weakest of free-speech protections, and no long-term relationship or commitment to a university community or permanent faculty. The long-lamented academic job market woes of fresh Ph.D.s are the most obvious consequences of this casualization of academic labor. It's not so hard to find teaching gigs, even in the most glutted of humanities disciplines, but it's extremely difficult to find a decent long-term job, or even a full-time position at a single university.

But the career challenges of recent Ph.D.s are only the tip of the iceberg. A sustained look at the casualization of academic labor suggests that it is in fact the rot at the heart of the new corporate university system, relentlessly compromising the core values of traditional university life. Those who wish to keep the academy from being entirely remade in the image of the corporation—and those who would merely like to find a decent job waiting at the end of the Ph.D. rainbow—must reverse this trend. And if doing so might be challenging, at least it looks straightforward. Unions, after all, are designed to take bad jobs and make them better. But perhaps the most insidious effect of casualization has been to erode the ability of those who teach in higher education to do anything about it. For the replacement of good jobs with contingent labor has also created power struggles among faculty members.

The Scope of the Problem

Since the advent of the tenure system in the early twentieth century, a mix of full-time tenured and tenure-track faculty, temporary full-time instructors, and part-time adjuncts has done the teaching at American universities. The balance has now shifted, however, toward the contingent end of this spectrum. By the estimation of the Department of Education's National Center for Education Statistics, the percentage of part-time faculty doubled from 22 percent in 1972 to near 45 percent at the end of the century. And this increase has not simply come out of the expansion of the aggregate teaching force. It is not the augmenting of an intact core of tenure-track positions with more disposable labor, but rather the steady slicing and dicing of good jobs into many smaller bad ones. And it continues apace: from 1993 to 1998, even as student enrollments were projected to steadily increase for the next decade or more, some 40 percent of all colleges and universities actually reduced the size of their full-time faculties, often by replacing regular positions with multiple adjunct slots.[1] Even a brief consideration of these numbers is startling enough. Since less than a fifth of positions in the general economy are part-time, they place university teaching, often assumed to be one of the cushiest jobs on the planet, in the ranks of the most casualized of occupations.

What about the tenured sinecures that so dominate the public perception of academic work? Don't most professors have a virtual guarantee of lifetime employment and protection from decades of poor teaching evaluations and scholarly sloth, providing that they can refrain from committing major felonies? Well, actually, no. Life on the tenure track is not nearly so cushy. And in any event, the tenure system encompasses a small and ever-shrinking portion of the academic teaching force. Hirings outside the tenure track have grown so dramatically that today less than a third of those who teach in American lecture halls and seminar rooms are encompassed by the tenure system. The institution is now sufficiently eroded by years of such hiring to be vulnerable to direct assaults. In the mid-90s, for example, Vermont's prestigious Bennington College simply ended the institution, firing 26 of its 79 tenure-stream faculty, including all instructors of foreign languages and literatures, musical instruments, sociology, politics, economics, and art history. The University of Minnesota came close to effectively ending tenure as well, backing away from its plans only after a faculty backlash and a strong threat of unionization.[2]

But the aggregate national statistics and the growing irrelevance of tenure only hint at the full dimensions of the academic employment crisis. The Department of Education's studies significantly understate the number of contingent faculty. By relying on institutional and faculty self-reporting, the study likely misses thousands upon thousands of adjuncts who are virtually unknown to their colleagues. Since so many adjuncts are hired (and fired) at the discretion of department chairs, without a formal search or application, they leave little institutional trace of their work or employment. The gap between the Education Department's data and the results of a similar study by the Coalition on the Academic Workforce suggests some of the difficulties of measuring the numbers and amount of work done by contingent teachers. Where the data reported by institutions themselves indicate that full-time faculty taught 71 percent of undergraduate courses, information gathered by the coalition found that full-timers were doing only 48 percent of the teaching. No wonder that the estimates of adjunct lecturers in the United States ranged from two hundred thousand to more than four hundred thousand. Nobody knows for sure.[3]

And just who counts as a faculty member in such measurements? This is a more fundamental question ignored by most surveys of higher education. Surely an endowed chair who teaches only one or two classes each academic year should be counted, and just as surely an adjunct paid by the course. But what about other instructors, like a graduate student who teaches discussion sections of a large lecture course or who leads her own seminar? This is where the full picture of academic employment patterns grows blurry. There are more than two hundred thousand graduate students who teach in some capacity. If their ranks are added to the calculation of the full-time/part-time ratio, then the numbers start to look quite different: around a third of instructors are on the tenure track, and as many as one half have only part-time positions.

The language used to describe graduate student teaching has not kept pace with the reality that they shoulder a substantial portion of the burden of undergraduate teaching. Most university administrators will tell you that teaching assistants and other student teachers are "apprentices" kindly provided with teaching opportunities as a part of their own graduate education, a tutelage that ends with their happy assumption of the greater duties and rewards of a faculty member. "Most of Brown's departments require teaching experience as a part of the degree," a spokesman for Brown stated in response to a unionization effort by its TAs. "It's deemed to be part of the educational process." Taking this reasoning at face value, the Department of Education reports with a straight face that graduate students taught only a minuscule 1 percent of courses in higher education.[4]

Even a brief look at the scope and nature of graduate student teaching reveals this to be a colossal oversight. An apprentice would teach in or at least close to her field of expertise; graduate teachers are used to meet the demands of undergraduate enrollment. They thus teach far from their fields, and even outside of their disciplines. They teach heavily subscribed courses like history surveys and basic language sections, even though their dissertations (and thus their supposed future job prospects) are far likelier to concern narrow periods and specific bodies of literature. An apprentice in the humanities would theoretically begin with more basic skills, such as grading, would progress to offering writing instruction, delivering lectures, and leading discussion sections, and conclude by teaching his or her own class. In the real world, most graduate teachers do the same basic work, especially the grading and basic language instruction most unappealing to senior faculty, over and over and over.

Most important, the rhetoric of apprenticeship begs the question of why so much teaching is done by graduate students. The simple answer is that they are an easy source of cheap, flexible, and highly motivated teaching labor. Universities' internal documents make this abundantly clear, even as their public stances (and legal responses to union drives by their graduate students) deny it. The "Teaching Fellow Program," reported a Yale University Committee in 1989, "represents a significant fraction of the undergraduates' classroom experience; it is an integral part of most graduate students' education and financial support; and it provides an essential support for faculty in a research institution with a strong commitment to undergraduate teaching."[5] As early as 1976, the university's official historian, George Pierson, noted the "drift away from a full-time professional teaching faculty," represented by the "large fringe of graduate students, lecturers, and visiting faculty who were coming to constitute almost a third of the very substantial corps of men and women now instructing in Yale college."[6]

Since the mid-70s—and perhaps even before—research universities with large doctoral programs have turned to employing graduate teachers to do the work created by rising enrollments and curricular changes. Thus graduate teaching has increased in lockstep with the proliferation of adjunct teaching positions. Although this trend is hard to quantify because it has escaped the attention of most higher education researchers and their studies, university documents provide a clear explanation of its causes. At Yale (where more than a decade of organizing and considerable outside attention have led to greater scrutiny than at other schools), graduate teaching seemed to make up for a lack of tenure-stream faculty as early as the beginning of the 1970s. Consider the following student-faculty ratios:

| | students per faculty member | |
	ladder faculty only	including graduate teachers
1968–69	8.82	7.6
1975–76	11.28	7.7

Continued enrollment growth and curricular changes only exacerbated this trend. "In the late 1970s," stated an internal study of graduate teaching, "a perception at Yale and elsewhere that the level of expository writing had declined sharpened interest in providing both basic and advanced instruction in writing." Who provided this new instruction? "[S]pecial 'Writing Intensive' sections of selected lecture courses across the curriculum [employed] Teaching Fellow IIIs to enhance the writing opportunities of students in those courses." New courses in the English department devoted entirely to writing "are taught by graduate students." Several years later, a foreign language requirement "produced in many of the foreign language departments increases in enrollments . . . [that] created a significant need for the use of graduate student teachers." Instead of hiring more ladder faculty—or even keeping the numbers of faculty positions constant—universities have instead chosen to employ graduate students to teach thousands upon thousands of sections, seminars, and labs. No wonder so many graduate programs have continued to admit Ph.D. students even when unable to secure academic jobs for their graduates.[7]

So an accurate measurement of the part-time/full-time ratio must include the work done by graduate teachers (who, when unemployed after receiving their Ph.D.s, can reflect back on their years of "apprentice" teaching and revel in the delightful irony). An examination of research labor must similarly address the burgeoning ranks of postdocs. Although postdoctoral positions date back to the birth of the modern American university in the 1870s, in the last few decades universities have in effect replaced regular faculty positions with far cheaper and more "flexible" postdocs. The last decade has seen particularly explosive growth: from 1992 to 1999, there was a 20 percent growth in the number of these positions, even as the academy cut the number of regular science faculty (eighteen hundred positions vanished from 1991 to 1995 alone).[8]

Since postdocs have not confronted their employers with organizing drives, as have graduate students, universities have remained more honest about the roles that they serve. "One of the reasons postdocs have become increasingly popular," stated the University of Southern California's president, "is because a postdoc is less expensive than a PhD student—you have to pay the PhD students' tuition plus a $15,000 stipend . . . and the postdoc spends 80 hours a week or more on research while the PhD has to go to class." "There's no question that you get the biggest bang for your buck by using postdocs . . . to fund high-quality research," similarly gushes a Carnegie Institute scientist.[9]

The difficulty of enumerating adjunct faculty and the exclusion of postdocs and graduate student teachers from higher education employment surveys mean that the academic employment picture is darker—probably much darker—than most have realized. A precise measurement of the percentage of faculty who are full-time or contingent employees will require the factoring in of the hundreds of thousands of graduate students and postdocs. This is easier said than done: universities do not keep much of the data necessary, and so will have to be canvassed on a department-by-department basis. The beginnings of such an effort have been made. In 1999, I and other members of Yale's graduate-student union attempted to measure the relative amounts of teaching done by ladder faculty, non-ladder faculty, and graduate students in the university's humanities and social sciences. We measured every weekly classroom "contact hour" between instructors and students in Yale College classes in the previous fall semester. Every lecture, small seminar, and lab or discussion section was apportioned to one of the three categories. Seen from the perspective of the work necessary to make any university's undergraduate classes run—the lecturing, the leading of discussions, the labwork—the use of casual labor is vastly more advanced than generally acknowledged. At one of the nation's premier (and wealthiest) universities, tenure-track faculty accounted for a mere 30 percent of weekly teaching labor, adjuncts 30 percent, and grad students the remaining

40 percent. Merely replacing the labor of its own graduate students would require Yale to hire hundreds of real faculty members. Similar data from New York University showed that teaching assistants accounted for 54.8 percent of all class hours taught in the College of Arts and Sciences, the university's primary degree-conferring school for undergraduate education.[10]

It is when such numbers are extrapolated to the academy as a whole that the full dimensions of the use of casual labor begin to become apparent. How many faculty positions might it take to replace the labor of the more than two hundred thousand graduate teachers? None of the national research or higher education organizations with the capacity to answer this question have asked it, and a national study of undergraduate teaching contact hours by graduate-student unions proved too difficult to coordinate. So nobody knows.

Just how underestimated casualization is will remain unclear until national studies measure the actual work done by instructors, as we did at Yale, rather than tallying the number of faculty positions. Whatever the final result, however, such a measurement is likely to make us all rethink the long-familiar "job market crisis." Most discussions of the prospects of new Ph.D.s lament their difficulty in gaining tenure-track jobs, noting the high number of applicants (well over a hundred) for most positions, and close with an urgent call to reconsider the number of students admitted for doctoral study. The underlying assumption is that once the supply is brought down close to the demand, most Ph.D.s will have no trouble finding tenure-track jobs.

This assumption is terribly mistaken. The job prospects of new Ph.D.s constitute an employment crisis, and have for more than twenty years. (In the 1977–78 academic year, my own father taught eleven courses in eleven months for $11,000, an experience insufficiently lucrative to make him stay in academia). But it should not be called a "job market crisis," because there seems to be plenty of work to be had, even though there is theoretically an "overproduction" of Ph.D.s. Aspiring professors will teach repeatedly as graduate students (and often as adjuncts at other universities in the later stages of their program) and will generally experience little difficulty in cobbling together a set of adjunct gigs into full-time employment. Finding a tenure-track job is the difficult feat.

So the employment crisis—most of it, perhaps all of it—is not the product of the iron hand of supply and demand, but rather the result of universities' decisions to slough off work that should be done by regular faculty onto adjuncts, postdocs, and graduate students. This explains why the repeated predictions of university administrators and senior faculty that the "job market crisis" would be ameliorated by the next wave of retirements, or the next demographic bulge of students, have failed to come true. These hopeful predictions are reminiscent of the old Communist dogma that socialism was just a few years off, a tomorrow glowing but a short distance from the misery and ugliness of the present, or the market utopianism promising that Angola or Argentina can be just as prosperous as Belgium or Japan if only the government will fire a third of its workforce, sell its phone company to a multinational, and privatize its pension system. They assume that we are in the hands of inexorable forces which will eventually work to our benefit if we only allow them to, and are tough enough to take our medicine in the meantime. If they had cared to take a closer look, these Pollyannas would have seen that at the height of the long-awaited baby boom retirements in the mid-1990s, only one out of three tenure-track slots was replaced by another tenure-track appointment. Instead, they urged students to continue flocking to doctoral programs, confident that the market would soon work its magic.[11]

The truth is that as long as there is no force willing to check the willingness of academic employers to take advantage of their own teachers and graduate students, universities will continue to rely on casual labor. Financially pressed institutions, especially the community colleges that current data suggest rely most heavily on casual professorial labor, find faculty compensation an irresistible target of budget-cutting. But the fact that even universities with endowments of billions and billions have such undersized regular faculties indicates that the move away from full-time faculty should be understood as the counterpart to the widespread business practices of downsizing and outsourcing. If your food service is a lean and mean operation run by Marriott and its army of minimum-wage employees, and you've outsourced your janitorial work, what sense does it make to apply a completely different rationale to your teaching or research staff? Moreover, corporations' practice of hiring people as "independent contractors" rather than employees—thereby relieving themselves of the obligation to provide such luxuries as overtime wages, health insurance, pension plans, or unemployment coverage—has an eerie parallel in universities' insistence that graduate students and postdocs are not "real employees" with a legitimate claim to an adult wage or the legal right to form a union.[12]

Life on the Casual Side

If too few adjuncts debate the ultimate cause of their difficulty in finding a regular job, then it's probably because they're busy. Very busy. Although higher education scholars and major professional associations such as the American Physical Society and the Modern Language Association have only recently begun to gather anything beyond cursory information about the salaries and duties of such faculty, there is some information about their status. A comprehensive survey, conducted in 1995 by the newsletter *Adjunct Advocate*, found that "adjuncts continue to be paid an average of just $2,000 per course, and to teach some six courses per year to about 150 students. The average adjunct also works at two institutions each semester, has no job security, no resources for professional development, and usually no health-and-pension benefits." More recent investigations confirm this basic picture, revealing that 75 percent of part-timers are paid less than $3,000 per course and fewer than a quarter have health insurance coverage from their employers. Postdocs are materially better off, generally paid in the low $30,000s and have the advantage of traveling to only one workplace. But less than a third of the top twenty-five research universities provide their postdocs with dental or disability insurance, maternity/paternity leave, child care, a retirement plan, travel expenses for attending conferences, or even life insurance. Since fully a third of science Ph.D.s three to four years out of school (and nearly a fifth of those five to six years out) were still in postdocs, even the relatively better-off science graduates who land a decent job will do so only once they're well into middle age.[13]

Some of these hundreds of thousands of gypsy teachers and perpetual postdocs are no doubt content with their lot, happily teaching a course in accounting or journalism as a refreshing supplement to their own careers. But that so many work for so long for such meager benefits reflects both their devotion to teaching and their yearning for a tenure-track or otherwise secure position. Most of my peers see their teaching and research as as much a calling as a profession. They're reluctant to switch lines of work just because another job would pay more or offer greater security. This devotion, of course, perversely makes them all the easier to exploit. "As long as people continue to work for those wages, and you get quality people," said one foundation director in a frank if anonymous discussion of postdoctoral salaries, "why raise the wages?"[14]

And so a constantly increasing proportion of part-time faculty actively seeks full-time jobs, making competition for these positions all the more fierce. A growing number of these aspirants have Ph.D.s, extensive teaching experience, and even scholarly publications to their credit. " 'Publish or perish' used to mean that one had to publish a monograph or several scholarly articles to get tenure," notes David Allen Harvey, a Ph.D. recently hired into a tenure-track position. "[N]ow it seems to mean that one must have a strong publication track record to get a tenure-track job in the first place." Harvey sees this as a confirmation that hard work eventually pays off—the "door to full-time employment may appear to be locked, but if one pounds on it enough times, it will eventually cave in." It might, but the ballooning qualifications of adjuncts also means that they will spend yet more years of their lives with no job security, no health care, and ridiculously low wages, even after the completion of their "apprenticeship."[15]

You can, of course, make a living as an adjunct. Thousands of people do exactly that for years and decades on end. Jill Carroll, an adjunct lecturer and self-described "entrepreneur" in my hometown of Houston, Texas, goes so far as to assert that the right attitude can easily make a string of temporary appointments into a satisfying and even modestly profitable career. "Adjunct lecturers will not succeed," she chides, "if they perpetually think of themselves as victims of the academy, or the market, or capitalism, or university corporate interests, or whatever." Carroll's annoyingly chipper attitude marks her advice as part of the "free agent" culture of contemporary capitalism. Downsizing and the loss of reliable jobs shouldn't bother us, this line of thinking goes, because they're actually setting us free from the stodgy bosses and stifling bureaucracies that insist on loyalty and demand social conformity. Enlightened new businesses and their "associates" (the preferred terminology for "employee") have embraced the old countercultural mantras of constant change, freedom, experimentation, enthusiasm, and an obsession with newness. So we can give up the gray flannel suit and lifetime employment for a belly-button ring and a series of consulting gigs. Carroll is a strident advocate for the academic version of this free agency. In the end, she asserts, being a successful adjunct is nothing short of liberation: "Freedom means no one institution owns you. You work for yourself, not for them. . . . This is freedom."[16]

Much of the practical advice that Carroll pushes through her company, Adjunct Solutions—build up a core of widely taught introductory courses, live in an area dense with schools, make yourself known to all department chairs and deans, aggressively pursue venues like continuing education and prison courses, and budget carefully—is perfectly rational, even necessary to make ends meet. But her assumptions about the amount of work and the sacrifices required to teach the ten or twelve courses annually that are necessary to generate a decent income are profoundly naive if not downright dishonest. Grading and preparing class discussion for five separate courses, Carroll estimates, will take only thirteen hours a week. Her one hour a day commute time is low for many of us who teach at only one university, and ridiculous for almost all who teach at two or three. (As Alexis Moore's essay in the next section makes plainly obvious, the lack of an effective public transit infrastructure in sunbelt cities like Houston and Los Angeles means that commuting time can't even be spent in desultory and frequently interrupted reading or grading.) Her suggestion that a profitable and secure "free-lance" adjunct career will take only forty hours a week after a few tougher years of getting established allots no time for actually reading books, something that many of us find not only enjoyable but also essential to our craft.[17]

Adjuncts who are not selling career advice are generally less sanguine about the costs of their jobs, as some of the essays in section 2 indicate. Carroll's annual income of more than $50,000 is largely made possible by the fact that four of her twelve courses are taught at Rice University, which pays a whopping $5,500 for each, perhaps twice the national average. No doubt Rice's provision of health-care benefits takes something of the personal edge off of her acknowledgment that "those whose comfort zones have been honed on permanent jobs, fixed income and reliable pension plans" will experience "anxiety" during their efforts at self-liberation as adjunct teachers. The experience of adjunct Keith Hoeller in Washington State is much more typical. After growing tired (and perhaps anxious?) of teaching a dozen courses at multiple institutions for a grand total of $25,000 a year, he managed to find the spare time to file a complaint against the regional university accreditation association for failure to enforce its own standards on overreliance on casual labor. Hoeller is not an extreme case: adjuncts working the equivalent of full-time or more than full-time jobs have been known to qualify for food stamps and to sleep in homeless shelters when attending academic conferences.[18]

The scant material rewards of adjunct labor are stretched even thinner when experienced in the context of significant student debt and the life cycles of young adults. With average time to degree completion rising steadily for decades—thanks in large part to the grim prospects on the job market, and the consequent ratcheting up of expectations for assistant professor applicants—students are taking on more and more debt while in graduate school. By the late 1980s, when the academy finally began attempting to measure graduate student indebtedness, initial surveys revealed that the average Ph.D. candidate left school with around $10,000 in debts. The average, however, masked the balancing effect of students who took on no debt, either because they attended particularly well-funded programs or had access to spousal or other family income. A subsequent study revealed that by the mid-90s, fully 40 percent of doctoral students borrowed an average of more than $21,000. Combine these figures with undergraduate indebtedness and dismal prospects for a good job, and it's hard to disagree with Cary Nelson and Stephen Watt's argument that "today's graduate students will be hit hard by a kind of 'double whammy': not only a difficult time finding a job in the profession to which they have sacrificed close to a decade of their lives but also a decade of repayment that will extend the penury of their student years long into their middle age."[19]

In most fields, spending more than a few years as an adjunct is the kiss of death in the search for a real job. You may as well walk around hiring conventions wearing a scarlet "A." Part of this is a simple matter of caste: incredibly, despite decades of dismal job prospects, hiring committees (made up of tenure-stream faculty, of course) will assume that there must be something wrong with an applicant unable to secure a job after several years of trying. This is widely known, and so many applicants actually eliminate mention of some of their teaching experience from their CVs.

A less perverse but equally inexorable liability is the almost complete lack of support for scholarly research. Very few universities award travel stipends, lab grants, or research funds (to say nothing of paid leaves) to their adjuncts. Even many outside grants require their recipients to already hold a "regular" academic job. Teaching a dozen or more courses over both the regular semesters and the summer leaves virtually no time for research. "The idyllic life of the prestigious scholar that many of us envisioned as we began our doctoral programs," Jill Carroll flatly declares, "is simply not available to most of us." That's not for lack of ability or devotion. "We know firsthand that the adjunct professors being hired today have excellent potential, because they have been our graduate students," writes Joyce Appleby, former president of the American Historical Association. "We have participated in their development as scholars while helping to nurture their love of history and teaching. We also know, if we reflect upon our own experience, that their potential is slowly drained, year by year, without the support for their scholarly development that we have written into our own working conditions." Since an active research program is a prerequisite for most tenure-track jobs, after a few years this potential is likely never to be realized.[20]

Almost all adjuncts face steep financial challenges, very heavy teaching loads, and dwindling prospects for secure academic employment. These burdens, however, are not equally shared across the spectrum of the professoriate. Women and minorities began entering the academic job market in significant numbers about thirty years ago, just when the political economy of higher education headed south. Oceans of ink have been spilled and thousand of little wars fought over affirmative action and higher education's "culture wars." But the specific effects of a widespread casualization on diversity in higher education have received far less attention than they deserve. Though women make up about 36 percent of the full-time teaching force, they comprise just half of the part-timers (more, actually, if statistics included TAs). They are much likelier to receive their doctorates in the most casualized of disciplines, such as English, than in the relatively better-off physical science or business fields. Women are thus more exposed than men to the personal and financial costs of adjunct teaching or perpetual postdoc servitude. Moreover, graduate school and immediate postgraduate employment fill up the years when most couples start families. Given the lack of health-care benefits, low pay, and long hours of adjunct and post-doctoral positions—to say nothing of the still prevalent unequal division of household work—many women find academic work flatly incompatible with childrearing.

Casualization has similar effects on the careers and lives of nonwhite academics. A disproportionately high percentage of African American Ph.D.s, for example, holds doctorates in education, one of the lowest-paying fields. All racial minorities are much likelier to work at two-year colleges, the institutions with the highest use of part-time labor. African Americans, for example, constitute 6 percent of instructors at public two-year colleges, for example, but only 3.2 percent at public research universities. So casualization may be as important a factor as outright discrimination in limiting the prospects for women and minorities to secure a decent place for themselves in the academy. And surely much of the backlash against affirmative action in academic hiring is driven by the desperation created by dismal job prospects for all.

Beyond Academic: The Social Costs of Casualization

In the end it's no surprise that academics suffer from university employment practices, just as people in virtually every other profession have watched secure, full-time jobs be replaced by a string of temporary and part-time positions. More of us face dismal working lives than most of the public, or even most professors, realize. But because higher education serves—or ought to serve—purposes beyond employing witty and talented people, there is reason for deep worry even for those not overly concerned with the fortunes of the coffee-and-Kafka crowd.

Surely one of the reasons that universities exist is to create knowledge and discover information that is socially useful to students and society at large. As long as we live in an industrial economy, we will need advanced technical and scientific knowledge, with all of the "basic" research into more fundamental processes of nature that that requires. As long as society needs to perform complex calculations or build new structures, we need mathematicians and architects. As long as we rely on natural resources, or care about the welfare of anything other than *Homo sapiens*, we need to have biologists and ecologists. As long as we read literature, or place our own lives in the stream of the past, or disagree about politics and policies, we will need the humanities and social sciences. The rub, of course, is that people as a whole don't agree about these things, and experts may disagree more. That disagreement is essential to intellectual inquiry—and in the case of questions that bear on ethics and public life, it is a precondition of a democratic society.

And so free speech is not only an attribute attached to individual academics (or anybody else), but rather necessary to make teaching and research actually serve a purpose beyond the gratification or advancement of whoever's performing it. A school where teachers and researchers tremble in fear that colleagues, administrators, legislators, donors, or even students or the public may disagree with something they write or say in lecture is only the shadow of a university. But most adjuncts had better tremble, if they want to be employed next semester. "The teachers who must go, hand in hand, every year . . . indefinitely into the future, to ask if they may stay," says the American Association of University Professors policy on non-tenurable appointments, "are not teachers who can feel free to speak and write the truth as they see it." The more cautious will "avoid controversy in their classes or with the deans and department heads on whose good will they are dependent upon for periodic reappointment." A blistering course evaluation, a political disagreement with a regular faculty member, a perceived personal slight: any of these can easily get you fired in a hurry.[21]

Professors, of course, have no more reason than anybody else to expect freedom from evaluation or scrutiny of their work. In fact, the tenure system is primarily a way of enshrining professional self-regulation, not of ensuring lifelong employment. Academics should be evaluated only by other experts, the reasoning goes, just as doctors set standards for medical schools and the criteria for the legal practice of medicine. Shifting political fortunes or the arbitrary will of a hostile dean or angry trustee will less frequently interfere with peer evaluation of teaching ability and research accomplishments than in the case of typical at-will employment. Whether there are other viable—or even better—ways of protecting academic freedom is an issue that we address in the conclusion to this volume. But it is clear that the erosion of tenure has grim consequences for free speech and the protection of the curriculum from idiotic "streamlining." At Bennington, for example, the pattern of firings reveals a clear retaliation by the president and board against faculty who had opposed earlier restructuring proposals. Twenty-three of the twenty-six faculty who signed a 1992 petition against the denial of tenure to one of their colleagues were fired after the elimination of tenure, as were prominent faculty opponents of past curricular restructuring. When the University of Minnesota proposed massively altering tenure in 1996, the administration sought to insert a contractual clause that reeks of the big-brother practices of the private sector, where freedom of speech is a joke. Professors could be dismissed or sanctioned, the university proposed, for failing to demonstrate "a proper attitude of industry and cooperation with others within and without the university's community."[22]

If the institution of tenure provides tenure-track faculty with far greater freedom of speech than in almost any other line of work, there is no reason to think that landing a tenure-track job makes a person a better teacher than his or her colleagues who didn't. Indeed, given the heavier weight allotted scholarship in tenure and promotion decisions at leading universities, getting a good job may actually make you a worse teacher. And since virtually all long-term adjuncts do is teach, they're likely to develop their teaching skills more quickly and to adapt them to a wider range of venues. Nevertheless, since adjuncts have no long-term relationship with their employer, their fellow teachers, or their students, an adjunct faculty as a whole cannot mount a first-class curriculum. "It is difficult to develop a coherent curriculum, maintain uniform standards for evaluating students' performance, or establish continuity between and among courses," notes the AAUP, "when major academic responsibilities are divided among 'transient' and regular faculty." How can you have a community of learning, any sense of shared purpose, or the synergy that is at the heart of a great college education, if you don't even have faculty and students who know one another?[23]

The specific working condition of adjuncts makes it extremely difficult to sustain excellent teaching. Grade inflation and other forms of pandering to short-term student interests are a constant temptation, since reappointment often hinges on zero complaints and high evaluations. Schedules are so crazy and teaching loads so heavy that keeping up with new research is difficult. Years and years of falling behind in a field, of course, eventually makes your teaching outdated. Even those instructors fresh from graduate school, who can easily translate current knowledge in their fields into the classroom, must dumb down assignments if they are to keep up with their hundreds of students in multiple classes at multiple institutions. "[T]he challenge for you as an adjunct," Jill Carroll tells her readers, "is to streamline both the creation and the grading of course assignments for efficiency and quality." Specifically, essay questions should "push the students to synthesize and critically evaluate *as well as* make it easy for you to quickly scan for key phrases and ideas in their answers . . . know exactly what you want from the students in their answers, write the questions with that in mind, and then evaluate their answers with a view toward those specific items."[24]

Like the rest of the survival techniques that adjuncts must adopt, these steps are eminently rational. Predictability, uniformity, and hurried "scanning" will make your job easier. But ultimately the logic of efficiency and the logic of education are at odds. Powerful writing is not a simple matter of the ritualistic invocation of key phrases or the process of conforming to a pre-set mold—if it were, the efforts to design computer programs to grade essays might actually have succeeded. Grappling with course material is not the same as regurgitating Carroll's list of specifics. The culture of one educational institution is not the same as another. Nor are student expectations, abilities, or preparedness. Administrators seeking flexible and interchangeable labor must treat their adjunct teachers as standardized production inputs, and these teachers in turn have every incentive to internalize this logic. What this false standardization gains in efficiency, however, it more than loses in educational quality.

Classroom instruction is not the only way that universities teach their students. The institution that encourages vigorous intellectual debates on ethical and political issues, but refuses to release information on its own investment policies, for example, sends an important message about the limits of free inquiry and the "proper" bounds of political questioning. In my experience, students are keenly aware of the status of their instructors. At a prestigious research university like Yale, the strange combination of teaching assistants and academic luminaries sends the clear message that education is only about mingling with the famous and catching some nuggets of wisdom while on the way to a high-paying job with the diploma thus acquired. (And in this job, no doubt they will encounter another servant class awaiting their commands.) At almost all institutions, exchanges with one's peers in a discussion section, learning new techniques in a lab, or struggling over writing are not actually critical parts of becoming an educated person. Why else would poorly paid instructors whom you may never see again be hired to lead them? How could something important happen in venues led by such obviously unimportant people?

This message only furthers the logic of casualization, of course: university education, it suggests, is not about what happens in class, but about what you can do with your credential. Just go to enough classes and do enough work to get your degree (or, at high-powered places, meet the right people): it might land you a better job than the poor schmucks who taught your classes.

The Faculty, against Itself

So casualization creates enormous costs for educators and education itself. But there's something deceptive about dwelling at length on the hard lot of adjuncts and the declining respect for liberal education: it obscures the facts that there are winners—big winners—in the restructuring of academic employment. Despite the focus of this chapter on teaching labor, it's worth remembering that a third of full-time faculty report that teaching is not their primary duty. The time that these faculty spend on research and administrative duties is made possible by the employment of cheap adjunct labor to meet the resulting teaching needs. It is thus no coincidence that the teaching expectations for ladder faculty at eminent universities declined in the late 1970s to the now-standard load of two courses or fewer each semester. This process of substitution is most directly visible when ladder faculty take a sabbatical or other research leave. Their courses are most often taught by adjuncts paid somewhere between $2,000 and $3,000 for each course, a small fraction of the equivalent pay for the person being replaced. And even when more elite faculty are teaching their normal load, adjuncts are most likely to teach the lower level, "basic" courses that are less "sexy" to teach—and further removed from the research agendas of senior faculty. A "shrinking Brahmin class of professorial-rank faculty enjoys academic careers and compensation commensurate with advanced training," noted a conference of ten disciplinary associations a few years ago, "while a growing class of 'untouchable' educational service workers can obtain only poorly remunerated semester-to-semester jobs that offer no career prospects."[25]

The faculty who most directly benefit from the casualization of academic labor are those who teach at research universities with large doctoral programs. Ph.D. candidates do most of the "gut" teaching, almost entirely staffing entry-level composition courses and running the discussion and laboratory sessions (always heavy on grading) of large lecture courses. In these formats, faculty need only deliver lectures (generally already well developed) several times a week, with a minimum of time actually spent with students. Their small teaching loads and the resulting time freed for research and publication are thus directly made possible by the labor of their own graduate students. Once again, university studies prior to the current rash of graduate student organizing were quite open about this point. "[A] number of departments have reduced the number of courses expected of full-time ladder fac-ulty," a Yale committee reported in 1989, "in part in response to the decrease in teaching loads at universities with which Yale competes for faculty." This reduction "has also contributed to an increase in the amount of teaching done by graduate students," it concluded. A Monopoly-like board game developed by a former academic who was denied tenure offers a more poetic description of this dynamic. Various cards—that indicate being published in the "New York Review of Each Other's Books," getting a research grant, or securing a course load reduction—help players advance to tenure, the game's object. Al-though the "most frequently used desirable card is represented by a kiss planted on the rear end of a donkey," a graduate assistant card, which indi-cates "someone to do your work," is also a valuable commodity. But watch out: a "Would you like fries with that?" card, which indicates "that the grad-uate student has left to enter a workforce that has no use for his academic skills," can cancel out your advantage.[26]

The severe bifurcation in the fortunes of faculty members makes it much more difficult for them to respond to the casualization of academic labor. At a minimum, the social gulf between ladder faculty and adjuncts means that the former—who have considerable power within their institutions—are simply unaware of the working lives of their less fortunate colleagues. They may not even know who they are—just the strangers who sometimes use the collective office down the hall, or somebody in jacket or dress they occasion-ally see leaving a classroom. As a consequence, ladder faculty are often un-aware of just how much of the teaching labor of their institution is accounted for by gypsy scholars. "Who are these people?" a senior professor friend of mine wanted to know after we released the results of the Yale teaching labor study. A brilliant scholar and gentle soul, he simply had no idea who was doing a considerable portion of the teaching in his own department.

Sometimes, of course, this ignorance is willful. Many of those on the winning end of the academic class divide know that some of the benefits of their position are made possible by the hard and poorly paid labor of others. Faculty at research universities are particularly aware of the contribution of their teaching assistants, as shown if by nothing else than their loud cries of outrage when strikes confront them with the true workload their lecture courses require. Such knowledge, of course, does not necessarily lead to soli-darity. Corey Robin's article in this collection (chapter 7) vividly demon-strates how faculty at Yale crushed their own students' strike, often in flagrant contradiction of the views they professed in decades of scholarship. Self-declared radicals and liberals were just as likely to join this effort as were more conservative professors, suggesting that the academic "culture wars" of the last decades have obscured the more fundamental academic class divide.

Even when such blatant hypocrisy is not at play, however, the interests of tenure-stream faculty prevent a more vigorous professional response to the use of casual labor. Every discipline has at least one professional association, an organization that publishes a prominent journal in the field, runs a large annual meeting, articulates professional standards for scholarship and teaching, and that often represents the field to the government and the public at large. What these organizations generally have not done—at least not effectively or vigorously—is to address the yawning academic class divide. As Cary Nelson points out in this volume, the "shame" factor and the legitimation of collective action that these associations could provide might be quite powerful. So why have they been so lethargic, in the face of decades of degradation of the craft? Perhaps because of the power of senior faculty within these organizations. Professional associations "have not acted against members who exploit adjunct instructors," writes longtime adjunct P. D. Lesko. "Were they to do so, I am sure that we would see a tremendous outcry from tenured and tenure-track faculty members. Yes, to put it bluntly, they are the ones who benefit tremendously from the use of adjuncts."[27]

Sporadic small-arms fire is more characteristic of the academic class war, however, than are the still infrequent open struggles between adjuncts and tenure-stream faculty. The running friction between the two groups generally takes the form of condescension from senior faculty, or of their outright blaming of adjuncts for the teaching problems created by adjuncthood. Although they are much better off and generally know it, established faculty are also often aware that in the long run they have something to fear from gypsy teachers. They could easily be replaced, after all, with dozens and dozens of enthusiastic and dedicated teachers willing to work for wages far below their own.

Adjuncts, on the other hand, are not in much of a position to take out their frustration on their higher-ups. But much of the disillusionment with the tenure system among younger teachers is the product of their sense that they have as much to fear from their "colleagues" as from administrators. A recent survey indicates that nearly 40 percent of young faculty agreed with the statement that "abolition of tenure would, on the whole, improve the quality of higher education." And who can blame them? Designed to be a bulwark protecting the entire profession from harmful outside interference, the tenure system is instead experienced by some as a pernicious hierarchy within the profession itself, one that gives inordinate power to senior professors.[28]

The widening gulf within the professoriate is an appropriate closing fugue to an examination of the casualization of academic labor. Just as is true of the use of casual labor in the economy as a whole, academic restructuring has benefited some even as it has hurt many. A tenure-track job at a major university today is in many ways a mighty cushy job. Despite the ritual whining of these faculty about their salaries, the idiocy of their colleagues, the ineptness of their administrators, the ignorance of their students, and so on, very few people on the planet exercise as much control over their daily working lives. This shrinking minority of the professoriate works long and hard, but on subjects of their own choosing; they have to be in a classroom or in their office a scant few hours a week. They can teach their classes, most of which are in areas of their own choosing, as they see fit. They have substantial time for their own research and reading—indeed, probably more time than their counterparts several decades ago. Those with tenure can lose the motivation to update their teaching or continue their scholarship with no fear of being fired.

As winners of the academic lottery, perhaps senior faculty members should feel content about the direction of the academy. But with the exception of uniquely smug and dysfunctional faculty cultures at places like Yale, they don't. In the first place, this is simply because they have too many friends, spouses, and students who live on the other side of the academic class divide to ignore the high human costs of the casualization of academic labor. It is also because many see the logic of the corporate university degrade their own work and twist their own students' expectations. But above all, it is because in the end most teachers have a reflexive commitment to the values of liberal education and an appreciation of their emancipatory potential. Most everybody I know who does what I do pursued a career in higher education for the best of reasons: not just that it would land us a cushy job, but that we would work with our students as they struggled to gain basic reading and writing skills, that we would help them open their eyes to new ways of seeing the world, and that we would ourselves discover important new information or techniques.

We do a good job of it, too: people come from all over the world to study with us. What truly rankles those who grasp the monstrous dimensions of academic downsizing is not just that it has made the lives of many of our friends and colleagues so unreasonably difficult, but also that it insults the higher purposes of what we do. This sense of outrage—not of entitlement for ourselves, but of anger at the corruption of our calling—is what will help all professors realize that casualization threatens both the economic security of academics and the dignity of our calling. As graduate students keep rattling the cage, as adjuncts become more mobilized, and as ladder faculty finally wake up and smell the coffee, perhaps we will find that a shared commitment to the value of education can unite us.

SECTION TWO

Laboring Within

As section 1 indicated, the growing prominence of online education, the rise of for-profit universities like the University of Phoenix, the use of corporate management techniques such as merit pay, and the growing use of casual teaching labor are dramatically transforming the academy. Higher education looks and feels much different than it did a generation ago, for students, teachers, and administrators alike.

The essays in section 2 take us into the heart of these transformations, not so much by explaining how they came about, but rather by presenting their human side. They all focus on a number of questions: What is it like to teach in the modern university? What do the increased attention to efficiency and the casualization of labor mean for the workaday lives of hundreds of thousand of instructors? How do new management practices alter relations among teachers? To what extent are teachers and students forced to reconsider the purposes of education and the significance of their role in it?

Kevin Mattson begins by describing his transition from graduate student to adjunct teacher. Like so many who received Ph.D.s in the last decade, Mattson watched the sweeping intellectual ambitions of his graduate study collide with the reality of adjunct teaching. Prepared for membership in an elite guild, where he would steadily climb the ladder from apprentice, to journeyman, and finally to master practitioner, he found himself instead in danger of becoming a permanent journeyman. Living for ideas, the original intention behind getting his Ph.D., gave way to living for work—the constant writing and rewriting of lectures to tailor them for the different institutions, class lengths, and students, the perpetual drives and interminable bus rides. Rather than a liberating example of free-agent enterprise or academic entrepreneurship, his work was just that: work. And not at a particularly dignified or rewarding job. Mattson concludes by arguing that accepting teaching as a form of labor will allow teachers to see their jobs as bound up in a larger political economy, freeing them to unite with others who believe in the dignity of work.

Although his stint as an adjunct teacher has defined the way that Mattson thinks of academic labor, many more teachers must patch together careers and lives out of such fleeting positions. Alexis Moore takes us deep into that world. Like Mattson, she had high hopes for the enrichment that her craft and teaching might bring to her students and her own life. Graduate study and years as an adjunct have made it possible for Moore to train students in art and to practice her own craft. But the low wages and lack of benefits and job security have exacted a high personal and financial cost. Getting to actually know students is difficult when you're only on campus for one or two classes a week, don't have an office, and aren't likely to be back next semester. Collaborating with colleagues on a coherent set of courses is difficult if you never meet the other adjuncts, or if the ladder faculty treat you as though you're in a different caste. Like many on the losing end of the academic class divide, Moore suffered few illusions about her situation. Convinced that she was being exploited, she turned to organizing with her fellow adjuncts. And that is exactly when the terrible logic of casual labor became most evident: not only did she face the predictable opposition of her employers, but full-timers and the union that represented them were also unsympathetic and even hostile. Adjuncts, it turns out, must grapple as much with the ignorance and selfishness of their more fortunate colleagues as with their employers. Casualization has not only deprived talented and devoted teachers of decent employment, but it has made it more difficult for them to organize.

Corey Robin describes another incident of conflict within the ranks of teachers, this time between Yale graduate students and their own faculty advisors. Having become an essential part of their university's academic labor force, graduate teachers were intent on gaining union recognition to address their concerns about class size, teaching conditions, and pay. After administrators refused to honor the results of a union election, they voted to withhold their grades until negotiations began. The tragedy of the grade strike, it turns out, was that senior faculty turned on their own students, writing negative letters of recommendation, blacklisting them, and supporting kangaroo court trials. What began as a confrontation between labor and management ended as a nasty and uneven fight between some of the best-paid and most eminent scholars and their would-be successors. Robin shows how senior faculty came to wholly identify their interests with those of their employer, often in flagrant violation of the principles enunciated over many decades' worth of publications. Even as they articulated what they thought was a "conservative" defense of the traditional virtues of the academic community against the supposedly bottom-line thinking of unionization, these professors in fact acted decisively to crush a major challenge to the effects of casualization on working and teaching.

The last essay in section 2 takes us squarely into the experiences of tenure-track faculty members. Joel Westheimer tells the story of his dismissal from New York University after becoming the only junior faculty member to openly support graduate student unionization. Despite repeatedly strong evaluations and a publication record that earned him numerous internal and external fellowships, Westheimer found previously supportive administrators suddenly cold and critical after he testified on behalf of the graduate students to the National Labor Relations Board. Overruling the unanimous recommendation of both his own department and all seven of his outside referees, the university fired him. Westheimer explains his dimissal as not only an example of the frequent employer use of firings to combat union drives, but as a product of the internal restructuring of faculty governance created by corporatized universities. Administrators, department chairs, and even regular faculty members have all too many incentives to place obedience to the dictates of their higher-ups over academic freedom or even free-wheeling academic inquiry itself. Joel Westheimer found the values of the corporate university to be more and more powerful the higher up the academic ladder he climbed.

The picture that emerges from these essays is familiar in outline but perhaps novel in important respects. After decades of downsizing, the guild argument of graduate training holds precious little water. Graduate teaching is for most people the first of many experiences in the casual academic labor force. Work in this labor force is difficult, debasing, and usually dead-end.

This is bad enough for the tens of thousands of adjunct teachers, and a relatively familiar tale for both academic and nonacademic audiences. But it's only the tip of the iceberg. What these essays also show is how the corporatization of the university has not only diminished the material circumstances of adjunct teachers, but has even more insidiously corrupted traditional academic values. Professors are supposed to take pride in their teaching expertise and to bring their scholarly acumen into the classroom. But if they want to ensure harmonious relations with deans and other university managers, they must stifle any criticism of the obvious fact that hiring a small army of temporary instructors makes it impossible to mount an excellent curriculum. Even scholarly accomplishments, as

Joel Westheimer's chilling story reveals, can become liabilities in more corporatized departments.

The increasing adoption of a corporate model has not harmed all faculty, as we saw in section 1. Alexis Moore's and Corey Robin's discussions of faculty response to organizing drives make this painfully clear. When push comes to shove, the winners of the academic lottery are just as interested in crushing such drives as are the executives of contemporary universities. Corporatization is thus not something entirely imposed from outside the university: faculty are complicit in the transformation of the modern university.

At the same time, even the faculty with the most secure jobs have seen their work deeply affected by the new model for the university. For one thing, the glutted job market has made it easy for universities to demand more work from tenure-track faculty. Standard course loads at teaching-oriented institutions have been increasing, and it is now easy to see jobs advertised with five or more courses a semester. Other institutions have ratcheted up their research expectations for tenure, insisting on a book or book contract, even though several articles would have done the job just ten years ago, and dismissing those who don't meet increasingly stringent standards of scholarly progress after just three years. These heightened expectations have significant ripple effects throughout the careers of young academics.[1] They exacerbate generational tensions, since many professors voting in tenure cases apply standards that they themselves could not have met. Moreover, even Ph.D. candidates must think carefully about the short-term marketability of their research projects. Intellectually ambitious projects that will require more years to come to fruition are now the kiss of death. Gaining tenure does not exempt one from these pressures. Instead, merit pay systems, discussed in section 1, simply perpetuate them.

Teaching itself also bears the mark of the corporate university. Students are now catered to, treated as consumers to be pleased, rather than as budding citizens to be challenged. Admissions offices have become marketing departments, competing for student tuition dollars and high SAT scores not so much through academic rigor, as by offering a variety of lifestyle amenities that have made many campuses, as one professor quips, look like "a retirement spread for the young." Students bring this mentality into the classroom, expecting not so much intellectual challenge and vigorous debate as pleasing and entertaining discourse. "The culture of consumption never criticizes them, at least not overtly," writes Mark Edmundson of his students. "In the current university, the movement for urbane tolerance had devolved into an imperative against critical reaction, turning much of the intellectual life into a dreary Sargasso Sea. At a certain point, professors stopped being usefully sensitive and became more like careful retailers who have it as a cardinal point of doctrine never to piss the customers off."[2] Quantified student evaluations, modeled after consumer surveys and often directly linked to promotion and merit pay, ensure that the supersensitive are rewarded and the overly challenging punished.

These essays taken together indicate the wide-ranging effects of corporatization on the working lives of professors. At the same time, however, their authors are not in full agreement about the aspects of university life that lead faculty members to resist the imposition of the corporate model. Those whose material circumstances are directly diminished—graduate students and adjuncts—have the most obvious incentive to resist the casualization of labor, itself the most obvious effect of the corporate model. And all of the essays imply that a commitment to important scholarship and excellent teaching should lead professors to reject the current transformations of the university, even if many don't.

But what actually makes well-paid professors with job security stand up for their less fortunate colleagues, or speak out about the sacrifice of quality education to bureaucratic expedience? Academics and labor activists offer different answers to this question. Kevin Mattson points to both tradition and novelty; he largely accepts the view of the purposes of higher education inculcated in his graduate training, but wants academics to also acknowledge their craft as work and part of a larger political economy. Joel Westheimer similarly presents his unfair dismissal as part of a larger corruption of teaching and scholarship. Other critiques, however, are less comfortable with the so-called "traditional" academic values. Some scholars locate the depoliticization of academic inquiry—and thus of academics—in the political exigencies of the cold war, though they may recognize that the later hegemony of the corporation has deepened it. For most who would identify themselves with the academic left, the intellectual developments of the last several decades, especially the rise of poststructural analysis, are the main factors which will lead professors to challenge orthodoxy and reemphasize inquiries into ends as well as means. Corey Robin does not explicitly join this conversation. Nevertheless, his discussion of the oceans of hypocrisy that lie between the actions of Yale professors during the grade strike and their left-leaning scholarship implicitly argues with the notion that the New Left's scholarly impact is of any help at all in resisting the corporatization of the university.

How professors might be politicized to challenge the corporate model is beyond the scope of this section. Instead, all of these essays call our attention to the lived experience of the contemporary university, to what it is like to work and teach as a graduate student, longtime adjunct, or tenure-track professor. In so doing, they show us that the transformation of the academy is more profound than most have recognized and has undercut the ability of faculty to resist it.

CHAPTER 5

How I Became a Worker

Kevin Mattson

I'm sure there were more depressing things than coming out of graduate school with a Ph.D. in history in 1994. But at the time, I couldn't think of many. I had heard all the warnings of the "bad job market" when I was in graduate school, but I hadn't realized what an oxymoron the term "job *market*" was. All that talk sounded abstract up to the point of getting my Ph.D. (unlike other graduate students, I had not taught very much as a teaching assistant). But with Ph.D. in hand, it hit me: the restructuring of academic employment, the rising use of graduate students as teachers, the exploding use of adjuncts was now going to crash in on my own life. I put out my applications and got a few nibbles, but no bites. I was told by one person who interviewed me for a full-time position that I had been beaten out by someone who had published four books (all I had was my piddly little dissertation). So I did what most people did then and now: I scraped up as many small teaching gigs as possible. Patching them together into a nice employment "package" with no health insurance or office, I became what was called back then an "expressway professor." It sounded so hip, so futuristic. And so I embarked on the noble profession that was quickly becoming neither.

I had entered graduate school with the pretenses of becoming an intellectual, hopefully free from the snotty connotations that word often carries with it. It meant more than smoking cigarettes in cafes, talking about Foucault and film theory. For me, it meant living for ideas—debating the bigger questions of the day. It meant thinking about things that are too often forgotten about while struggling to make ends meet—questions of ethics, values, and politics in the broadest sense of the term. It meant going beyond figuring out what worked in life—what got us success. As Randolph Bourne, a social critic at the turn of the century and a person who embodied the ideal of a young intellectual, put it, the intellectual life entailed "a restless, controversial criticism of current ideas, and a hammering out of some clear-sighted philosophy."[1]

Of course, being an intellectual requires a great deal of free time, freedom from the pressures of survival. And it didn't take long to discover that, as an adjunct professor, I wasn't so much an intellectual as a worker, albeit it one who worked with his mind mostly. Preparing lectures for classes I had never taught before made this clearest. I plowed through my notes only to find that much of the stuff read during graduate school prepares you poorly for teaching undergraduates, especially those low on motivation, skill, and cultural capital. So I read tons of new, much more basic stuff just to get the requisite information for a lecture. I'd write it up and then edit it so that it could safely fit within the time frame. Because my classes met for different lengths of time (at one institution, I taught an hour and a half class, at another an hour and five minutes, and at another fifty minutes), it was hard to streamline things. Everything had to be written for each individual class, which often made it that much more tedious. The hours taken up by writing these lectures meant that the actual classroom meetings with students constituted the smallest part of my work life. Most of my time was spent in a cramped apartment, writing lectures, often rehearsing them (in hushed tones so neighbors wouldn't think me strange), and reading what I could to prepare for the next lecture.

Perhaps the toughest thing was the grading. Looking back on this, I can't help but remember one of my favorites among the posters that came out of the Yale graduate student organizing campaign. It depicted a young woman sitting next to a large mound of exams, sweating profusely, a look of utter desperation in her face. She was thinking to herself: "This isn't labor, this isn't labor, this isn't labor . . ." Of course, it is: ask anyone who has struggled over a pile of six-page papers written by undergraduates with minimal writing and reasoning skills. What always struck me when I faced a poorly written paper was just how underprepared the students were. And sooner or later, it became evident why: they were being taught by overworked and underpaid adjuncts like myself, precisely those who often tried to help them with their writing but found it difficult to do without an office or time to meet students. Needless to say, if you take the time to try to work with students on their writing, you soon realize that there's really nothing intellectually stimulating about the process. It's just plain work. Unfortunately, I actually liked my students enough to care. I worried about many of my students who wrote so badly that they would undoubtedly flub an application letter. I worked hard at improving writing skills—which seemed not just a prerequisite for getting a job but a prerequisite for being a citizen capable of reasoning and arguing with fellow citizens. So I graded and met with students about their writing. I once spent an hour and a half with a student, going over subject-verb agreement, the difference between a dependent and independent clause, and correct punctuation. We never once talked about the *substance* of her paper—her argument or her ideas.

The thing that struck me most was the unpaid time that eats into your day and consciousness—for example, the driving from one campus to another in a car that you pray won't break down. I quickly learned that "dead time" had to be taken advantage of; while driving, I had to think of my next lecture, the one I had to write that night. Sometimes I'd take buses to get from one job to another, thinking the whole way about my next lecture. The other people on the buses were mostly maids, janitors, and low-paid office workers. That told me something. It felt ridiculous when my students would call me "Doctor Mattson."

I remember one of the more humiliating experiences of this time vividly. It drove home how little control I really had over my work. Hired as an adjunct at a community college, I was to be paid a stellar $1,200 for teaching one course. There was no chance of reappointment, no chance of really anything at all coming out of this, other than a personal i.d. number I could use to make Xeroxes, as long as I was willing to stand in line for a half hour. The course was taught in a downtown shopping mall that had gone ratty. The community college thought that by locating a branch there, it could pick the place up a bit. The school was then on the third and fourth floors, so students could enjoy the fine cuisine of the food court just one floor down or perhaps shop for clothing between classes two floors below. The blurred line between consumerism and education that everyone talks about was not even a line anymore.

I remember the first conversation with the person who had just hired me. "You're probably used to grading pretty difficultly," he practically whispered to me on the phone. "Huh?" I asked. "Well, you've graded at a harder school than this one and you're probably used to a higher caliber student . . ." His voice drifted on without ever coming to any conclusive point. "What are you asking of me?" I asked. "Well, you're probably the sort of grader who gives low marks when the paper you're reading isn't all that . . ." There was the drift again. I shot back: "Are you asking me to inflate my grades?" There was silence; to describe it as awkward is an understatement. Then there was the timid "Yes." The conversation was over.

So there I was in a shopping mall, teaching for $1,200 a course for which my boss told me to sacrifice any sense of ethical responsibility. Then I got a call telling me that an outside person would evaluate my teaching. Now, re-call, there was no chance of getting any other teaching gigs through this in-stitution. Worse yet, the last time the school had hired a permanent faculty member—get this—was *1967*. And now I'm being told that someone is going to evaluate my teaching and that this could possibly stand against me. This was the last surrender of control. The class was not even mine; it be-longed to the bosses who could exterminate my employment anytime (or, more likely, just let the semester run out and wave bye-bye). Who were these people to judge me?

*****

What kept haunting me during this year as an adjunct was my graduate school education. I had always been told that graduate school was a special sort of "training," something like the old guild system of the medieval age or of eighteenth- and early-nineteenth-century America (academics love thinking they live in a world that time has passed by). The system was to work this way: You proceeded from apprentice (graduate student) to jour-neyman (teaching assistant) to master artisan (professor). Unfortunately, my Ph.D. was in history and I had actually read histories of the guild system as it once operated in America. The analogies between my experiences as an ad-junct professor to those of nineteenth-century journeymen made me wince. During the 1820s and 1830s in cities like New York, journeymen found themselves incapable of becoming master craftsmen; instead, their "training" became longer and longer stints of employment and hourly wages, and their only option was to sell their labor to master craftsmen who looked increas-ingly like small factory owners. That never stopped the master craftsmen sit-ting at the top from talking about the virtues of the old guild system, even as they helped to destroy it. The last thing these master craftsmen wanted was for the journeymen to start thinking of themselves as workers and start form-ing unions—precisely what they did, as numerous historians of early labor unions have made clear. As an adjunct unable to find full-time employment in academia (what I had been trained for), I felt as if I was becoming a perma-nent journeyman, selling my labor (teaching) power to others. The appren-ticeship analogy thus ironically fit my experiences all too well.

At the same time, I was reading about professors being paid enormous salaries at some institutions. There were the big names who hit the lecture circuit, demanding exorbitant amounts of money for their supposed words of wisdom. Conservatives like Paul Kenendy and leftists like Cornell West could pull in 10K for an evening of easy work. I would read these stories, and it didn't seem to me that their lives and mine were all that separate. I imagine that the journeymen of yore looked at the most successful craftsmen of the nineteenth century the way I looked at the "rock star" intellectuals of my own time. These professors needed graduate students and adjuncts to do the bulk of the teaching so they would have time to jet around the country talking about radical politics or the new American empire or whatever. These disparities no longer shocked me. They seemed a part and parcel of my own work's degradation.

One of my three jobs was at the institution where I had got my Ph.D. There were professors there who would talk openly about their own past as they watched me whiz in to teach my course. One of them told me about receiving his Ph.D. in the 1960s. He told me he had five job offers out of graduate school, and simply took out a map and decided which place he wanted to live. That was that. When he told me this story, I just stared dumbfounded at him. There really was something like a guild system operating in the past, I thought to myself, some system by which you were trained and then rewarded with almost guaranteed employment. Of course, it was a modern version of the guild system, reliant as it was on a Keynesian–New Deal support of state schools and the famous GI Bill now gone defunct. Nonetheless, there were older faculty who had some memory of a better time—something that made my whole experience that much worse. When there exists something in the very recent past like that, when it can be explained in simple conversations about a person's life, its memory burns all the hotter.

Regular contact with tenured professors drove home the generational aspect of the problem. Here I was, a member of Generation X—a term I hate but use—talking to well-fed baby boomers blathering about their jobs. The more I talked with baby boomer professors, the more I realized that I and my fellow Gen X'ers had missed the bountiful years. As the corporate marketers used to point out, Gen X is the ironic, slacker generation. We're the hip and all-knowing generation that has watched far too much television, becoming jaded about practically everything in life. We're the generation that postpones the "adult trappings" of life, often leaching off the earnings of our baby boomer parents. But really we are the *contingent labor generation.* Irony didn't come from nowhere, after all. Nothing makes you more ironic than working some sucky job; actually, nothing makes you more ironic than being highly overeducated and working some sucky job. Generation X academics are the first to grapple with the brunt of academic employment's restructuring. Just compare us with the baby boomers who trained us. It dawned on me when I was an adjunct that we were really witnessing historical change here—none of which was very good.

Of course, when people undergo a historical labor transition like this, they often look for new ways of thinking about the whole thing. I could have embraced the new philosophy of my generation represented in magazines like *Fast Company*, a rag that started coming out when I was doing my adjunct stint. Writers like Daniel Pink argued that the "organization man" of the 1950s was dead. People were now busting out of that mold and becoming "free agents." It all became a story of liberation—from the gray flannel suits of the past to the energetic, independent, creative *ubermenschen* of the present. Instead of relying upon our employers—let alone the government—to provide us with things like health care or a retirement package, we were supposed to come up with these things on our own by privately investing in the stock market. Job security became an oxymoron. At first appearance, I was something of a free agent or at least "flexible" (another overused term). What isn't flexible about teaching at three different institutions at the same time, taking on all the bit parts I could find, even seeking them out? (Yes, I actually was "interviewed" for all of these positions: the less said about that the better.) But there was no chance that I could actually become a free agent in the deeper sense of that term, that is become empowered (as the trendy language goes), become *truly free*. What was I to do, start up some university out of thin air? I couldn't act like an entrepreneur, there was no capital, there was no possibility. I was stuck. Free Agent blather sounded like a crude justification for restructuring employment such that working as an adjunct became some liberation from the past—a past in which people got health insurance, had offices, felt anchored to an institution where they could nurture relations with students and other faculty, and got paid reasonably well. The talk of Free Agentdom made it sound like I had all the options in the world. But I really had only two options—to organize or leave it all behind. I thought about the first option but then settled for the latter.

Organizing, the ultimate rejection of the free-agent philosophy, was the right thing to do. Weirdly enough, though, it wasn't obvious at first. Though I considered myself a leftist, I had no real experience in organizing for a labor union (I had done community and political organizing but not labor organizing). More important, most of the places I worked would have been extremely hard to organize. For instance, at one school I taught, adjuncts were completely isolated from other adjuncts. It wasn't some Foucauldian conspiracy, it was just that adjuncts rarely met other adjuncts, even when, ironically, we shared offices. The fact was that when I was at one school, my "fellow workers" were at another institution; when they were at that institution, I was at another. It was like working at a workerless workplace, more so because you never knew if an adjunct was going to stay on for the next quarter or semester. You never had a clear sense of the people you should organize. The isolation and anomie were bad enough for your work life; for organizing, it killed all possibilities. "Solidarity" was a joke. When I finally tried my hand at organizing administrative employees five years later at Rutgers University, the experience made clear what was missing as an adjunct. In organizing administrative employees, you simply found out where someone worked and got them at their desk. There was no such thing for adjuncts, at least not if you yourself were an adjunct.

Nonetheless, I started to call around about organizing as an adjunct. During the days that I dreamed about becoming a member of a labor union (but never for too long, since I was always preparing the next lecture), I would drive home and, on my way, pass construction sites that were seeming to pop up all over the city. I'd see what I considered "workers" jackhammering away, the sort of scenes depicted in WPA murals or works of socialist realism. I remembered how as a young guy I had wanted to get in touch with the "working class." Call it a bizarre Marxist youth fad, which it was. So one summer, I unloaded fish off of ships on Cape Cod. I'd haul heavy boxes around with whiskey-swilling workers. It was dangerous and dull work. It soured me on the working class as being anything more than, well, working class. Ironically, here I was now, Ph.D. in hand, and I felt more like a worker than I did in that fish factory. I now knew what it meant to not just work hard but to be fearful that you might not get enough money to make the rent and that this work was truly *your future*—that there was no escaping it. In Cape Cod as a sixteen-year-old, I knew I could go back home and find comfort. Now things were different.

But there was still a barrier between me and the construction workers. I knew that. I could speak proper English; I could sound "sophisticated." I didn't work with my hands. I was *white collar*. Needless to say, the difference seemed, well, marginal now. Sure I was white collar, but then again so was my mom. When she got divorced—"displaced housewife syndrome," they called it back then—she took her B.A. and got a job doing social research. It was high-skilled quantifying work, the tabulation of statistics and the correlation of large data sets—white collar work par excellence. And she was making five bucks an hour. She slaved away. I remember her coming home and complaining about the same sort of bosses that I could imagine these construction workers complained about.

*****

I spent only a year doing that adjunct stint, leaving at its close for slightly brighter prospects. Nonetheless, that year of work has defined the way that I think of academic labor ever since. After I left those gigs, things became a bit clearer. After all, there was a slight resurgence of the labor movement with John Sweeney's ascendancy at the AFL-CIO. In 1996, academics at Columbia even put on a "teach-in with the labor movement." Eventually this gelled into the organization known as Scholars, Artists, and Writers for Social Justice (SAWSJ). Some of the original organizers wanted to return to some sort of Popular Front alliance between workers and thinkers—two sectors of society that they saw as separate from one another. At the original Columbia teach-in (which led to numerous other ones), baby boomer academics sweated as they thought about how they could "help" unions organize. For instance, the sociologist Norman Birnbaum pondered the connections between "intellectuals and unions." He explained that there were some "general conditions under which intellectuals were induced to ally themselves ... with the labor movement." One such condition was "some form of systematic economic or spiritual distress affecting the educated directly." As this baby boomer academic saw it, such a condition was "lacking."[2] When I read these words, I practically hemorrhaged. And I kept hearing it again and again from the leaders of SAWSJ—*how can we help the labor movement*, they would ask, as graduate students and adjuncts in the audience scratched their heads. These baby boomer scholars who wanted to help out John Sweeney were clueless; none of them realized that all they had to do was walk out of their offices, down the hall, and help adjuncts organize into a union. At the least, they could discover that there really *was* "some form of systematic economic distress affecting the educated directly."

After I came to Rutgers University, I helped out on a botched campaign to organize administrative employees, of which I was one. The weird thing was that Rutgers had a union for "custodial" employees and even for professors, including adjuncts and graduate student TAs. The administration kept referring to us as the "non-bargaining" unit—one of the most bizarre and humiliating appellations I could imagine. This group of employees was quirky because it included everything from highly educated workers (research directors with Ph.D.s) to secretaries. The university had decided to cut back on standardized raises, instead implementing merit pay and thereby encouraging everyone to compete for raises from what was a smaller and smaller pot of money. Plenty of people were pissed. At least this time, I could find my fellow employees sitting at their desks and cubicles. But I was startled by a question many of them asked before they would sign a card to hold an election: "We're not going to become a part of that labor union that represents the janitors, are we?" God forbid, I would always think to myself, that we librarians, research directors, and secretaries would actually consort with such trash—that was always the not-so-hidden message behind these comments. We lost the campaign, and I realized something then: It's never going to be easy.

It was even harder trying to explain to people outside the university why we were trying to organize. Most of them would lift their eyebrows and snort something about how people in the state university had it easy. When I talked about how the administration was gutting reward systems and, in my humble opinion, lying about what they were doing, someone would inevitably make some comment about children in sweatshops. It seemed almost impossible for me to explain what we were up to without sounding as if I was *whining*.

I see things differently now. It's 2002 (the dot.com bubble has burst) and more people are waking up to the fact that just because you're white collar, educated, or a brain worker doesn't mean things are easy. Just read Jill Andresky Fraser's *White Collar Sweatshop*. You can get it all here: the longer days, insidious "rankings and ratings" done at workplaces, unpaid time (cell phone calls on the train home), lack of health insurance (or just plain bad insurance policies), rise of contingent labor, and a decline in loyalty toward the workplace that these things prompt. When I read the book, I immediately thought back to my adjunct days. Fraser also talks about how the American Medical Association tried to organize medical doctors into unions so that they could better fight the degradation of care within health maintenance organizations (HMOs). She discusses how skilled technical workers went on strike at Boeing. Hell, even the "permatemps" at Microsoft—those contingent laborers denied full-time benefits but working full-time hours—are organizing a campaign. Organizing adjuncts and future adjuncts (graduate students) doesn't seem all that weird or exceptional any longer. It seems perfectly sensible.

In thinking about this, I am reminded of how during the 1930s, Marxists were getting quite excited about the "proletarianization" of the white-collar classes. Social critics like Lewis Corey thought that as white-collar workers woke up to their exploitation and fall from grace, they would identify with the working class and rise up in social revolution. Marx was right, he suggested, the revolution really *was* around the corner. Well, I can't think of a time when the professoriate has been more proletarianized than today. But Corey's prediction seems as silly now as it was back then. Adjuncts aren't going to unite with janitors and seize the state anytime soon. I'd really prefer that they not think about seizing the state, to be honest. I'd rather they see that they often face the same plight in life—employers who would like to pay them as little as possible—and then partake in a long-term reformist struggle to improve the lot of all workers.

A sense of humility on the part of adjuncts and other white-collar workers facing tough times would be a good start to this process. We need to face
the reality that we *are* workers and should be able to understand that others
also lack control in their work lives and feel unrewarded for the work they
do. If we did that, I'm sure many Americans could understand our plight,
since it's so many other people's plight. By speaking of ourselves as laborers,
academics might even be able to renew an idea that is increasingly threatened—the old American belief that all work is dignified. Though the populist language of a commonwealth of producers seems to have been
consigned to the dustbin of history, most Americans still believe that work
should be rewarded and that productive labor helps create a better society.
Academic laborers can help renew this idea by expanding our conception of
work to include that which takes place in higher education institutions and
serves the public. In the end, we're all in this together.

CHAPTER 6

The Art of Work in the Age of the Adjunct

Alexis Moore

For as long as I can remember I have loved to paint and draw. Throughout my college years I pursued the visual arts—painting, drawing, photography, and art history. My experiences with certain professors helped me to define my path as an artist and later on as an art teacher. While enrolled as an art student at the University of California at Santa Barbara in the late 1970s, I was advised by one professor in particular to investigate the art world of Los Angeles. As my studies advanced, my interest in art-making only grew stronger. I was developing my own hand, finding my own voice. The same professor encouraged me to apply to graduate school in visual art, assisting me in creating an entire body of new work for a portfolio. During the early 1980s, art and the politics of the times drew me into making large sculptural "installations" (using a gallery space, props, sound, and/or video) to make visual statements. I left the paper and canvas behind for a less tangible kind of artwork.

I had never thought much about making artwork just to sell it, however, and therefore I needed to find alternatives to make money and to pay the bills. Graduate school gave me the opportunity to continue making art and, at the time, although I had not thought much about teaching, getting a master's degree in art could open up this possibility. I naively thought it could also lead to the ability to get work at a living wage. Two decades later, that goal is still a struggle.

In retrospect, I see that the working life of graduate school should have given me an indication of what lay in store. In 1980 I moved from Santa

Barbara to a warehouse and studio space in downtown Los Angeles to attend graduate school at UC Irvine. I was given a teaching assistantship, working for an art historian. I can recall my first real experience teaching as a graduate student, when the professor I worked for called me on a Saturday morning, just three weeks into the term, to invite me to lunch. I was suspicious, naturally, because such requests usually meant I was going to be asked to research something, or do "extra" work. But, as most graduate students, I was at her beck and call. (I used to drive her to campus, some forty-five miles, while she sat in the back of my 1969 VW van and worked.)

When I met her that Saturday, I noticed she had a large manila envelope in tow. Upon sitting down, she dumped the envelope, containing more than one hundred slides, onto the table, and announced that she was off to New York for two weeks to do some research. These were the slides I could use to augment my lectures. I thought, at the time, why can't I go and do the research in New York and you stay and teach. Well, needless to say I don't remember much about lunch that day. My head was spinning with the work I had to do to prepare. I had never lectured before, and this class had more than one hundred and fifty students, was in a large lecture hall, with a stage and microphones. Remember, I was a studio artist, not a student of art history.

Looking back, I suppose I could thank this professor for giving me my first experience teaching, with little time to worry about it or, for that matter, to even get nervous about it. I did fine, and in retrospect actually enjoyed the experience. What I never imagined was that this surreal experience would be the first in a long career as an artist who does academic piecework to survive.

Upon graduating from UC Irvine with a master's in fine arts, I was invited to return to the university as a part-time lecturer. I was still living in downtown Los Angeles, and by this time, having blown up the engine in the old VW bus, I was driving an aqua-colored 1965 Mercury Comet station wagon. I remember commuting to class through the downtown "slot" in the summer with the heater blasting in 90-degree air so the old car wouldn't overheat. I jumped at the chance to teach at the university and to gain the experience I needed for pursuing my own teaching jobs. For five years, I taught foundation and intermediate drawing classes in the painting and drawing department at the university. Little did I know that the driving had only just begun.

After leaving Irvine, I decided to try to get a teaching job at one of the many colleges in the Los Angeles area. It was clear that adjunct teaching was not going to make me rich—how could it, at just $2,800 per class?—but it was better than working as a waitress or for an art-moving company. I successfully landed my first job at a community college, where I was able to teach one class. I wanted more, of course, but in the community college system in California, part-timers can teach only 60 percent of a full-timer load. Working more than that would qualify them for benefits and access to a full-time, tenure-track position. In my area of studio art, classes meet for five or six hours per week. Since just two classes puts us close to the 60 percent limit, most community colleges limit art teachers to one class. This is just the sort of trick that companies like Wal-mart have honed to an amazing degree—making health-care benefits depend on working a certain number of hours that are never quite obtained.

The Endless Commute

I have often thought if I were to run into someone on the freeway, it would probably be another part-time colleague going to her next class. There are thousands and thousands of us. According to current data from the Community College Chancellor's Office, there are 36,900 part-time faculty and only 16,860 full-timers in the state's community college system. Because we are limited in the number of hours we can teach at a single institution, we must take teaching jobs at several schools. So "bumping" into a colleague is a real possibility. Many of us teach at up to five institutions a semester. I have headed out to a class only to realize that I was going to the wrong school on the wrong day.

What began as a necessity soon became my life's routine. I applied for full-time teaching jobs, but the prospects of landing a tenure-track position in the mid-1980s were extremely remote. Not much full-time hiring was going on, especially in the visual arts. So I taught one or two classes and used the rest of my working time for my own art. I also had a low-paying part-time job as a designer for a picture framer, which proved to be somewhat more stable than the teaching jobs I was getting. I settled into the pattern of having to wear several hats, and driving and driving and driving, in order to make a living wage.

If you think that you might like this type of migratory work, living in a place like Los Angeles provides the perfect setting. L.A. County alone is more than two thousand square miles and has an extensive web of hundreds of miles of freeways. Crisscrossing the freeways, I have taught at six community colleges, two universities, and two private colleges, in Los Angeles, Orange, and San Bernardino Counties over the last seventeen years. Although officially a part-timer, usually, I have taught up to eighteen hours a week in the classroom, far more than the equivalent of a full-time load.

Working at as many as four different schools in one term, I have taught as far away as fifty miles and as close to home as four.

In the process, I have become a road warrior. In 1995–96, for example, I drove more than a hundred miles twice a week in order to piece together work at three area colleges. I covered a giant triangle throughout the day: heading to a morning class while eating my breakfast; to an afternoon class, at a different college, while eating my lunch; and to a night class at yet a third college, while eating my dinner. I figured out how to eat yogurt, drink a hot liquid, and tune in the traffic updates while I drove. I became experienced at avoiding heavy traffic on certain freeway interchanges during peak traffic hours, often reading my map book to find alternate routes. Once, after finishing a class at 10:30 P.M., some fifty miles from home, I found the freeway had been shut down for some unknown reason. The bumper-to-bumper traffic was routed off the freeway, and after driving in these conditions for twenty miles out of my way, I arrived home at 1:30 A.M.

Working for Dignity

Because of the nature of this kind of transient teaching, "part-timers" like me face a complex set of issues that differ from the lot of full-time faculty who teach at a single institution. Some of these issues are logistical: having too many keys for departments and classrooms (which often have to be turned in and reissued every semester) to calendars that do not coincide with one another. Several years ago, for example, I taught at two colleges where, for four years in a row, I could never take a spring break completely off because the sessions didn't coincide from school to school. Examination schedules overlap from one school to another, which can make being at all of them difficult or impossible. The trend toward a shorter semester with "inter sessions" at the community colleges further bungle part-time faculty schedules. We have to pass up certain teaching opportunities because of conflicts with calendars at different schools. This trend seems purely economic for the colleges, which are able to offer more classes to more students, in a fast-track, diploma-mill fashion. Like other issues, however, this one is driven by divisions among faculty members. Many full-time instructors want this compressed schedule because they can teach more classes in a shorter time and make more money. The outcome is that part-time faculty will be bumped from classes, and so the gap between the academic classes will further widen.

Faculty guidelines, deadlines for paperwork, keys, and parking restrictions are only a few of the added job-related issues that part-time faculty must understand and keep sorted out each semester at each institution. Another is the many payroll deduction plans for retirement. In California there are several plans, depending on the college or university. I currently have accounts in four different retirement plans. The regular change in employers requires numerous phone calls and massive paperwork.

Part-time faculty are not compensated for any teaching-related activities done outside of the classroom, even tasks like writing letters of recommendation, reviewing portfolios, or helping students with applications. Once someone asked me to write down all of the "extra" tasks that I perform. I came up with a list of fourteen items in my field of studio art, everything from displaying student work in galleries to graduate student critiques (I had taught some grad classes as well). Often we can't do these so-called "extras" because we simply don't have any space to work with students. One of my current jobs provides office space, with a whopping one hour per class of paid office time per week. I am even given a telephone—but must share it with seven other part-timers. There is no voice-mailbox so students can leave messages. Even this is remarkable. At the six community colleges I have taught at I have never had an office space, even to share. Once a dean at one of these institutions came up with the bright idea that he would give the part-timers "access" to telephone voice-mail so students could leave messages. Part-time faculty were asked to use a telephone in the art office (or you could access it from home) and dial a personal code to access the system.

Many of us refused to give out the telephone numbers to students, not because we didn't want students to call us, but because it amounts to doing work outside of the contract, for which we are not paid. In a large metro area like L.A., a subsequent issue also arises for faculty who live outside of the local dialing area. If they call from home, they would be charged long distance and thus would actually end up *paying* to do this extra work. E-mail accounts for adjuncts run into similar problems: answering e-mail is a job-related task, and our students should be able to rely on instructors to stay in touch. But whereas full-timers are compensated for such work, we are not. Every time a part-timer does any of these things, and does them for free, she is essentially subsidizing this exploitive system. Not only are we cheap—we are often working for free.

Most of the means by which full-time faculty can seek redress for their grievances are not available to adjuncts. We don't sit on university committees and are generally unlikely to have personal relationships with administrators or department chairs. While full-time faculty may be able to address work-related issues through their unions, part-time faculty concerns are often not represented at all by collective bargaining agreements. We are likely to belong to multiple unions but to receive few benefits from this representation. Currently, for example, I am a member of two faculty unions, paying total dues to both. While I feel it is necessary to join and maintain membership in a union, this cost, for part-time faculty, can be quite high, especially if you work at several schools with different union representation at each. Many part-timers never join unions because it is just too expensive.

After years in the trenches, many part-timers grow tired of the low pay, endless commute, and lack of basic respect from their employers. But we often don't know what to do about it. Many of us are new to the teaching profession and are afraid lest our concerns and complaints fall on deaf or unsympathetic ears. Often as not, our full-time colleagues stifle any complaints. "Put up and shut up" and "you should be happy you have the work" is the prevalent attitude. Many of my colleagues, even though they may have been teaching for years, try to steer clear of ANY interaction with other faculty or administration types. And many won't join the faculty union out of similar fears. I have been told by full-time faculty to "be careful" because the dean and college administrators know who is in the union because they control the payroll deductions for union dues through the accounting office.

Such scare tactics, however Neanderthal, do provide some part-time faculty another reason not to join the union. Furthermore, the slender prospect of full-time employment may be held over your head to make you shut up. Hiring committees are staffed by full-timers, and if they see you as a "complainer" you will have no chance. They even have input into much of the part-time hiring that takes place.

Behind all of these fears lurks the simple fact that we can easily be put out of work. For part-timers, an assignment or load sheet does not offer a guaranteed job. The conditions under which a part-time faculty member takes an assignment may vary from college to college, but generally, the agreement is contingent on many circumstances: *if* the schedule isn't changed, *if* enough students enroll in the class, *if* a full-time faculty member doesn't want to teach this class, or *if* enrollment doesn't drop below a set number by first census. You could also lose your job if someone in the department or administration finds another instructor thought to be "better." The school can simply decide to replace you then and there, without cause, and with just a few days' notice.

Even once you've been assigned a class, most colleges have the right to let part-time faculty go at any time and for no reason. Why? There is no due process for part-time faculty. Administrators don't have to give us a reason for letting us go. Unless a full-time faculty committee or a considerate dean uses a (usually unwritten) system of seniority for rehiring of part-timers, we are randomly plugged and unplugged from the system. And in fact few colleges use a seniority or "careful consideration" clause when hiring part-time faculty. We are disposable and vulnerable.

Organizing and Its Challenges

In 1999, after years of feeling like an outcast and growing wary of the migratory nature of the part-time teaching profession, I had the opportunity to meet a handful of like-minded adjuncts at a local community college. Like me, they were tired of being exploited by unfair pay and denial of benefits, among other things. This amazing group of five or six people began holding meetings on campus, and I went to one. I immediately felt as if I had finally found my long-lost sisters and brothers.

The administration at this particular community college is known for not budging on faculty pay issues. Part-timers had very low hourly pay, no health benefits, and no paid conference hours. This is a unionized campus, but rather than being part of the solution, the union was a big part of the problem. The college has a history of a low faculty participation in the union on campus; in early 1999 there were more than 1,250 faculty (about 900 of them part-timers), but fewer than 225, 15 of whom were part-timers, were union members. Union leaders had an overly cozy relationship with the administration. Reelected for twenty years straight, they kept the faculty in the dark, kept the dues very high, and discouraged joining in order to protect their own position. Over the years, from time to time, pockets of faculty tried to change the union board but were stonewalled at every turn.

The group that was trying to change the situation on this community college campus consisted of five or six part-timers and a couple of helpful full-time faculty. Our job was formidable: we had a hostile union to contend with, could rely on only a few full-time faculty to support us, and were up against an entrenched administration that had no interest in addressing our needs. If we could gain power, however, we knew that our working conditions could be substantially improved. The college's faculty pay was among the lowest in southern California, but was in one of the richest districts in the state.

Our small group didn't even know most of the other part-timers. So we decided that the first priority was to survey them, to find out who they were and what their priorities were. The responses were not surprising: pay equity, office or conference hours, health benefits, seniority, and rehire rights were the most important issues. We paid out of pocket for the survey and spent hours distributing and tabulating the results. We delivered an in-depth proposal, including an equity chart, to the union leaders. They responded by sending us a memo scolding us for doing this and, further, told us they would reimburse us for our printing costs if we would deliver to them the raw data from the survey. We ignored this request. They had refused our many attempts to meet with them, or even to give us the names of part-time faculty union members. The union even kept its budget secret from us. Our group also began to address the board of trustees at this time, trying to educate its members to our needs and concerns. We continued to meet regularly and planned an effort to lower the dues through an initiative to the union constitution.

We also reached out beyond our campus, researching union dues at other community colleges in the area, and corresponding with the state level of the union. During this time, we managed to raise membership of part-time faculty in the union significantly, although the dues were still very high. The local opposed us at every step of the way. It denied our request for membership cards and tried to block us from distributing information to faculty through faculty mailboxes. We again ignored the union and proceeded with our plans. In an effort to educate students and other faculty on campus, we staffed an information table in the college quad for a week and compiled more than three hundred student support signatures on our behalf. We also started the Coalition News, a newsletter about our efforts, and distributed it campuswide. We joined the faculty senate and began to report to it on part-time faculty issues around the state.

In October 2000 the district sent a memo to full-time faculty—it didn't even bother to inform adjuncts—with its final offer in contract negotiations. Needless to say, it included no gains for part-time faculty. Meanwhile, we went to the Public Employment Relations Board (PERB) to request records to inform us about the finances of the local union.

The combination of the school's intransigence and our organizing efforts led faculty to demand changes from the college and the union that was supposed to be representing their efforts. Many faculty, both full-time and part-time, were beginning to grow short on patience with the college administration. We tried to turn up the heat at every step. When a student supporter researched and wrote a lengthy paper on the financial inequities at the college, the administration forbade him from distributing leaflets with the key facts and information. We publicized the repression in local and national media, including the *Chronicle of Higher Education*. Later that same month, in an effort to bring further attention to the situation, the staff, faculty, and many students marched and drummed around campus in protest of the failed contract negotiations. Many of us began to show up at the board meetings en masse.

At the same time, we also pressed our case to the union. During a lunch-hour rally, our part-time group launched our dues-lowering initiative. Union officers tried to prevent several faculty from signing our petition. One union representative told a faculty member not to sign and blocked me physically from talking to him. Although the initiative was technically un-successful, the union later decided to lower the dues anyway. We had be-come too powerful to ignore altogether.

Mounting this effort on one campus made us all aware of efforts under way elsewhere in California. Later that semester, the Part-time Faculty Committee held a meeting of the California Part-time Faculty Association (CPFA) at our campus. The CPFA educates faculty in California on legisla-tive affairs related to the part-time temporary faculty in higher education. The organization's insights and e-mail capacity has helped our own efforts. Its meeting brought local politicians and advocates for part-timers from around the state to our campus and focused further attention on our specific problems.

Although contract negotiations went to impasse near the end of the school year, in May of 2001, elections were held on our campus for certain positions on the executive board of the union. For the first time in the his-tory of the college, a part-timer was elected to the board. Although part-time membership in the union is still quite low, and we know that we still have a lot of work ahead of us to organize more part-timers, it is gratifying to see the victories that we have won. The new leadership seems open and more democratic. Our committee continues its work.

*****

Decades after driving my advisor to her classes, I still fly on the freeways of Southern California to teach art at multiple institutions. The drawbacks of this path are all too obvious. I still have to pay out of pocket for my health insurance. I still have low pay and no paid office hours at the community college where I have taught for seven years. I still must work at other jobs in order to make a living wage. I have a car which has more than 155,000 miles on it. The many hours of union work bring me no monetary composition.

But my career is not without its rewards. Despite the degrading attitude of my employers and all too many of my full-time colleagues, the teaching itself has always been rewarding. It has made me a better artist and has given me the satisfaction of helping others to discover and develop their own abilities. I frequently receive cards about the art exhibitions of former students, and it is deeply moving to have a former student return to show me his or her new work. Now that I have made common cause with so many other part-timers, I have yet another reason to keep struggling to steal some respect for my work.

CHAPTER 7

Blacklisted and Blue
On Theory and Practice at Yale
Corey Robin

And this is it—this is Yale, he said reverently, with a little tightening of breath.

—Owen Johnson, *Stover at Yale*

On December 7, 1995, graduate student teaching assistants at Yale University voted to go on strike. If Yale did not recognize their union, the TAs would not hand in their final semester grades. Since its beginning in 1990, the fledgling union had been a periodic irritant to the university, jabbing the campus with short strikes and mass demonstrations, extracting discrete concessions, but never winning full union recognition. From its long history of opposition to organized labor, the university had learned that the best strategy to counter unions was to affect a posture of Olympian disregard.[1] Like a great Saint Bernard lumbering through the alpine snow, Yale fixed on its distant goals—a $1.5 billion fund-raising drive and a gradual reduction of full-time faculty and staff—never appearing to cast a sidelong glance at the passing protest or occasional picket. In fact, so indifferent to student unrest did the university seem that the union's greatest fear going into the grade strike was that the administration would not respond at all.

The TAs miscalculated. Awakened to the possibility that graduate students might at last establish a union on campus, the university vowed to crush the strike. Faculty and administrators threatened to block striking TAs from ever again teaching at Yale. The administration announced that faculty advisors should feel free to use students' strike participation against them in letters of recommendation. The university brought three union leaders up on disciplinary charges, which carried the possible penalty of expulsion; since two of the three activists were foreign students, this meant probable deportation. Almost immediately, the strike began to collapse, and on January 14, the day the university had set as its final deadline for the TAs to hand in their grades, the union ended the strike.

Both the grade strike and the university's response to it have since been overtaken by subsequent events, particularly the successful and near-successful graduate student organizing drives at NYU, Columbia, Brown, and other universities.[2] But for participants in the grade strike—I was the lead organizer of the union at the time, having taken a leave from my graduate work in the political science department—and for those who worry about academic freedom, Yale's efforts to defeat the strike, particularly its threat of negative letters of recommendation, remain something of a mystery. How was it that a university renowned throughout the world for its traditions of liberal learning, humane politics, and thoughtful interchange could have resorted to blacklisting? How could French professors Denis Hollier and Chris Miller, literary critics who have written sympathetically about poststructuralism and postcolonialism, have signed and sent a letter to their students stating that strike participation "could legitimately be taken into account in faculty evaluations of a student's aptitude for an eventual academic career"? How was it possible for teachers and scholars to violate basic academic norms, outlined most clearly in a 1970 statement of the American Association of University Professors: "Evaluation of students . . . must be based on academic performance professionally judged and not on matters irrelevant to that performance, whether personality, race, religion, degree of political activism, or personal belief"?

Not only did the Yale professoriat break all the rules of academic fair play, but it also threw off the stylistic strictures that normally govern academic conduct in the Ivy League. Literary scholars and intellectual historians who pride themselves on their detachment and individualism, on their good taste and idiosyncratic sensibilities, rushed to join the militant ranks of union busters. Shy bookworms turned into holy warriors, quiet skeptics into defenders of the faith. Though the response to the grade strike certainly had its rational components—the TAs, after all, were threatening the university with an unprecedented challenge—there was something emotive, almost unbalanced, about the faculty's actions. Theirs was no mere effort to stop a strike; it was a playground crusade by men and women who in other circumstances would have avowed their commitment to tolerance, genial discussion, and reasoned disagreement.

The faculty believed their reaction to the strike was entirely justified, a legitimate response to a tactic that was, in the words of one political science professor, an "abomination." The grade strike, they claimed, denied undergraduates their right to a grade, earned through hard work and tuition payments. Unlike a regular teaching strike, the grade strike held the university hostage to a "terrorist act," in the words of another professor. It was not a strike at all (few professors or administrators made this argument at the time, but this was how the university later defended its actions in court); it was an act of theft, a piece of perhaps brilliant but undeniably vicious industrial sabotage. One didn't argue with terrorists; one defeated them.

And yet, however deeply felt, this assessment of the grade strike's illegitimacy does not fully explain the faculty's actions. Besides the fact that few professors made such a claim during the strike itself, it doesn't quite jibe with what everyone in academia knows about the normal practice of grading. As the TAs pointed out at the time, professors usually pay little attention to grading and recommend that their TAs not waste their time doing it. One professor in my department told his TA to read only the first page of her students' papers, while another expressed to me his surprise that I spent much time grading at all. Grading is a burden happily relinquished by the faculty, which is why TAs invariably do it. Moreover, during the strike itself, several professors coped with the sudden shortage of hands by making up their students' grades. Some professors handed out three-by-five cards in lectures, asking students to write down the grade they thought they deserved, which professors then assigned as final grades. Other professors assessed students solely on the basis of their midterm grades. Given this long-standing and makeshift cynicism about grades, why was the Yale faculty so exercised about the strike, particularly when the administration could have easily solved the problem by simply recognizing the union?

But if the faculty's reaction to the grade strike cannot be explained by their heartfelt opposition to an unsavory tactic, was it merely, as some have suggested, a defense of their material privileges, an altogether predictable response of the powerful to the powerless? Isn't Yale just another company in a company town, doing what corporations always do in the face of strikes? Every year there is a strike somewhere in America broken by illegal and illiberal means. When menaced by the concerted action of their employees, what employers don't resort to desperate, often invidious, measures? Why should we expect Yale to act any differently from a textile mill in North Carolina or a hotel in Las Vegas?

But whatever their similarities, a university is not, in the end, a factory or a hotel; it may be obsessed with money and power, but it is also obsessed with Joyce, Eliot, and Pound. Like so many elite universities, Yale claims to represent something higher, nobler—its motto is *lux et veritas*, light and truth—and the preferred instruments of a plant manager in Ohio somehow seem out of place amid the translucent marble of the Beinecke Library, which houses everything from a Gutenberg Bible to the letters of Langston Hughes.

And yet, perhaps it is the very presence of these relics of high culture at Yale that ultimately explains the university's response to the grade strike. Imagining themselves the beneficiaries and custodians of a cultural patrimony extending back to ancient Greece, the Yale faculty believed that they were not merely defending their power against an upstart union. They thought they were engaged in a pitched battle between Western civilization and its enemies. In ways the TAs never quite appreciated, the grade strike was more than a clash about contracts, hours, and benefits; it was a struggle over Yale's grandiose self-conception, its fantasy of the relationship between itself and high culture. The striking TAs were telling the world that learning and civilization depend upon the tedious work of low-paid, often dissatisfied employees, while the university insisted that higher education—at least at Yale—was a sacred vocation that did not partake of the grubby or the profane. Persuading anyone, including a Yale professor, to give up his romance is never easy, but when that romance mixes power and pedigree with imagination and ideology, things can get downright nasty.

Yale's response to the grade strike, then, is not a story of individual mean-spiritedness or even conservative fanaticism. It is a story of how a devotion to the highest ideals of learned civilization was fused with a devotion to elitism and privilege, and how a challenge to the second seemed, in the minds of the university's defenders, to spell the inevitable doom of the first. The grade strike was in fact an ordinary strike, but it was an ordinary strike that occurred in an extraordinary place.

The Romance of Yale

Despite the admission of women and a century of other social transformations, Yale in 2002 remains, in one critical respect, little different from Yale in 1902. It is still a gentleman's college, a learned estate where youthful minds amble among the colonnades of Western civilization. Small colleges dotting the campus evoke that medieval fellowship of students and scholars forged long ago at Oxford and Cambridge, while letters of Latin and Hebrew carved into the facades of campus buildings suggest to one and all that even the gods of ancient Rome and Israel went to Yale.

Admissions brochures at Yale offer snapshots of thoughtful intimacy between students and professors, deftly portraying the university's marriage of promised power to inherited culture. Every June, students graduate from Yale, ready to embark on their journey to the commanding heights of the international political economy. But before they go, they must be certified as fully trained in the liberal arts by a Yale professor. Yale is this communion of privilege and poesy, a stately mansion where the professor stands proudly at the apex of the knowledge class, while the student stirs hopefully on the threshold of the ruling class.

There is just one problem with this picture: It isn't true. As at most universities throughout the United States, Yale undergraduates are taught, by and large, not by senior or even junior faculty but by TAs and adjunct instructors. The nation's future power elite no longer encounters Western civilization in the cozy office or cramped seminar room of a learned scholar. Instead, they acquire Shakespeare, physics, and Plato from an overworked, underpaid trainee.

Of course, it's hardly news that professors don't teach. But at Yale, the truth is not easily admitted. In 1995, the TA union published a study demonstrating that TAs and adjuncts were performing roughly two-thirds of the teaching to the faculty's one-third. In response, an English professor posted the report's cover in the department lounge with the title—*True Blue*—scratched out and the words "Untrue Blue" angrily scrawled across it. Yale president Richard Levin simply denied its conclusions, claiming that graduate students were responsible for only 3 percent of the teaching; in the face of all the evidence, he blithely declared his numbers fact, the union's fiction.

Yale wants to claim that the brightest still train the best, but it can attract the brightest only by promising them that they won't spend much time doing so. So it is forced to juggle, often unsuccessfully, the imperatives of a modern research university with an upstairs, downstairs self-image. It's a difficult act, resulting in the occasionally hilarious spectacle of Yale administrators and faculty dressing up mediocrity as pedagogical innovation and finding in the bottom line a wellspring of education reform.

Not long before I arrived at Yale, for instance, a graduate school administrator by the name of Chip Long recommended that TAs could save time performing their duties if they didn't reread books assigned to their students that they had read in college and if professors demanded fewer writing assignments. Long's muse was accounting, but his rhetoric was Arnoldian:

"It would surprise me," he reflected, "if there weren't courses out there which could fruitfully, usefully, responsibly reduce the amount of writing they require from students." On another occasion, the English faculty decided to assign twice as many students to each of the sections of the department's much lauded composition course, which had produced the likes of William F. Buckley and Peter Matthiesen. The faculty claimed that the TAs could do twice as much work in the same amount of time if they merely stopped providing written comments on student essays. When the TAs complained that the department was trying to provide education on the cheap, the faculty insisted that the cutbacks were not about saving money. Not writing anything on a student's paper, they explained, would better "sustain the student's desire to write."

The grade strike threatened Yale for the same reason teaching assistants threaten Yale: It reminded the university that the great chain of being linking Plato to professor to student had been broken, that the undergraduate's main point of entry to Western civilization was no longer a tweedy scholar but a financially strapped graduate student. Former Yale president Benno Schmidt has admitted that "graduate students have never been treated as a proud or enriching part of undergraduate education." Indeed, other university administrators have compared graduate students to gypsies and rats, the classic unwelcome guests of Europe. With its overtones of Old World hostility, this dark iconography reveals just how distasteful some of Yale's leaders find TAs. For not only do TAs force the university to fess up to its own accounting needs, but they prod the institution to remember that education is not just the transmission of knowledge but real work, that it must be paid, that it takes time and energy, that it is more than an exercise in breathless self-improvement. That was the message of the grade strike, and it was not particularly welcome.

The Romance Fades

On December 5, just two days before the TAs voted to strike, two graduate students publicly revealed that they had been blacklisted by their professors. A Ph.D. candidate in the English department discovered that Richard Brodhead, a beloved English professor who also happened to be dean of Yale College, had spoken negatively of her union activity in a letter of recommendation. Brodhead praised her abilities as a teacher and scholar, but criticized her union involvement in a lengthy paragraph. She was an enthusiastic union member, he wrote. Perhaps too enthusiastic. She was "a poor listener" on the question of unionization, lacking those skills of diplomatic accommodation and tactful silence that academics so prize. She had "shown poor judgment in the choice of means" that she—and the union—had used to push for reform. (Two years earlier, she had led the campaign to inform alumni donors about the previously mentioned changes in the English department's composition course.) The picture was clear: though intellectually qualified, this student was uncooperative and unprofessional, a troublemaker who would only raise a fuss in an otherwise tranquil academic setting.

The second graduate student was in the classics department. In 1992, he had served as a TA for Donald Kagan's course on ancient Greece, and Kagan was his advisor. At the time, Kagan was also dean of Yale College. A strike was called that spring, and this student informed Kagan that he would honor the picket line. As Kagan later recalled to the undergraduate newspaper, "I told him that [striking] was his right, but that if he didn't meet his classroom responsibilities I would advise him to think twice about asking me for a recommendation." The student refused to change his position, and as promised, Kagan refused—three years later—to write on his behalf. The student was never able to get a university position and wound up teaching high school in Philadelphia.

These revelations on the eve of the grade strike provoked an agonized discussion at Yale. With two out of three successive deans of Yale College outed as blacklisters, professors and administrators were forced to confront the ugly fact that violations of academic freedom were not quirky aberrations, irrational recriminations of a rogue professor, but an institutional practice. When I asked Jim Ponet, a rabbi at Yale whom I consider a friend and occasional mentor, to speak out publicly against these incidents, he asked me a series of sharp questions: What was the relationship between Brodhead and the student? Had he informed her that he would write a negative letter? (He had.) Did he owe her a letter of recommendation? These questions weren't surprising; Jim delighted in acrobatic moral deliberation. But in this case, all the Talmudic back-and-forth was merely preparatory to his decision to remain silent. After thinking it through, Ponet explained to me, he had decided that Brodhead and Kagan were acting within their rights. These students had the right to speak out against the university and even to strike, he said, but the deans had their rights too: to speak their minds—or, presumably, not to speak their minds (Kagan after all refused to write a letter)—and to evaluate their students as candidly and honestly as possible. Brodhead was evaluating the student as a citizen of the university, and that was a legitimate topic for a recommendation. Was it not dangerous to insist that professors write recommendations in a certain way? Would that not constitute a form of censorship as chilling as the one I was decrying?

I didn't say anything at the time. I was too stunned. But in retrospect, I see that there is so much wrong with Ponet's argument that I wonder now how he could have made it. It's a well-recognized principle of moral philosophy—and of common sense—that if someone has a right to something, the rest of us have an obligation to honor that right. If students have the right to speak out against the university or to strike, which Ponet acknowledged they did, then the faculty have a duty to honor those rights, not to do anything that would abridge their exercise. How was it possible to claim that the English student had the right to speak out against department practices, and then claim that Brodhead had the right to respond by ruining her career?

But, for Ponet, this argument only begged a second question: Why was Brodhead's letter not a form of expression, a form of pure speech, rather than an act of blacklisting? After all, Brodhead had merely written a letter offering his opinion. Was that letter not just as much protected speech as the student's letter? What Ponet was forgetting was all those cases of pure speech—perjury, libel, harassment—that society rightly has decided are forms of actionable harm. A negative letter of recommendation is more than mere expression. It's a harmful act, a form of retaliation whose only function, in this case, is to silence speech that a professor finds threatening.

Ponet is an extremely intelligent man who is committed to academic freedom and dissent. He even supports unions. But like so many other liberal faculty, Ponet believes in Yale. He loves it. He went there as an undergraduate. He fondly remembers radical young professors maturing to middle-aged skepticism and tenure. He welcomed the ascension of President Levin and Dean Brodhead because they promised to restore Yale to its former liberal greatness, to the days when President Kingman Brewster stood up for the rights of African Americans by publicly declaring that Bobby Seale could not receive a fair trial in New Haven. Ponet marvels at the wonderful collections in Beinecke Library, debates with other faculty whether that literary splendor justifies Yale's sizable endowment and consequent stinginess toward the city of New Haven, and then concludes that it is the very raising of such heterodox questions that makes Yale such an exalted place. How could Ponet believe in Brodhead-the-blacklister and Yale at the same time?

What was so difficult for Ponet and other Yale professors to understand in December 1995 was perfectly clear to academics around the country. Around this time, more than three hundred faculty from around the country signed a petition addressed to President Levin stating that "graduate students' choice of how or whether to participate in the unionization drive should have no bearing on their treatment in class grading, qualifying exams, TA hiring decisions, letters of recommendation for job candidates, or any other aspect of the academic relationship between graduate students and faculty or administrators." A few of Yale's most liberal faculty signed the petition—Michael Holquist in comparative literature, Sara Suleri-Goodyear in English, Ian Shapiro in political science. Each of these individuals would eventually help break the strike, some using the very means proscribed by the petition.

The Romance Ends

As soon as the graduate students voted to strike, the administration leaped to action, threatening students with blacklisting, loss of employment, and worse. Almost as quickly, the national academic community rallied to the union's cause. A group of influential law professors at Harvard and elsewhere issued a statement condemning "the Administration's invitation to individual professors to terrorize their advisees." They warned the faculty that their actions would "teach a lesson of subservience to illegitimate authority that is the antithesis of what institutions like Yale purport to stand for." Eric Foner, a leading American historian at Columbia, spoke out against the administration's measures in a personal letter to President Levin. "As a longtime friend of Yale," Foner began, "I am extremely distressed by the impasse that seems to have developed between the administration and the graduate teaching assistants." Of particular concern, he noted, was the "developing atmosphere of anger and fear" at Yale, "sparked by threats of reprisal directed against teaching assistants." He then concluded:

> I wonder if you are fully aware of the damage this dispute is doing to Yale's reputation as a citadel of academic freedom and educational leadership. Surely, a university is more than a business corporation and ought to adopt a more enlightened approach to dealing with its employees than is currently the norm in the business world. And in an era when Israelis and Palestinians, Bosnian Muslims and Bosnian Serbs, the British government and the IRA, have found it possible to engage in fruitful discussions after years of intransigent refusal to negotiate, it is difficult to understand why Yale's administration cannot meet with representatives of the teaching assistants.

Foner's letter played a critical role during the grade strike. The faculty took him seriously; his books on the Civil War and Reconstruction are required reading at Yale. But more important, Foner is a historian, and at the time, a particularly tense confrontation in the Yale history department was spinning out of control. The incident involved teaching assistant Diana Paton, a British graduate student who was poised to write a dissertation on the transition in Jamaica from slavery to free labor, and historian David Brion Davis. A renowned scholar of slavery, Davis has written pathbreaking studies, earning him the Pulitzer Prize and a much-coveted slot as a frequent writer at the *New York Review of Books*. He represents the best traditions of humanistic learning, bringing to his work a moral sensitivity that few academics possess. Paton was his student and, that fall, his TA.

When Paton informed Davis that she intended to strike, he accused her of betraying him. Convinced that Davis would not support her academic career in the future—he had told her in an unrelated discussion a few weeks prior that he would never give his professional backing to any student who he believed had betrayed him—Paton nevertheless stood her ground. Davis reported her to the graduate school dean for disciplinary action and had his secretary instruct Paton not to appear at the final exam. In his letter to the dean, Davis wrote that Paton's actions were "outrageous, irresponsible to the students . . . and totally disloyal." The day of the final, Paton showed up at the exam room. As she explains it, she wanted to demonstrate to Davis that she would not be intimidated by him, that she would not obey his orders. Davis, meanwhile, had learned of Paton's plan to attend the exam and somehow concluded that she intended to steal the exams. So he had the door locked and two security guards stand beside it.

Though assertive, Paton is soft-spoken and reserved. She is also small. The thought of her rushing into the exam room, scooping up her students' papers, engaging perhaps in a physical tussle with the delicate Davis, and then racing out the door—the whole idea is absurd. Yet Davis clearly believed it wasn't absurd. What's more, he convinced the administration that it wasn't absurd, for it was the administration that had dispatched the security detail. How this scenario could have been dreamed up by a historian with the nation's most prestigious literary prizes under his belt—and with the full backing of one of the most renowned universities in the world—requires some explanation.

Oddly enough, it is Davis himself who provides it. Like something out of *Hansel and Gretel*, Davis left a set of clues, going back some forty years, to his paranoid behavior during the grade strike. In a pioneering 1960 article in the *Mississippi Valley Historical Review*, "Some Themes of Counter-Subversion: An Analysis of Anti-Masonic, Anti-Catholic, and Anti-Mormon Literature," Davis set out to understand how dominant groups in nineteenth-century America were gripped by fears of disloyalty, treachery, subversion, and betrayal. Many Americans feared Catholics, Freemasons, and Mormons because, it was believed, they belonged to "a machine-like organization" that sought "to abolish free society" and "to overthrow divine principles of law and justice." Members of these groups were dangerous because they professed an "unconditional loyalty to an autonomous body" like the pope. They took their marching orders from afar, and so were untrustworthy, duplicitous, and dangerous.[3]

Davis was clearly disturbed by the authoritarian logic of the countersubversive, but that was in 1960 and he was writing about the nineteenth century. In 1995, confronting the rebellion of his own student, the logic made all the sense in the world. It didn't matter that Paton was a longtime student of his, that she had had many discussions with Davis about her academic work, and that he knew her well. As soon as she announced her commitment to the union's course of action, she became a stranger, an alien marching on behalf of a foreign power.

Davis was hardly alone in voicing these concerns. Other respected members of the Yale faculty dipped into the same well of historical imagery. In January 1996, at the annual meeting of the American Historical Association, several historians presented a motion to censure Yale for its retaliation against the striking TAs. During the debate on the motion, Nancy Cott— one of the foremost scholars of women's history in the country who was on the Yale faculty at the time but has since gone on to Harvard—defended the administration, pointing out that the TA union was affiliated with the Hotel Employees and Restaurant Employees International Union. Historians at the meeting say that Cott placed a special emphasis on the word "international." The TAs, in other words, were carrying out the orders of union bosses in Washington. The graduate students did not care about their own colleagues, they were not loyal to their own. Not unlike the Masons and Catholics of old. It did not seem to faze Cott that she was speaking to an audience filled with labor historians, all of whom would have recognized these charges as classic antiunion rhetoric.

One of the reasons Cott embraced this vocabulary so unselfconsciously was that it was a virtual commonplace among the Yale faculty at the time. At a mid-December faculty meeting, which one professor compared to a Nuremberg rally, President Levin warned the faculty of the ties between the TAs and outside unions. The meeting was rife with lurid images of union heavies dictating how the faculty should run their classrooms. It never seemed to occur to these professors, who pride themselves on their independent judgment and intellectual perspicacity, that they were uncritically accepting some of the ugliest and most unfounded prejudices about unions, that they sounded more like the Jay Goulds and Andrew Carnegies of the late nineteenth century than the careful scholars and skeptical minds of the late twentieth. All they knew was their fear—that a conspiracy was afoot, that they were being forced to cede their authority to disagreeable powers outside of Yale.

Cott, Levin, and the rest of the faculty were also in the grip of a raging class anxiety, which English professor Annabel Patterson spelled out in a letter to the Modern Language Association. The TA union, Patterson wrote, "has always been a wing of Locals 34 and 35 [two other campus unions] . . . who draw their membership from the dining workers in colleges and other support staff." Why did Patterson single out cafeteria employees in her description of Locals 34 and 35? After all, these unions represent thousands of white- and blue-collar workers, everyone from skilled electricians and carpenters to research laboratory technicians, copy editors, and graphic designers. Perhaps it was that Patterson viewed dishwashers and plastic-gloved servers of institutional food as the most distasteful sector of the Yale workforce. Perhaps she thought that her audience would agree with her, and that a subtle appeal to their delicate, presumably shared, sensibilities would be enough to convince other professors that the TA union ought to be denied a role in the university. The professor-student relationship was the critical link in a chain designed to keep dirty people out. What if the TAs and their friends in the dining halls decided that professors should wash the dishes and plumbers should teach classes? Hadn't that happened during the Cultural Revolution? Hadn't the faculty themselves imagined such delightful utopias as young student radicals during the 1960s? Recognizing the TA union would only open Yale to a rougher, less refined element, and every professor, even the most liberal, had something at stake in keeping that element out.

In his article, Davis concluded with these sentences about the nineteenth-century countersubversive:

> By focusing his attention on the imaginary threat of a secret conspiracy, he found an outlet for many irrational impulses, yet professed his loyalty to the ideals of equal rights and government by law. He paid lip service to the doctrine of laissez-faire individualism, but preached selfless dedication to a transcendent cause. The imposing threat of subversion justified a group loyalty and subordination of the individual that would otherwise have been unacceptable. In a rootless environment shaken by bewildering social change the nativist found unity and meaning by conspiring against imaginary conspiracies.

Though I don't think Davis's psychologizing holds much promise for understanding the Yale faculty's response to the grade strike—the strike, after all, did pose a real threat to the faculty's intuitions about both the place of graduate students in the university and the obligations of teachers; nor did the faculty seem, at least to me, to be on a desperate quest for meaning—he did manage to capture, long before the fact, the faculty's fear that their tiered world of privileges and orders, so critical to the enterprise of civilization, was under assault. So did Davis envision the grotesque sense of fellowship that the faculty would derive from attacking their own students. The faculty's outsized rhetoric of loyalty and disloyalty, of intimacy (Dean Brodhead called the parties to the conflict a "dysfunctional family") betrayed, may have fit uneasily with their avowed professions of individualism and intellectual independence. But it did give them the opportunity to enjoy, at least for a moment, that strange euphoria—the thrilling release from dull routine, the delightful, newfound solidarity with fellow elites— that every reactionary from Edmund Burke to Augusto Pinochet has experienced upon confronting an organized challenge from below.

Paton's relationship with Davis was ended. Luckily, she was able to find another advisor at Yale, Emilia Viotti da Costa, a Latin American historian who was also an expert on slavery. Da Costa, it turns out, had been a supporter of the student movement in Brazil some thirty years before and was persecuted by the military there. Forced to flee the country, she found in Yale a welcome refuge from repression.

Where Did All the Romance Go?

Eloise Pasachoff arrived at Yale in the fall of 1995, fresh out of college, to begin her Ph.D. in English. A first-rate student, she excelled in the classroom, particularly in Annabel Patterson's seminar that fall on John Milton, Andrew Marvell, and John Locke. In her final evaluation of Pasachoff's work, Patterson wrote, "An almost unqualified series of H[onors] papers is no small achievement, given the continuous demands of this pattern of assignments." Patterson also commended Pasachoff for "the close attention you pay to textual details, and the energy and naturalness with which you ask questions, especially in class." She then paid what she probably assumed was the ultimate compliment to the young graduate student: "For what it's worth," Patterson wrote, "these are the symptoms that one would remember in guessing that you would be a good teacher, and passing the message on to prospective employers."

Had Patterson's evaluation ended there, it would have seemed no more than a bit of generous encouragement to a promising student. But it went on, and as it continued, Patterson's praise began to disclose a darker intent. For Pasachoff was not only an excellent student. She was also a union activist who organized support for the grade strike among her fellow first-year students in the English department. After Patterson expressed her willingness, when the time came, to "remember" Pasachoff to future employers, she appended the following paragraph:

> All these things being so, it would be cowardly of me if I did not add that I truly hope you will neither have a return of Miltonic vocation doubt [Pasachoff had earlier confessed to Patterson her uncertainty about pursuing an academic career] . . . nor get caught up in campus politics to your own detriment. If you would like to talk about the issues of involvement in early January, just give me a call. My sense is that Milton, Marvell and Locke would all have been dubious about acting in these circumstances.

Having just promised to put in a good word for Pasachoff, Patterson now advised her not to continue her involvement with the union. Patterson's breezy suggestion that Pasachoff call her to discuss "issues of involvement" intimated a kind of deal: You, Pasachoff, give up your agitation, and I, Patterson, will see to it that you are taken care of. It was perhaps not the crassest exchange of vows, but it did recall that famous opening scene in *The Godfather* where Vito Corleone agrees to beat up the attackers of an undertaker's daughter in return for a "service" that Corleone says "some day" he may "call upon" the undertaker to perform. Even at this most sordid of moments, Patterson felt the need to invoke the great men of Western civilization—Locke, Milton, Marvell. At Yale, Plato meets Puzo, and neither is worse for the wear.

Or perhaps not. For Locke was a great defender of natural rights who argued on behalf of religious toleration, participated in a failed assassination plot against a repressive king, organized an unsuccessful rebellion, and generally made life uncomfortable for himself—all for the sake of conscience. Milton, author of *Aeropagitica*, one of the most beautiful defenses of the independent imagination in the English language, thought there was nothing more distasteful than the spoon-fed mind, the flabby intellect that went unchallenged. Intelligence was made muscular by hardship and adversity; the most dangerous threat to a thinking person was comfort, ease, and all the promises of the good life that Patterson was now so bent on peddling. As Milton famously wrote:

I cannot praise a fugitive and cloistered virtue, unexercised and un-
breathed, that never sallies out and sees her adversary, but slinks out
of the race where that immortal garland is to be run for, not without
dust and heat. Assuredly we bring not innocence into the world, we
bring impurity and much rather: that which purifies us is trial, and
trial is by what is contrary.

Patterson is a noted scholar of Milton's work. That she could invoke the
author of these words to justify political retreat for the sake of personal
advance cannot be explained away as ignorance. Not even cynicism or
hypocrisy accounts for such a stunning piece of advice. Something more
mundane is at work here, revealing the bizarre nexus of ideas and power,
theory and practice, that is Yale—that is, indeed, the practice of higher education at so many elite universities around the country.

With the exception of David Brion Davis and Donald Kagan, all of
the faculty discussed here came of age during the 1960s or just afterwards.
Their work demonstrates the influence of progressive intellectual currents,
including feminism, poststructuralism, even Marxism. Richard Brodhead's *Cultures of Letters*, a collection of critical essays about nineteenth-
century American literature, is clearly inspired by multiculturalism and
modish sensibilities about race and gender. Brodhead draws liberally
from the work of Foucault, and his discussions unite figures of high
culture such as Henry James with less celebrated women and African-
American writers. Denis Hollier, one of the authors of the infamous
French department memo mentioned earlier, travels within radical French
literary circles; postmodern luminary Jean-Francois Lyotard wrote the
introduction to Hollier's book on Sartre. Nancy Cott is a pioneering figure
in women's history who has inspired generations of feminist historians.
Annabel Patterson is most explicit about the influence of the 1960s on
her work. In *Reading between the Lines*, she discusses at length the for-
mative role that decade played in her development as a critic and scholar.
Although she now suggests that we should "break away" from the 1960s,
she insists that her desire to do so is "trivial in comparison" to the
"larger sense of empowerment" she received from the political struggles
of that era.

The faculty at Yale who crushed the grade strike juggle two heartfelt
commitments: a devotion to high-minded liberal principles and an equally
strong devotion to Yale. Although they see themselves as the bearers of an
exalted tradition of humane learning—which envisions in education an

ameliorative path to freedom and progress—they are ineluctably pulled by a not-so-exalted tradition of elitism. Knowledge and privilege are, for them, necessarily fused; one cannot have the one without the other. And so, despite their best intentions, the faculty float every day further and further from the spirit of Socrates, Mill, and Freud. It's not that they don't care about ideas. It's just that for them a job at Yale is an idea.

CHAPTER 8

Tenure Denied

Union Busting and Anti-Intellectualism in the Corporate University

Joel Westheimer

It was supposed to be a dull day downtown. On September 28, 1999, I rode the subway to the court building where I would offer testimony to a hearing officer from the New York regional office of the National Labor Relations Board. I was to testify, of my own volition, on behalf of New York University graduate students who were seeking to join a union, then return uptown to teach my afternoon class in NYU's School of Education. When I entered the room where the hearing was to take place, however, it was easy to tell that the stakes were high. I already knew that NYU had hired the same high-profile law firm used previously by Yale and presently by Columbia University. But to my surprise, not one but three lawyers for the university were present along with two high-ranking university officials, each dressed in a carefully pressed suit and tie: the vice dean of my school and NYU vice president, Robert Berne. Then there I was, a young, untenured assistant professor, dressed in rumpled khakis. I was called to the stand, and lawyers for both sides began with prepared questions. The hearing room grew increasingly tense, the questioning increasingly fierce.

Ten months after the trial, I would submit my application for promotion and tenure. Soon after, Ann Marcus, dean of the School of Education, would overturn the unanimous recommendations of both my own department faculty and all seven outside experts chosen to judge my case that I be granted tenure. By August of 2001, less than two years after testifying against the university's interest in denying graduate students the right to form a union, I would be fired.

Both events—my testimony and the violation of principles of faculty governance that led to my being fired—relate to my own academic research on democratic communities in education. Studying the democratic purposes of schooling, in both elementary and high schools as well as in colleges and universities, has always been compelling to me because the gap between rhetorical and substantive democracy can be so large in these institutions. But although I have always felt strongly about issues of democracy and community in education, this essay is personal and difficult to write. It is an essay I never imagined writing. This essay concerns how both my academic freedom and, indeed, my legal protection under the National Labor Relations Act were violated by the administration of New York University. I write this account because I believe it is important to examine up close the ways university administrators—who are increasingly modeling themselves after corporate executives—respond when grass-roots efforts to reassert democracy and pursue just working arrangements on campuses begin to gain strength. The focus here is on my case at New York University, but the implications reach farther: campuses across the country, including Columbia, Brown, Yale, Penn State, University of Maryland, University of Pennsylvania, University of Illinois, and UNC-Chapel Hill, all have active teaching assistant, and sometimes adjunct and even tenure-stream, faculty organizing campaigns. This essay is as much about their struggles as it is about those at NYU because, though immediate circumstances will vary, one disturbing trend remains constant: as university administrations increasingly look to the bottom line and displace educational goals with economic ones, the democratic ideal of the university will suffer, and so will our faculty and students.

The graduate student organizing drive that ended in an embarrassing defeat for the NYU administration was a victory, I would argue, for the university as a whole. As Lisa Jessup describes in the next section, NYU graduate assistants are now affiliated with the International United Automobile, Aerospace and Agriculture Implement Workers of America (UAW) and have recently negotiated their landmark first contract, which included higher salaries, health benefits, paid professional development courses, proper appointment procedures, and fee waivers. All of these were unimaginable until their successful organizing drive, labor board suit, and, finally, union representation. Now adjunct professors at NYU are also gearing up for a major organizing drive to improve their working conditions, and not one but *two* unions are each hoping to represent them. These victories, however, were not without costs.

Union Busting in the Corporate University

When NYU graduate assistants first started organizing their union, I joined faculty colleagues in supporting the assistants' right to choose a union. I did so because I know firsthand the value of the hard work they perform for the university. When I heard some members of the NYU administration claim that a union would damage relations between graduate students and their faculty advisors, and that a union would be harmful to the teacher training graduate students receive, I felt a particular need to speak up—as an education professor who specializes in the subject of community and democracy—to correct these fallacies.

As a faculty member, it is not for me to say whether or not graduate students should choose to unionize. But I *can* say that the vast contributions they make to the university constitute "work" and that honoring that work through a collective bargaining agreement will make the university a richer, more just, and more collegial place for all of us. Most important, as a faculty member who sees the work graduate students do in teaching, in research, and in service to the university community, I can say that the choice of whether to unionize should be theirs.

As the graduate assistants began their organizing campaign, the NYU administration naturally wanted to collect evidence for the argument that teaching assistants (TAs), and research assistants (RAs) are not university employees protected under U.S. labor law, but rather are *only* students who—because they are learning through their work—do not have the right to form a union. These were exactly the arguments put forth by Berkeley in the early '80s and Yale in the '90s to prevent their respective graduate student organizing committees from being legally recognized as employees of the university and, therefore, gaining the legal right to organize. Early on in its antiunion campaign, the administration of the School of Education at NYU sent a letter to some faculty asking for "job descriptions" for our research assistants. The letter asked a series of questions that began with the benign "Describe what your research assistants do." But the questions quickly became shameless to anyone with any knowledge of the university's position on graduate assistant unionization. One such question: "How do you supervise, mentor, guide and evaluate [graduate assistants]? Include how often you meet with them individually, how you orient them, how you

review their work, whether they work with others as part of a team, etc."
That university officials would ask professors how they "supervise, mentor,
guide, and evaluate" their RAs is not only underhanded—in that it unwit-
tingly enlists professors in the administration's antiunion campaign—but it
is troubling because it does so by exploiting professors' own insecurities.
Imagine a professor responding this way: "Actually, I don't mentor my
graduate assistants all that much, and they spend most of their time photo-
copying and grading student papers; sometimes they go to the library and
get books for me or file papers, or answer the phone, or fix my computer."
No, we are far more likely to say—and the administration and their law
firms know this—that we do a terrific job of mentoring and guiding our
malleable young students, and that students' experiences with us are always
valuable, always educational, and so on.

Yet it should be clear to any professor that the work graduate research
assistants and teaching assistants do on research projects or in teaching
classes—while it has a learning component to it—is nonetheless clear and
significant employment. That is, a significant portion of their job is a job,
and not related to their course learning any more than the work of research
associates at a think tank, government office, or corporate research department (all of whom are guaranteed the right to organize under U.S. labor
law) is not "work" even if they are (of course) learning while doing it. Previous chapters have detailed how university departments and professors benefit from the work that research assistants offer by helping with research
projects. Teaching assistants similarly may learn something while teaching,
but this learning does not diminish the fact that the university employs
them to teach its courses (and generates revenue from their labor). That is
why teaching and research assistants should enjoy the right to have an officially and legally recognized graduate student organization to speak on their
behalf, one to which the university is legally required to listen.

But what makes this administrative tactic particularly effective is the
fact that the working relationship between graduate research assistants and
professors is generally multilayered and complex. Often, for example, a professor will simultaneously employ a research assistant as well as serve on his
or her dissertation committee. This means that the professor and the graduate student will spend a great deal more time together than the time for
which the research assistant is paid. For the purpose of responding to administration questions like these, then, it became important for faculty to
state explicitly that they were responding only to the *working* relationship in
the context of the time for which the research assistant is hired since other
educational interactions take place outside of this time frame and are similar

to interactions faculty would have with *any* student in a graduate program—whether they are employed by a research grant or not.

How did I respond to fox-dressed-in-sheep questions from the administration like the one above? I summarized the previous arguments, always being careful to note that I was speaking only of the work the students do *as part of their research assistantship.* I also copied my written response, including the commentary on the inappropriate nature of the questions, and distributed it to several other faculty throughout the school. I didn't know it at the time, but things were about to change dramatically for me and my application for tenure at the university.

Soon after the university began collecting information to be used to counter the graduate student organizing drive, the question arose of whether I would testify before the National Labor Relations Board for the graduate students. For reasons I've already mentioned, I felt a particular obligation to speak up to counter the administration's claim that the faculty/student relationship would be adversely affected by unionization. I had already joined other faculty at NYU in a petition urging the administration to allow students to exercise their democratic rights and vote on whether they wished to have union representation.[1] After consulting with colleagues, in the fall of 1999, I testified at the NLRB hearings. In a brutal cross-examination, NYU's lawyers barely let me speak. Each of my attempts to respond to questions from the UAW lawyers was abruptly cut off with attempts to discredit my basis for any knowledge for the questions I was being asked. For more than two hours they told me that I wasn't at the university long enough to know anything, that all my testimony was hearsay because it came from faculty meetings and memos, and that—as recorded in one Al Pacino-esque moment with the NYU lawyer screaming at the top of his lungs—"HE KNOWS NOTHING!" I came in thinking the whole day was to be painfully tedious and boring and I left feeling as if I had appeared in what surely must have been an episode of *Law and Order.*

Despite the frequent objections of NYU's lawyers, I did get to offer testimony on several points that the graduate student organizing committee relied upon to make their case before the labor board. I thought my testimony might make a small addition to the growing mountain of evidence that graduate teaching and research assistants conduct work that should be deemed employment and that they, therefore, have the right to organize. What I did not know at the time was that the dean of the School of Education at NYU would shortly testify before the labor board in direct opposition to my testimony supporting graduate assistants' right to organize. And, naively perhaps, I did not imagine that taking a public position in opposition to university administrators would brand me a "troublemaker" and leave me vulnerable to dismissal.

I was, as it turns out, the only untenured professor university wide to testify. In May 2001, Associate Dean of Faculty Gabriel Carras told me by telephone that the dean had overturned the unanimous recommendation of both my department faculty and all seven external reviewers and had denied my tenure bid on the grounds that my scholarship was inadequate.

This news came as a surprise. Though one is always nervous in anticipation of tenure decisions, my scholarship was one area in which I felt confident that I had amply met the requirements of the university. I had also been assured by colleagues at NYU and elsewhere that, while tenure decisions can be enigmatic, I did not need to worry about my record of scholarship.

I am uncomfortable listing my credentials, and I will do so now in the briefest possible terms to serve the argument of this essay. Since I began working at NYU six years ago, I received the highest possible merit ratings awarded by the school each year—exceptional merit. Each year, only about 20 percent of faculty in my department (including full professors) receive "exceptional merit" evaluations. Before submitting my application for promotion and tenure, I published a book with Teachers College Press, ten journal articles, several book chapters, essay reviews, newspaper editorials, and reports. I had been invited to lecture on my work nineteen times at universities including Cornell, Harvard, Stanford, and the University of Toronto. And I had presented papers at academic conferences twenty-seven times.

Between 1996, when I started at NYU, and 2001 when my tenure and promotion bid was reviewed, I received five awards and fellowships. External awards included Cornell University's Millman Promising Scholar Award for Educational Research awarded to only one person each year from a national competition of scholars.[2] Dean Marcus nominated me for this award, and she had to choose only one nomination from the entire 180-some members of the School of Education faculty. In an NYU publication, she stated: "This award underscores the significance of [Westheimer's] work as a scholar. . . . His inquiries . . . are informed by a sophisticated understanding of educational practice. His work is skeptical, rigorous and lucid."[3] I also received an internal award: in 1997, I received the Daniel E. Griffiths Award, given to only one faculty member, for the best scholarship in the School of Education.

Moreover, in each of the years prior to my labor board testimony, my annual reviews by both department faculty and university administrators were positive:

1996:
- "[Westheimer's] teaching is exemplary."
- "[He has] established a record of professional activity and involvement which is local, regional and national."
- "[Westheimer's] prospects for tenure are excellent."

1997:
- "Students in his [courses] wrote extensive midterm and final reviews that were uniform in their praise."
- "His research record is admirable."

1998:
- "Through his research and publications, [Westheimer] now has a national reputation."
- "His teaching, research, and scholarship remain excellent."
- "Professor Westheimer is making excellent progress towards promotion and tenure."

1999:
- "Professor Westheimer presents a total picture of quality university teaching."
- "His productivity and professional activities are exemplary for an assistant professor."
- "[He is making] excellent progress towards promotion and tenure."

I received those last reviews in May 1999. Then, in September, I testified.

The administration's view of my performance changed quickly. My department chair, Mark Alter, and Dean Marcus, turned hostile and disparaged my research and service to other faculty members. In July 2000, Marcus wrote to me about concern over my "willingness to commit fully to the needs of our programs," without specifying what this might mean. It was the first ever mention of any such concerns. And a senior faculty member in my department with close ties to the department chair told me that although my teaching was "masterful," there was concern that I needed to be more of a "team player," "more collegial," and to go along "with the direction of the department and the school."

My department faculty's Tenure and Promotion Committee wrote in my 2000 review that they found my teaching to be "inspiring," that I had done "exemplary work," and that my scholarship was "a model for assistant professors." Still, Alter for the first time downgraded my rating from "exceptional merit" to merely "merit." Furthermore, I was assigned an onerous administrative workload that neither I nor any of my colleagues had ever been assigned before. After I requested a shift in my 2001 teaching load from spring to summer, Alter wrote the following in a November 3, 2000, memo to me listing my administrative responsibilities for the term: I would "oversee the continuing professional development of teacher Summer activities . . . oversee the implementation of course work related to all teacher education programs . . . assume responsibility for the middle school extension including recruitment, advisement, and course development . . . oversee the implementation of the doctoral committee's recruitment plans . . . coordinate all advisement for both graduate and undergraduate students . . . ensure that incoming and continuing pre-service and in-service students are advised regarding their programs, course schedules and their registration . . . Plan and supervise orientations for incoming Fall students . . . oversee the coordination of summer field activities including student teaching and field observations [and] serve on [any] committees that meet during the summer."

After the denial-of-tenure phone call from the dean's office, the deans spent a week trying to get me to withdraw my application for tenure and simply resign. They told me it would look better on my CV to quit rather than to be terminated. They didn't mention that when you withdraw your application you also forfeit your right to file a complaint with the labor board or pursue any other legal or administrative remedy. I decided not to withdraw.

Shortly after, the NYU chapter of the American Association of University Professors (AAUP) submitted a petition signed by more than sixty NYU professors calling upon the administration to reexamine my tenure application. At the same time, all seven of my external referees, five past presidents of the American Educational Research Association (AERA), and a total of twenty-seven senior scholars in the National Academy of Education signed a statement to NYU raising concern that my tenure case may have been judged on the basis of political activities and calling upon NYU to reconsider my application and to ensure that tenure proceedings not be used as retaliation. Then a broader petition with more than seven hundred signatures was collected. After reviewing my case, the associate secretary of the AAUP national office also sent a strongly worded letter to NYU president Jay Oliva expressing concern that my academic freedom had been violated. Senior education faculty from Stanford University, the University of Washington, Columbia University, the University of Wisconsin-Madison, the University of Illinois-Chicago, and others also wrote letters or phoned the dean's and president's office to voice concerns over academic freedom raised by my case. Then a Workers Rights Board hearing was convened by community leaders, and a report was issued titled "Right to Organize and

Academic Freedom at New York University" detailing the board's finding that I was denied tenure "in retaliation for testifying against NYU on behalf of the union rights of graduate student employees before the National Labor Relations Board." In November 2001, several wonderful colleagues under the leadership of Robby Cohen organized a conference on Democracy and Education at NYU on my behalf. As one newspaper reported it, "Distinguished faculty from some of the nation's top universities gathered Thursday afternoon [in] a show of support . . . honoring [Westheimer's] scholarship and research in the field of education." Other newspaper and journal articles highlighting the suspicious nature of NYU's actions appeared in the *Chronicle of Higher Education*, the *New York Times*, the *Villager*, *Dissent*, *Academe*, and the *Washington Square News*.[4]

The result of all of this public inquiry? NYU did not respond to the charges. It was now seven months after the dean had issued her decision to fire me, and it would still be several months more before the federal government would charge NYU with illegal retaliation.[5] But the dean of the School of Education, the associate dean for faculty affairs, my department chair, the president and the vice president of NYU had little or nothing to say.

The Marriage of Anti-Intellectualism and Anti-Unionism

At this point, one might conclude from my experience at NYU that, although universities' corporate practices may be offensive, they don't really intrude on the day-to-day life of faculty except during exceptional circumstances such as union drives. In fact, however, the increasingly corporate logic of the university has a more far-reaching and insidious influence. These universities can be quite good at one of their primary goals—making money. And money, coupled with the kind of attacks on democratic faculty governance that characterize corporate university culture, can translate into perks for faculty that administrators dole out in return for complicity—low course loads, easy research money, travel budgets, computers. It is easy to speculate where such a convergence might lead: if you're "good" faculty, you are rewarded; if you're bad, you are cut off from plum teaching assignments, research money, and, possibly, tenure. But ultimately, what faculty—and especially junior faculty—are being asked to give up is their own intellectual independence. The creeping corporate climate of some university departments can easily lead to the substitution of bureaucratic allegiance for scholarly inquiry as the cornerstone of academic life.

In some cases, the effect on the intellectual life of a department might be plain to see. In some schools, faculty-elected department chairs—who traditionally served terms of a few years and then eagerly returned to their intellectual pursuits within the department—have been replaced by chairs *appointed* by university higher-ups with no or at best perfunctory input from department faculty. Some stay in these positions for a decade or more and have little interest in scholarly inquiry. A colleague at a midwestern university reported that her department chair, who had been appointed before my colleague was hired, had suggested to the faculty that research questions that the department wanted investigated should be agreed upon by a committee (of senior faculty and administrators) and posted on a website and that faculty should align their research with one of those questions. Requiring research to be streamlined according to central criteria—doubtless related to funding opportunities—makes perfect sense if one treats an academic department as a profit center. But it turns scholarly life into something less than we all hope it to be.

At times, the mere fact that department faculty are pursuing an active, diverse, and uncontrolled set of research agendas may be perceived by department administrators as a negative development. At first glance this seems paradoxical, since nearly every department explicitly proclaims the promotion of such agendas as one of its primary missions. However, as in other bureaucracies, the corporatized department may come to place a higher priority on control and predictability than on the inherently messy and uncontrolled nature of intellectual life. Intellectual independence manifest in independent research may end up seeming threatening to departmental hierarchies. At NYU, my department had features that have proved worrying in many similar situations and ones that may seem familiar to some readers—an upper cadre of faculty/managers who conduct little if any new research and ground their prestige and security not in refereed publications but in close relationships with the school's administration. This is the classic form of a department whose leadership has been transformed along corporate lines. Too often, while such departments continue to recruit promising scholars on the basis of their research production, department leaders, many of whom may have largely abandoned scholarly life, are caught in a bind: they need such scholars to reproduce the department's reputation and grant-getting ability; but once there, these scholars may pose some level of threat to the order of business within the department (and to the security of the chair who has likely already traded the kind of professional security earned from scholarly inquiry and production for the kind won by allegiance and loyalty to university higher-ups).

Appointed chairs can slowly and steadily shift faculty focus from scholarly pursuits that advance a field to those that advance the chair, a possibility that is especially troubling to junior faculty who will be seeking tenure. External pressures on the corporate university, from donors and politicians, constrain and refocus academic research. So do internal incentives on the departmental level. As in much of university politics, junior faculty remain the most vulnerable. Disguised in language like "research consistent with the needs of the department" or "research that contributes to the mission of the department," anti-intellectual agendas punish independent thinking and reward docility.

In the field of teacher education, this most often takes the form of departments rewarding only research on the department's own programs (and preferably research that demonstrates how good these programs are). This is like coercing Columbia University historians to report a glorified history of Columbia University or UCLA sociologists to study happy social interactions at the campus student center. Yet asking education faculty to study their own education programs is sometimes called "progressive" and often encouraged by senior faculty and administrators. Professors doing the research may justify pressure from the administration to produce showcase research with the comforting notion that they are engaging in "action research" or "participant observation" (which are invariably deemed progressive regardless of the research question, aim, scope, or underlying values). I should be clear that my intention here is not to demean action research or participant observation as methodologies; indeed, many outstanding researchers have fought long and hard to have good research on one's own teaching or programs recognized as legitimate and valuable scholarship—which it certainly has the potential to be. I only note that in an increasing number of education departments, administrators and senior faculty are encouraging junior faculty (and often doctoral students in search of a dissertation topic) to research and showcase the department's own programs not for the pursuit of better scholarship but rather for the promotion of the department and/or its chair.

For junior faculty, the absence of scholarly discourse or spirit of intellectual inquiry in the department may seem, in the first years of service, disappointing but not tragic—meetings that are all procedure and no content, department chairs with egos but without intellectual convictions, senior faculty who have quit writing or never started. These departments might seem bumbling or unprofessional, but more or less harmless places to pursue one's own professional and scholarly interests. Until my recent experience with NYU, I had never worried much about this facet of poor management.

But these departments are the ones most vulnerable. Those faculty whose prestige and security derives from departmental service rather than from scholarly contributions are more easily pressed into antiunion campaigns. Having now seen how aggressive administration antiunion campaigns can be, I am made far more aware of the need for faculty to defend against the erosion of democratic faculty governance.

Though it is impossible to generalize from my experience (indeed, it is not entirely possible to know what drives decisions or organizational arrangements even in the department of which I was a member), it is worth noting that faculty governance in departments that have remade themselves along corporate culture lines can become little more than a parody of pseudo-democratic (or simply nondemocratic) governance in which faculty simply (and always) endorse administrative positions. As soon as a faculty member's independence comes into conflict with the power and control of the chair and the university administration, these departments snap into action. This is precisely (and belatedly) when it is discovered that the fact that faculty had little real engagement with intellectual life means that they are left vulnerable to the pressures for conformity and silence that characterize the corporate department and university. Faculty managers' and department chairs' only convictions remain those that do not ruffle the administrative feathers of those higher up. And the chill that blankets departments in which power has been centralized results in the further entrenchment of antidemocratic tendencies.[6]

Under these conditions, the university starts to look less like a place of free exchange of ideas and more like a Hobbesian Leviathan, a place that boasts, as former SUNY New Paltz president Roger Bowen warns, "a settled, conforming, obedient citizenry—not dissenters who challenge convention."[7] In these departments, junior faculty either conform, withdraw from departmental life after being tenured, or leave altogether. In the Department of Teaching and Learning at NYU, ten assistant or associate tenure-track faculty were hired in the past five years; of these ten, five have left the department and two are actively on the job market. Moreover, the department has now begun to hire primarily "clinical" and part-time faculty who remain always at the command of the chair and are left little time to pursue independent scholarly work; these clinical faculty are more easily pressed into serving the interests of administrators rather than those of open inquiry. There are many reasons people change jobs, to be sure. And whether the new hires reflect unionization concerns, budgetary concerns, or concerns over control is hard to say. The model of what might be, however, is hard to miss.

When the weeding is completed, the anti-intellectual mission of the antiunion university becomes clearest. The bottom line is raised to the top. Research that promotes the financial and hierarchical health of the administration is rewarded, and independent scholarly thought is punished. Institutions of higher education become ones of education for hire.

This is all the more ironic given the fact that university administrations often make the argument in campuswide antiunion campaigns that unions will *diminish* intellectual pursuits. "Unions are anti-intellectual" is the university's line. They argue that the union represents an intrusion of crass interests and power politics into an arena that should be about the integrity of ideas, that the university is dedicated to scholarship and excellence, and that unions ensure mediocrity because of hiring rules and procedures. Actual practice suggests otherwise. Anti-intellectualism and universal endorsement of the university's antiunion stance may far too easily go hand in hand. Undue administrative influence over research agendas, appointed department chairs and the further erosion of democratic governance, and the hiring of part-time and clinical faculty with no time for scholarly inquiry and little job security are all threats to both scholarly inquiry and university democracy. Anti-intellectualism and antiunionism are not opposites but rather reinforce each other. In fact, in the corporate university, due process protections afforded by faculty unions may be the best way to protect free and independent scholarly inquiry.[8]

Where Do We Go from Here?

I recognize that people in all types of jobs are threatened or punished for supporting the right to organize. Before I testified before the National Labor Relations Board, I thought hard about the possible risk to my career, but ultimately, I made my decision based on two assumptions. First, colleagues convinced me that my scholarship record was sufficiently strong that even if my testimony rankled some in the administration, they would be unable to find legitimate grounds for denying tenure. Second, I just did not believe that NYU was the kind of place where faculty could be punished for speaking out on behalf of something so mundane, so obvious, so unrevolutionary as the right of graduate assistants to choose whether they want a union. It turns out I was wrong on both counts.

On February 27, 2002, while I was writing this chapter, the federal government charged NYU with illegally firing me in retaliation for my testimony in favor of allowing NYU graduate students to unionize. The *New York Times* headline the next day read "Labor Board Rules that NYU

Denied Tenure to Union Backer." Following a four-month investigation, Celeste Mattina, director of the labor board's New York region, reported that "after balancing the information, we concluded that the real reason for [Professor Westheimer's] denial of tenure was because of his union activities."[9] By the time this book is in print, a decision will have been rendered by the board. Should the decision prove to be not in their favor, NYU, by any measure of past behavior, will appeal. It has already retained the same law firm used in its unsuccessful attempt to break the graduate assistant union. Sadly, NYU will also likely continue to fight ongoing unionization efforts by adjuncts and, perhaps one day, by faculty. If we estimate legal fees at $350 to $425 per hour (that's probably low), the cost to the university of an endless string of court litigation for its antilabor practices has been and will continue to be very high—money that could just as easily be spent on student financial aid, hiring new faculty, or raising salaries paid to adjunct professors. Indeed, the university seems more comfortable paying lawyers $350 per hour than research assistants $15.

The difficult professional lives that adjunct faculty face makes especially clear that organizing drives will continue. And unlike graduate students, adjuncts cannot be construed as laboring for part of their education as students, which is what makes their efforts to unionize particularly frightening to university administrations.

The economic logic of the university will be easy to understand: until the cost of fighting the unions exceeds the fiscal benefit of paying poverty wages, the antiunion campaigns will likely continue, to the detriment of academic labor, to the detriment of academic freedom, and to the detriment of both students and the ideal of the democratic university. It is imperative, therefore, that we continue to ask ourselves: How will administrators respond to workplace justice issues? How should faculty respond? We clearly must be aware of the scare tactics universities will employ, like hiring antilabor lawyers at escalating cost to the university budget and to campus morale. We must be aware of the internal chill factor: faculty are afraid to stand up for fear of retaliation or of being ostracized, or simply because intellectual and moral commitments have been suppressed. And we must be aware that the primary motivation for administrators is no longer a matter of reconciling competing interests in a democratic university, but, instead, the strict pursuit of a bottom line. It is this changing face of the university that I believe we have to fight against. As in so many other arenas in which democratic interests are pitted against economic ones, democracy seems to be losing.

I do not yet know how my case against NYU will end. I do know that I do not regret testifying on behalf of graduate student teachers' right to organize. I do not regret speaking out for the rights of adjunct faculty to make a living wage and be offered respect and dignity. These issues are too important, not just for me, but for the hundreds of thousands of academics—graduate students, adjuncts, and tenure-stream faculty—who are still engaged in the struggle over the right to organize, and who need to know that we cannot be cowed into silence by the unprincipled behavior of a handful of administrators. It is up to all of us—tenure-stream and part-time faculty, administration, students, and staff—to ensure that we move toward rather than away from the pursuit of democratic governance, of free and open inquiry, and of just working conditions for the entire university community.

We need to remind ourselves and the university administrations where we work of American education's historic ideal: to educate a democratic citizenry ready and able to pursue the common good. And how does one go about teaching democracy? By example, to start with. It's purported that Albert Einstein—a founding member of a faculty union in Princeton, New Jersey—put it this way: "Setting an example is not the main means of influencing another, it is the only means." There may be many approaches to pursuing education in the service of democracy, but they must all begin with reflection on ways we can remain democratic in our daily practices. That requires the strength to speak out that can come from joining together in the common cause of improving the conditions under which all of us work.

SECTION THREE

Organizing

"Organize, organize, organize." This familiar mantra of the labor movement grew in volume over the course of the last decade as full-time faculty, graduate student employees, and adjunct faculty began organizing for change on campuses all across the United States and Canada. The transformation of the academic workplace clearly had produced a transformation of the academic worker whose rights and voice—as both academic and employee—were sacrificed in the name of profit, efficiency, and quality assurance. In section 3 we present case studies that illustrate the successes and failures of organized responses to the forces of corporatization outlined in section 1 and illustrated in the personal narratives of academic experience in section 2. What is clear in all of the following essays is that the emergence of the modern academic labor movement is clearly connected to a larger project of reclaiming the university by protecting the integrity of academic work and guaranteeing the rights of all academic employees.

The case studies here are meant to delineate the ways in which academic activists have sought to resist the transformation of the academic profession and the academic workplace by seizing control of the debate surrounding higher education and the terms and conditions of employment for those laboring within. Not surprisingly, the diverse and rapid changes discussed in the first two sections have created innumerable challenges for those advocating and organizing for change in the academic workplace. While the calls to organize may have been familiar, the nature of academic work made clear that, in order to be successful, the techniques of organizing would have to be different.

The '90s saw an unprecedented growth in unionization and other forms of organized resistance to the effects that corporatization has had on higher education. The most active and publicized organizing has most certainly been that of graduate student employees. Forced to bear greater responsibility for undergraduate education, and with diminishing prospects for meaningful full-time employment upon completion of the Ph.D., graduate student employees began to see their present and future conditions of employment as inextricably linked. Unionization was seen as a way to finally redefine the relationship between graduate education and graduate student employment by challenging the apprenticeship model that university administrators use in order to continue the exploitation of graduate students. Unions have the power to do this by bringing employer and employee to the bargaining table to negotiate terms and conditions of employment in the academic workplace.

In recent years, state labor boards throughout the country have sided with graduate students on the employee/apprentice question and the role of collective bargaining in higher education. In December of 1998, for example, during a statewide drive by graduate student employees in the University of California system, the Public Employment Relations Board ruled that California's Higher Education Employer-Employee Relations Act (HEERA) "presents a framework under which the pursuit of academic excellence, the free exchange of ideas, the preservation of academic freedom, and collective bargaining all co-exist and complement one another." This assertion made clear that rather than disrupting education and undermining the collegiality necessary for a vibrant academic community—as those who clung to an apprenticeship model never ceased arguing—collective bargaining actually strengthens higher education and the academic profession by affirming its essential elements.

The first two essays in this section document two graduate student employee organizing drives. While one was successful and the other a sobering defeat, both illustrate clearly the many internal and external challenges to organizing graduate student employees. These essays deal with the range of questions, from affiliation to campaign strategy and beyond, that must be balanced in order to ultimately lead to a victory and a collective bargaining agreement.

The victory of Graduate Student Organizing Committee-United Autoworkers of America (GSOC-UAW) at NYU told by Lisa Jessup is the most recent success story and the first among private colleges and universities. While graduate student union victories continued to mount at public universities in the late '90s, the specter of *Yeshiva* and the National Labor Relations Board (NLRB) bureaucracy loomed in the private sector. The 1980 *Yeshiva* decision effectively ended faculty unionization in the private sector, but organizers and activists at private colleges and universities became increasingly confident that administrators would not be successful in categorizing graduate student employees as management. University administrations knew this. That they clearly made a conscious decision to fight NLRB recognition shows just how important this victory was for the academic labor movement.

Because of this, GSOC-UAW organizers were not facing just one hostile employer (the NYU administration) but a well-funded, well-organized administration machine intent upon destroying this union and the hopes of other private-sector graduate employee unions with it. Developing a broad base of support is critical for any organizing campaign; GSOC-UAW organizers made it even more central than usual to their own. They had to in order to combat the administrative efforts to undermine the union on campus, before the NLRB, and in the national media.

Jessup shows us the importance of developing and implementing a multifaceted campaign wherein victory results from internal and external organizing of all constituencies with a stake in graduate student employee unionization at NYU. While this most certainly begins, in typical fashion, with collecting cards and developing the support of those that will be in the bargaining unit, we see the importance of situating the struggle for recognition within a broader debate about the state of higher education and the rights of all workers to organize. Success here demanded that identified stakeholders and supporters be given manageable and meaningful ways to express support and, more important, to pressure the NYU administration. With activities ranging from petitions of support from faculty and "town hall" meetings to discuss the academic implications of unionization, to demonstrations for the right to organize involving elected officials and the AFL-CIO, GSOC-UAW succeeded in publicly framing the debate about unionization in its own terms. Though the fight for recognition and, ultimately, the arrival of the first contract was long and frustrating, the campaign strategy was successful in building and maintaining the support necessary for victory at NYU and potentially other institutions.

The GSOC-UAW victory at NYU seemingly paves the way for the next wave of successful graduate student union drives. The election loss for GradSoc at the University of Minnesota in 1999 can be equally instructive. As Michael Brown, Ronda Copher, and Katy Gray Brown make clear, the early stages of this campaign included a vision in which unionization was the key to enhancing the graduate student voice in both employment and academic debates and, in doing so, creating a more democratic university. Unfortunately, whereas GSOC-UAW's campaign strategy successfully built on a variety of internal and external organizing initiatives, GradSoc's vision for the union was ultimately lost in a campaign that emphasized the short-term achievements of signing cards and assessing support over the long-term goals of membership development and union building.

As Brown et al. document, many GradSoc organizers struggled with the union's message throughout the campaign. This became obvious as the election neared and an antiunion organization of graduate students challenged GradSoc's campaign. In responding, GradSoc realized that explaining why a union is necessary and beneficial is far more difficult than the very simple (and popular) anti–"big labor" rhetoric. Even the most pro-union organizers began to see that an organizing campaign is only as strong as the message behind it and the long-term plans before it. In the end, GradSoc organizers had failed to develop a campaign that would include a series of interim victories at each stage and in building momentum that would also build support for the union. Graduate students at Minnesota have clearly learned from this failure and have begun to reassess the future of organizing on their campus.

Though unionization was by far the most public of the activities employed by graduate students to address academic labor issues, collective bargaining was never seen as the only means of doing so. In the face of the growing academic labor crisis, graduate student activists began to seek power within the most conservative academic professional establishments. Cary Nelson documents one such case in which the insurgent Graduate Student Caucus (GSC) of the Modern Language Association (MLA) quite literally "took over" the MLA's agenda by forcing the organization to deal with the political, economic, and social forces responsible for creating an increasingly corrupt academic labor system. It is no accident that the MLA was the site of this first and most militant takeover. Full-time job prospects for graduate students in English and the modern languages had continued to diminish over the last decade, and terms and conditions of employment for graduate student employees in these fields continued to erode, while the elite leaders of the association chose to ignore the situation rather than use their position to address the crisis. In many ways, disciplinary associations like the MLA have clung to the very same apprenticeship model as university administrators. As a result, GSC activists were faced with the similar challenge of exposing the apprenticeship justification for exploitation as the fiction it had most certainly become.

Like the union drives going on all across the country, members of the MLA-GSC organized in the hopes of bringing a more democratic agenda to the work of the association. With graduate students and part-time faculty making up a growing percentage of the MLA, it was imperative that the organization respond to this growing constituency. Nelson's essay shows just how difficult changing the academic professional mind-set can be but how necessary it is if the academic labor movement is going to be successful. Nelson gives us a personal view of the inner workings of the MLA Executive Committee as it faced GSC initiatives. In doing so, he exposes the hypocrisy and resistance to change that have led to the failure of professional associations to take any kind of leadership role in addressing the effects that corporatization has had on our disciplines and our workforce. Moreover, he shows us that disciplinary associations do have an ethical responsibility to ensure that academic citizenship is a right and not a privilege and that members need to hold the leadership accountable to this goal.

As a full-time faculty member, Nelson also makes clear that graduate students are not the only ones fighting for academic citizenship. As we know, the transformation of the academic workplace documented in this collection has all but guaranteed that the terms and conditions of employment for graduate student employees will not change significantly upon completion of the Ph.D. Part-time and adjunct faculty in the Boston area realized that their rights as academic citizens would not be consistently met without taking responsibility for each other. Barbara Gottfried and Gary Zabel's essay discusses the unique approach taken by Boston's enormous but mostly invisible part-time faculty to organize for justice in the academic workplace on a regional level.

Using a social movement approach, part-time and adjunct faculty activists in the Boston area have responded to the many challenges of organizing contingent faculty by developing a model that emphasizes the collective welfare of adjuncts in the metropolitan region to overcome their isolation from one another. By organizing regionally and in concert with other activist organizations, these activists have been able to establish a citywide solidarity with one another and educate the public about the effects the casualization of the academic workplace has on not only the faculty teaching at area institutions, but the entire higher education community as well.

College and university administrators have not been the only targets, however. In an effort to create a more democratic university that guarantees the rights of all its citizens, Boston-area organizers realized that they would have to transform the undemocratic union structures that had been far too complacent in the very casualization they were now fighting. Zabel and Gottfried provide valuable insight into the ways that part-time and adjunct faculty activists strengthened their voices within their own unions to create the local change that provided the inspiration for a regional approach. Through the development of an "adjunct program" stressing fair wages, benefits, and other employment and professional rights for contingent faculty citywide, Boston organizers have moved closer to full citizenship rights for all academic employees.

Similar to the citywide approach taken in Boston is that taken by union activists at California State University (CSU), who realized that only a systemwide and statewide movement could resist the steady erosion of faculty rights. The example of the California Faculty Association (CFA) is slightly different in that it shows us an established faculty union attempting to *reor*ganize and rebuild after years of failing to develop a cohesive message in response to corporatization and its effects on the mission of the CSU. The "Future of the CSU" movement documented by Susan Meisenhelder is an attempt to unite the concerns of all California citizens, legislators, and members of the higher education community interested in preserving a vibrant state system that would be able to effectively serve the diverse needs of the state.

Like all large state systems, CSU has changed radically throughout the last decade. Increasing enrollments, outdated facilities, distance learning, casualization of the academic labor force, and many of the issues discussed in this collection combined to undermine the mission of both the CSU and the CFA. In an effort to take control of the higher education debate in California, CFA leaders developed an internal organizing program that, through its emphasis on quality education and a stronger faculty voice in the academic workplace, has been able to counteract the corporate rhetoric and managerial practices that have threatened the system.

The case studies in section 3 illustrate the diversity of approaches being employed by unions and other associations to combat the harmful effects of corporatization on the higher education community. This diversity is the best example of the strength of the contemporary academic labor movement, not only in the way it represents its range of participants but also in how these participants respond to the larger forces that now shape the university.

CHAPTER 9

The Campaign for Union Rights at NYU

Lisa Jessup

In recent years there have been countless articles written about graduate employee unionization. The Graduate Student Organizing Committee-United Autoworkers of America (GSOC-UAW) and its campaign to organize teaching and research assistants at New York University was the subject of many of them. Being the first private university in the country to successfully organize a union got our campaign a lot of attention. Normally it is difficult to get press to cover stories of workers trying to form unions, but there has been some caché to graduate employee organizing campaigns, producing many articles that spin the story in pretty much the same, overly cute way: Graduate students and autoworkers? Philosophers as shop stewards?

Graduate employees have been represented by unions for more than thirty years, beginning with the University of Wisconsin in the late '60s. In the years leading up to our drive, there had been a wave of public university organizing, and now our campaign has helped to prompt a second wave of organizing, especially in the private sector at universities such as Columbia, Brown, Cornell, and Tufts. At this writing, graduate employees on more than twenty-six campuses have recognized unions and are organizing at fourteen other campuses. They are more likely to be represented by unions than is the average American worker. Given that, we think it is time to put to rest the old articles on graduate students trading in their backpacks for picket signs or the "unlikely partnerships" between student employees and industrial unions.

In this essay, I outline how graduate workers at NYU fought for a union against many odds and won. The campaign was groundbreaking but for the most part was won the way most workers win and was fought by NYU the way most employers fight unions. University organizing does have its own set of circumstances that inform the day-to-day of the campaign: a large, wealthy employer run by an ever-growing administration and a board of trustees representing corporate interests; a diverse group of workers, sometimes with union contracts; a nonprofit status with a public image and relationships with the political and local communities; students and faculty who can become active around issues and help shape the community opinion. We took advantage of those circumstances as best we could. I hope that examining this campaign will be a useful tool for other workers who want to form unions in their own workplaces. I will provide a general overview of the campaign and also devote attention to specific aspects of the campaign, on our side and on NYU's, that are worth looking at in more detail. I pay particular attention to some of the nuts and bolts of the organizing, the legal case, the role of the faculty, NYU's antiunion campaign, and our creation of a broad network of support within the university and in the larger community.

Overview

GSOC-UAW's campaign to organize graduate employees started in the spring of 1998 and ended with a union contract about four years later, in January 2002. The contract, the first of its kind, provides significant improvements. The graduate employees' wages will rise 38 percent (with many doubling their pay), their health care will be fully covered (many used to shoulder the full cost), and they will have workload protections and access to a fair grievance procedure, to name just a few things that made the long fight so worthwhile. The pressing needs of graduate employees and their commitment to change helped sustain the long campaign at NYU.

During the spring of 1998, a group of graduate students decided to form an organizing committee and start working with Local 2110, UAW. By October of that year we were collecting signatures on union petitions, and we had commitments from the majority of the fifteen hundred graduate employees by the following April. Up until then, NYU really did not conduct an antiunion campaign. Although we did not expect the university to just sit down and negotiate with our union voluntarily, we did present them with the opportunity, once we reached majority in April of 1999. The university refused, and thus began the long fight for union recognition.

The fight on NYU's end consisted of spending literally millions of dollars prolonging the inevitable: delaying through hearings and appeals at the National Labor Relations Board; claiming that graduate employees were simply students and not entitled to form unions; running a public relations campaign on campus against the union; attempting to enlist faculty to pressure graduate students; and refusing to abide by a ruling and an election that mandated they recognize our union and bargain.

For GSOC, the fight was about constantly building our membership; maintaining momentum and enthusiasm among a group of new workers every year; creating and mobilizing a broad network of support with workers and students on campus, with labor, and with elected and community leaders; winning a legal decision on a local level; winning an election; winning a federal legal decision granting union rights for graduate employees throughout the country; and escalating our actions. In the spring of 2001, on the brink of a strike vote, the university agreed to recognize our union and to start bargaining.

I describe the campaign as long in the sense that no worker should have to go through what GSOC-UAW went through—justice delayed for almost four years because of the tactics, legal and otherwise, of the employer. However, we recognize that many graduate employee campaigns have taken much longer, some more than ten years. Graduate students at Yale, for example, have been actively organizing for union recognition for more than a decade. We believe that these long fights, coupled with the willingness of our members to take action, shortened the fight for us. We hope that our fight makes the process easier elsewhere. That said, I should add that the fight is unlikely to be easy anywhere. Since GSOC-UAW was recognized, both Brown and Columbia have used their tremendous resources to delay in the courts and attempt to reverse the federal decision granting union rights to graduate employees at private universities.

Phase I: Organizing for a Majority

In October of 1998, about forty graduate assistants committed to start working on the petition campaign to form the union. At this stage, the goal was to gather signatures onto union petitions from a majority of the graduate employees. The petitions themselves were worded in such a way that we could present them to the National Labor Relations Board for an election. Although we did ask the university to recognize our union voluntarily, we had no illusions that it would do so. We prepared from the outset to challenge the law at the NLRB—which did not recognize graduate teachers as being covered by federal labor protections—and, we hoped, to change it for everyone going forward. But first, more than eight hundred employees had to sign union petitions before the end of the spring 1999 term.

We had a staff of three half-time graduate assistants, a lead organizer, and the volunteer committee. Our plan was to organize one-on-one, that is, with organizers taking the time to talk to individual graduate assistants one at a time, to build support for a union and a strong community. We conducted training and also sent the graduate staff and volunteer organizers to the AFL-CIO's intensive three-day training, called the Organizing Institute. We did this throughout the course of the campaign. We needed not just to sign up a majority of grads, but to build as diverse an organizing committee as possible. Early on, our committee consisted only of students in the humanities. We decided to commence the petition campaign anyway and recruit a more diverse leadership as we went along. We could do that pretty easily at a university because everyone has free access to all of the buildings and departments.

Talking to strangers can be daunting, and most organizing committees try to find an easier way to sign everyone up, such as holding large meetings or leaving cards in people's mailboxes. GSOC was no exception. Organizers got used to approaching students individually, however, and doing so helped them to see the isolation in which most graduate students were working. Although NYU likes to speak of the "university community," at the outset of the campaign there was very little interaction among graduate students across departments. Now many graduate students who were involved in the organizing comment that a true community that transcends the immediate demand of organizing has emerged and that it could never have come together without the union.

Early on, everything we did had to be about building our membership. We were learning fairly quickly that some major issues were the poor wages and lack of paid health care, as well as an overall desire to have a say in governance of the university. There were some committee members who found the time-consuming organizing and reporting back to be boring and "numbers focused." Often our meetings would turn into debates about our organizing strategy. Other approaches—such as putting up posters or holding conferences or teach-ins about issues of academic labor—were more attractive to some, but we stuck to membership building. The concern was not about keeping things under the radar: this was not the kind of campaign you could hide from the employer. Public meetings take a lot of effort and tend to attract the same people every time you do them. Conferences on academic labor would not help us reach far into departments where people supported having a union but just didn't participate in conferences. Since then we have had teach-ins, a representation election, work-ins, conferences, and strike votes, but we still feel that to have the strongest and most participatory membership, such events need to be organized one on one.

By early March 1999, several hundred graduate employees had signed petitions. But we still needed to reach hundreds more. We decided the best way to get the signatures on petitions was to organize "blitz" fashion: recruit dozens of organizers to go out into departments with petitions and staff tables for a week. This would also be our first real visibility event. For "GSOC Week" graduate employees, some of whose activism had consisted solely of signing a union card, committed to more than four hundred hours of organizing. We also enlisted the aid of activists and other UAW members from Local 2110, Legal Services', and the National Writers Union to help us meet our goal in one week. That week we solicited the help of more than two hundred working members and five hundred graduate students in support of GSOC. We had a majority and were ready to start planning how to force the university to recognize the union.

Phase II: Going Public

Once we reached majority, we decided we needed a big event to demand recognition from the university, to "go public" and celebrate our success. We also worked quickly to involve a much broader community in our fight: faculty; undergraduates; labor on campus, in New York, and within the national AFL-CIO; elected officials; clergy; and local community organizations. We anticipated a protracted fight with a hostile employer, and we knew we needed to build a larger community that would have a stake in winning the campaign. We wanted to have a network of support on campus that would continue to last as we became established, and also to involve key individuals that could help pressure the university.

For months, individuals and groups on campus had been asking how they could help with the campaign. At that point, we were not holding actions or creating venues in which groups could express support—we were just trying to keep supporters informed of our progress. But when we realized that we would reach our goal that spring and started planning how to demand union recognition from the university, we started thinking in terms of events and community support.

Although we had a general idea of the kinds of things we could ask supporters to do—sign petitions, call or meet with administrators, speak up at events, rallies, demonstrations—we needed a different approach with the faculty because of the nature of their relationship with graduate students.

Prior to our recognition event, we met with a group of faculty to develop a plan for support. From other campaigns we had learned a couple of things about dealing with faculty members. At Yale University, as Corey Robin describes in the previous section, faculty had threatened and retaliated against graduate students for their union activity; and at the University of California, faculty support had been disappointing and lukewarm at best. We considered not enlisting faculty support. After all, how many workers ask their supervisors to support their campaign? It wasn't really support we wanted, but rather to prevent the kind of faculty behavior that had occurred at Yale. So even though we thought that NYU faculty might be more open to unions, we did not want, through asking for faculty *support*, to create a situation in which graduate students looked to their faculty for *approval* in a decision that was up to the graduate employees to make.

What we came up with was a neutrality campaign for the faculty. (We later asked the administration to adopt a position of neutrality—that is, to refrain from attempting to influence graduate employees' decisions on whether to join the union—but, like the notion of voluntary recognition, it seemed a long shot.) Initially, we wanted to do something that would involve a larger group than just the diehards on the faculty or the usual suspects. We developed a petition with language that addressed the "right to organize." The petition said: "After only seven months of campaigning, the overwhelming majority of graduate student employees at NYU have joined the union. . . . We, the undersigned, urge NYU to respect this fully democratic decision on the part of graduate student employees. . . . In particular, we urge NYU to adopt a neutral position and not to obstruct this democratic process." We anticipated that issues like choice and democracy would have broad appeal. The petition was something that very supportive faculty could work on (drafting, getting signatures, presenting to the administration) and that many more could feel comfortable signing.

The faculty group wrote the petition and circulated it just four days prior to our event for recognition, gathering about 65 signatures in the process. By the time that first petition (of four) wound down, we had collected about 120 faculty names in support of neutrality and the right to organize. For the event itself, we asked the faculty, members of the support staff and the maintenance workers unions, elected leaders, clergy, and members of the Yale graduate employees union (GESO) to join us in demanding recognition from the university. The event was a huge success, in part, because of the way the events unfolded.

The plan was to have our expanded organizing committee, along with supporters, present a letter to the university president, L. Jay Oliva, asking that the university recognize GSOC as a union based on majority support. We wanted the event to be visible: we would all assemble at the top floor of the library, carrying signs with the names of all of the departments where graduate assistants worked, and present the letter. Then we would descend the stairs quietly to hold a press conference out front.

Getting a hundred people with signs quickly up to the top floor of the library proved a little tricky, but soon we were all up there attempting to deliver the letter. The security officers, stationed outside the top administrators' offices, took the letter and asked us to wait. After a bit of back and forth we were asked to continue waiting, and earlier concerns some had about disrupting the library atmosphere melted away as we were asked to wait longer and longer. We brought up the press and the elected officials, the chair for higher education for the state assembly, a state senator, a city council member, and U.S. Congressman Jerrold Nadler. The press event turned into an impromptu rally with speeches, a reading of the faculty neutrality letter, cheering, and chanting.

At last, the university's labor relations representative, Richard Semeraro, came out and told us that the administration had the letter and "would respond." Council member Christine Quinn then shouted that we had a U.S. congressman there and asked if NYU would be willing to meet with the four elected officials present. After a short conference some members of the administration sat down with the four officials. The conference did not yield anything immediately for GSOC, but it was meaningful. Involving elected officials from the early days ensured that they would be somewhat invested in the process. The meeting put NYU on notice that whatever it did with respect to the union, it would be accountable not just to its workers but to a much larger community. It also sent a message that NYU's friends in office were our friends, too—we were not just a student group with a gripe, we were a strong union with the clout to mobilize support.

Phase III: NYU's Antiunion Campaign

The university responded to our demand for union recognition with a letter a week later: "The National Labor Relations Board (NLRB) is the agency established by Congress to resolve disputes concerning labor relations matters in private universities. . . . The NLRB has developed a comprehensive set of rules which provide a protected environment for the full and free discussion of all aspects of union representation which is especially appropriate in an academic community." It went on to say that there were two relevant cases before the labor board that would influence its ruling on graduate assistants at NYU. Additionally, it mentioned two old cases on the books from the '70s that denied union rights to student employees. The university went on to say, however, that "NYU has the same concerns expressed by the NLRB but will comply with the duty to bargain, as it has always done, if it is established by due process of law."

The cases they mentioned all dealt with "employee status." In order to use the labor board as the vehicle to get a union recognized or to file unfair labor practice charges, workers must meet the NLRB's definition of employee. The board does not grant union rights to all people who work, such as independent contractors, and has excluded certain types of workers from the protections offered by the National Labor Relations Act. In the Yale case, the labor board issued a complaint against the university for threats and retaliation for union activity, as described in Corey Robin's article in section 2. The union there had persuaded the regional board to look at the question of employee status as it dealt with the complaint. Yale had argued for dismissing the charges altogether, without dealing with the employee status issue, claiming the strike was a partial strike and therefore not a protected activity. A case involving Boston Medical also dealt with employee status of student workers, in this case, medical interns and residents who, as a class, had never been granted union rights under the NLRB. At that time both cases were before the NLRB in Washington.

We filed our petition at the labor board the next day. The university retained Proskauer-Rose, the law firm that had worked for Yale on the GESO unfair labor practice hearing and that also represents the Museum of Modern Art, Columbia University, and many other workplaces in our union. Proskauer engages in "union resistance" with its partners charging from $450 to $600 per hour. So, with two partners and two associates working for NYU, we estimated the firm earned a few million from the university for the years of hearings, briefs, and an antiunion campaign it was advising. NYU's first move to defeat the union was to engage in delay, through lengthy legal hearings and appeals.

The labor board would not dismiss our petition, as NYU had requested, but instead agreed to hold hearings on the question of "employee status." Even though graduate employees at public universities all over the country were unionized, NYU was a private institution. The university, both at board hearings and in its campaign against the union, made a lot of noise about the difference between state universities and private ones. It stressed at the hearings that we were seeking to overturn twenty-five years of precedent at the board and that the "law" should stand as is. But in fact, precedent consisted of only a couple of cases on the books, both from the '70s, and graduate employees' situations had changed radically since then. Universities had come to rely more on the labor of graduate employees and part-time contingent adjuncts. The real difference between graduate employees at state universities and private ones was not employee status, but rights: grad employees at private universities could engage in strikes, but most of their state counterparts were prohibited by state law.

Over the course of the hearings, NYU put deans, administrators, and faculty on the witness stand to make a case on "educational relatedness." Their argument was that all of the work being done by graduate students at the university is so closely related to their academic work that the work itself is simply education. So we made sure that our witnesses described such educational activities as blanching asparagus for departmental events, teaching seven semesters of Spanish I, booking hotel rooms for a conference, and Xeroxing and more Xeroxing. They also testified to the fact that at NYU teaching assistants perform more than 50 percent of the contact hours (i.e., classroom meeting times and office hours) in the College of Arts and Sciences and more than 80 percent of the core undergraduate curriculum.

On our end, we wanted to simply make the case that graduate employees provide a service for compensation under the direction and control of the university. That is the heart of the definition of a statutory employee under the law. Graduate assistants testified about their work, and faculty members testified about their reliance on graduate employees. All of the testimony—including that of Joel Westheimer, who describes his subsequent firing in section 2—helped to contradict the testimony of administrators.

The hearings dragged on for nine months. Some people have asked why we went "the legal route"—why we did not simply get NYU to recognize our union voluntarily and bargain. Voluntary recognition does not necessarily take less time or fewer resources. It usually takes serious action, like a strike, to force an employer to "voluntarily" recognize a union. We were prepared to get recognition one way or another, but we knew we had a good case and that it would have consequences beyond NYU. The downside to going the "legal route" is that it implies that the right to form a union is dependent on government approval. In essence, we were litigating while simultaneously running a campaign intended to make the university recognize us regardless of the legal outcome. This strategy led to some feeling on campus that although the university was engaging in delay, pursuing its legal options was somewhat legitimate because both sides were talking about this as a first, as history. As a result, moderates in the union drive were content to let the legal action play out a bit before considering a strike. Now that the NYU case has been litigated and decided on a federal level, however, it is unlikely that graduate employees will be content to let the issues play out in the courts as universities attempt to re-litigate employee status. Now it is much clearer that universities use the legal process only as a delay tactic.

We were still in hearings in the fall of 1999, and by then the university had started to try to use the faculty in its campaign against the union. That September, the administration wrote to the faculty what we came to call the "how to break the law" letter. It read: "It could lawfully be said by a faculty member, for example, that unionization of graduate students could lead to changes in the reliance of faculty on graduate assistants, that negotiation of a collective bargaining agreement would likely result in rules and restrictions . . . and given such restrictions, many faculty might find it necessary to re-evaluate their reliance on graduate assistants." The letter was disguised as a legal memo on the National Labor Relations Act's constraints on speech: no threats, intimidation, coercion, retaliation, or surveillance. Fair enough. However, this letter, in scripted detail, was a how-to for faculty to break the law and get away with it: "In general, stating that certain negative consequences 'will' result from unionization should be avoided. It can be said that selection of a union 'could' or 'may' have such an effect."

The letter was almost identical to one sent to Yale faculty about a year earlier by the provost there, Alison Richards. GESO organizers had been given one by a sympathetic faculty member, and they asked us to keep it quiet. When NYU's letter went out, we received dozens from faculty over the fax and did not intend to keep it quiet.

We wanted to expose NYU's tactics and pressure administrators to back off. In November of 1999, we held a legislative briefing for elected leaders and clergy so as to involve more influential people and step up pressure on the university. We knew that we would need more than a legal ruling to win this campaign. Typically, employers conduct their own worker-focused campaign to get workers to vote "no" for a union. We had to figure out a way to curb this kind of campaign on campus while continuing to build our membership with a new crop of first-time graduate employees. Given the success of our faculty neutrality petition, we decided that focusing on worker democracy and fairness would be the best message. Only this time our audience was much broader than faculty. We had already begun working with a small group of legislative leaders and seen what a difference they could make; while the administration had no qualms about dismissing students, they could not dismiss a U.S. congressman. Likewise, with the eyes of the community focused on it, NYU was limited in the kinds of ugly union-busting actions it could take.

We were able to get U.S. Senator Charles Schumer to cohost the briefing, along with the AFL-CIO. This briefing was also designed to make our campaign a "right to organize" or Voice @ Work campaign. The AFL-CIO's Voice @ Work campaign highlighted organizing efforts in which employees had chosen to unionize, but were being prevented through antiunion campaigns, legal delays, lack of legal protection, or other reasons. We know from polling research that the majority of Americans are opposed to the kinds of tactics that employers use to bust unions, but they are unaware of how pervasive these tactics are. The AFL-CIO uses press conferences, briefings, and other public forums for workers to tell their personal stories of struggle to help bring to light the way employers use unethical methods to thwart union rights on a regular basis. For our briefing, we took that "how to break the law" memo and emblazoned giant posters with quotes from it as props for the event. We used that letter to show the invited leaders that NYU was acting no differently than any other antiunion employer.

Communicating the experiences of graduate employees was crucial to gaining the community support that we needed. Not surprisingly, the importance of the work of graduate teachers was not immediately obvious to those outside of the university. The idea of "eggheads" organizing a union was enough to pique people's interest. In order to win their support and respect *as workers*, we had to tell them what grads did and why they were organizing a union. This was the first of three legislative and community events in which GSOC members described their work and the kinds of working conditions they wanted to change. Many of the guests were shocked to hear stories of grad students working sometimes more than forty hours a week and living in poverty, while racking up close to a hundred thousand dollars in debt.

When people hear the word "graduate student," many think "privileged." So not only were students faced with a university that did not recognize them as workers, but they were also faced with a broader community that was not making the connection either. And beyond that, there were graduate students themselves who, though poor, felt that they had other options and did not have much in common with other low-wage workers.

Grad students talked about who they are and what they do to get by (generally they are not rich or privileged, work two or three jobs and take out loans, are not supported by Mom and Dad, and sometimes are parents themselves), what they did at the university (50 percent of all teaching hours, 90 percent of all grading) and what they were facing at work (very little pay, no health care, uncertain future prospects, and a rich employer thwarting their right to organize a union). Graduate assistants spoke about being $40,000 in debt, or being the only people in their families to attend college at all, or being an international student with no access to loans, unable to make ends meet on $12,000 a year in New York City. All spoke about the university's campaign to deny them the right to organize a union.

Senator Schumer then ended the event by kicking off an "Appeal for Fairness" campaign, asking the university to be neutral, to not engage in an antiunion campaign or delays. The appeal said, "We want to urge you and your administration to allow these employees the dignity and respect to make this important decision free from interference from their supervisors, faculty and advisors." We continued to get legislators, labor leaders, and community leaders to sign the appeal, gathering the signatures of more than forty legislators, fifty labor leaders, and countless religious and community leaders.

In addition to hosting legislative and community briefings, GSOC members traveled the city and even the country telling our story. We traveled to Washington, D.C., to be part of the AFL-CIO Voice @ Work campaign. We made the rounds of local labor, community activist, city council and other political meetings. We went to UAW conventions and conferences to meet other UAW members and share the news of our campaign. And we participated in every major labor rally in the city. Participating in these events was important not only for garnering external support but for encouraging a broader group of graduate employees to take ownership of our campaign and become part of the larger labor movement.

Phase IV: Winning the Election

We concluded the hearings in late January of 2000, leaving the labor board just six weeks to decide our case if we were going to be able to hold an election that spring. In terms of organizing, we were working on a petition, asking GSOC members to be public in their support of the union, on a poster to be used prior to the election. We were also organizing for another public event, this time with President John Sweeney of the AFL-CIO, who is also on the board of directors of the Wagner School for Public Service and the Wagner Labor Archives at NYU. We also continued to work with the faculty on the issue of neutrality.

The first faculty petition had basically been ignored by the university. The university chose to fight the union on the question of employee status, framing the decision as an academic issue. But if the university's decision was truly an academic issue and not simply an employer tactic to fight a union, shouldn't faculty have been consulted?

The issue of governance was something that faculty could rally around. Some wrote a second petition, and many faculty spoke out in defense of unionizing at forums and "town hall meetings" set up by the administration to present its views on graduate employee unionization. This second petition called for the administration to respect faculty governance and pointed to particular actions taken and claims made by the administration against the union. It criticized NYU for its use of Proskauer-Rose, citing the firm's advertising of its antiunion advocacy. It also accused NYU of making unfounded claims about the harm a union could do to faculty-student relationships. The signers said: "We find it ironic that NYU has professed such concerns about impaired collegiality when its own clear disregard for faculty opinion in this matter violates even the most minimum standards of collegiality." The faculty reiterated its call to the administration to remain neutral and concluded: "At this point the administration must reconsider its firm adoption of an anti-union position. Furthermore, we call upon the NYU administration to open the widest possible dialogue with faculty and refrain from making any additional, unilateral decisions." This petition was signed onto by even more faculty than the first, and connected the issue of self-determination for graduate employees to the autonomy of faculty. The petition also prompted the university to adopt a watered-down version of shared governance that the university called "consultation." Consultation was largely a farce, with the university hand-picking groups of faculty to advise it on decisions it had already made, and the administration then defending those decisions at town meetings, which it would refer to afterwards as further vehicles for "consultation."

On April 3, 2000, the regional director of the NLRB ruled in favor of the union and ordered an election. The ruling was clear on employee status: "In applying the common law agency definition of employee to the graduate assistants at issue here, it would appear that they clearly fall within that definition."

It also addressed the university's claim that even if the graduate assistants were found to be employees, they should be denied collective bargaining rights for "policy reasons," namely that collective bargaining should not be granted because it could interfere with the mentor-mentee relationship and with academic freedom. The ruling said:

> It thus appears that the underlying rationale of the Employer's contention that academic freedom will be compromised by the obligation to engage in collective bargaining is essentially a rejection of the appropriateness of graduate students speaking through a common voice. . . . The asserted anticipated interference with academic free-

dom essentially appears to be a fear that collective action over graduate students' conditions of employment will be more influential and
powerful than individual action. The issue thus framed is whether
the NLRB should deny collective bargaining rights to employees
because of this anticipated impact of collective bargaining. This suggestion runs directly contrary to the express purposes of the Act."

The regional director concluded by stating, "There is simply no basis to
deny collective bargaining rights to statutory employees merely because they
are employed by an educational institution while enrolled as a student."

The board ruled that teaching assistants and some research assistants
and graduate assistants would be eligible to vote in a union election. It excluded research assistants in the sciences who received external funding to
do their own research. During the hearings, NYU had argued and put in
good evidence that the work RAs were doing was simply their own dissertation work. We thought that based on this evidence, they would not be
deemed to be employees, so we modified our petition to exclude them, lest
they be used as a basis to exclude all assistants.

NYU was unhappy about the ruling and recommenced its antiunion
campaign full on for the next three weeks. It sent a barrage of e-mail messages and held "town meetings" and departmental meetings, trying to set
them up as debates. It also refused to provide us with the legally required
"Excelsior list"—the list of eligible voters and their contact information,
which employers are required to provide to unions—citing the Family Education Rights and Privacy Act (FERPA). In recent years universities have
used FERPA to thwart unions on a variety of fronts. In our case, the university sent an e-mail to students eligible to vote in the election stating that the
Auto Workers were seeking contact information about them and asked if
they would like to opt out of providing it. To make sure potential voters
were fully informed of their "privacy rights," NYU hired people to telephone students at home about this issue. In violation of the NLRB's ruling,
NYU provided us the voter list with information missing for about a hundred students who had opted out. The list also contained more than a hundred ineligible MBA students whose titles were unclear, but who we knew
were not being paid by the university.

The administration drew much attention to the exclusion of the RAs in
the sciences, accusing the union of gerrymandering a unit to its liking. The
argument, while unconvincing to most graduate students, was recited ad
nauseam. Nonetheless, some faculty and students believed the university's
argument. That is the point of employer antiunion campaigns: to create an
upside-down world in which empowerment is really disempowerment,

unionized workers actually lose money rather than gain, and the right to vote is actually disenfranchisement. As we moved to an election, NYU's campaign quickly became garden variety. In the many e-mails and home mailings the university sent to potential voters, the administration wrote about dues, strikes, "flexibility," faculty-student relationships, and other things.

Divide and conquer, one of the oldest tricks in the antilabor book, characterized the campaign targeted at international students. NYU has more international students than any other university in the country. They had been a large contingent on our organizing committee from the beginning. This was for good reason: international students had the most to gain. Given that almost all of them were on visas that prohibited them from working outside the university, winning improvements on the job at NYU was the only way they could improve their lot. NYU saw an opportunity, however, to try to convince international students that a union would hurt them because of the position the UAW and the labor movement had taken on H-1B visas. These are guest worker visas granted to high-tech workers. Because they indenture an employee to a single employer and keep wages artificially low, they are a bosses' game. They also have nothing to do with unionization on a university campus. But in the intense atmosphere of the pre-election campaign, the issue was a live one. The UAW, along with many elected Democrats and the rest of the labor movement, had opposed the expansion of H-1B visas. The university tried to convince international students who might be applying for these visas in the future that our union did not care about the interests of foreign workers. Some students saw through this subterfuge, but others were swayed. After the end of our campaign, both Brown and Columbia trotted out this issue (now two years old) in an attempt to convince international students that it really is not in their interest to form a union in America.

The issue surfaced again in the final hours of the election campaign. The night before the election, a senior faculty member in the math/computer science department—one of the largest in the university, and composed primarily of international students—sent out a threatening e-mail. "The student visas (F1) are not exactly working visas," read the message. It continued:

> It is true that many students have temporary jobs to support themselves during their period of education. I do not know how the INS would view employment under a union contract. Difficulties often arise at the application for a Green Card. INS has its own rules which can be inconsistent with regulations of another government agency. These rules are becoming tougher every year, thus, I personally would recommend caution.

The message invokes the INS and its power just to make sure students got the message: voting yes could jeopardize your ability to stay on a student visa and to work in this country in the future.

We objected immediately seeing as how the professor's e-mail was purely a scare tactic; we demanded that the university either give us access to the university's e-mail system to respond or correct the mistake itself. The university did neither, and we ended up filing unfair labor practice charges over the threats. But we had already lost a significant number of votes in that department.

To organize for the election, we beefed up our staff temporarily, bringing in organizers from other campuses and from our union. The ruling gave us a unit we expected and we basically focused on holding on to our yes votes and trying to reach the people who were new to us when we got the voter list from the university. Holding the election in spring was to our advantage insofar as knowing our unit. There is some turnover between spring and fall, but most new people enter school in the fall. It had been a struggle for us each fall to get lists of working graduate students in each department and we never felt our information was solid until early in the spring term. To facilitate organizing, we divided the campus into four teams. General committee meetings were held weekly at this stage and focused on training organizers and developing strategy. With the teams we could have separate meetings with groups of a more manageable size to deal with assignments, report-backs, and organizing problems. We ended up using the team structure throughout the campaign.

For the election, we had a plan to distribute one piece of literature per week during the period up to the vote. We had a piece on what to expect from the university, the support poster with about 750 names on it, an endorsement booklet (with letters from Local 2110 shops, the clerical workers union at NYU, and elected officials including Senator Schumer), and a testimonial piece that basically said, "We've heard the university's arguments and we're still voting yes." More important, we planned a campaign of one contact per supporter during the three-week period prior to the election and then a contact each day of the three-day election until the person voted. Even though some of our supporters were annoyed about the push, it paid off, and when the election was over we had turned out more than 90 percent of who we predicted to be yes votes.

The election was held in the School of Business. The union had decided to challenge the eligibility of the MBA students the university had added to the voter list. When the university got word of it, it created a campaign inside the school, telling all students, regardless of their status, to vote. From union observers at the election we know that there were students coming in to vote with full knowledge that they were not eligible, saying, "I know I am not on your list but my faculty told me that if I want to vote you have to let me." At the end of the election there were 295 challenged ballots.

The university appealed the decision to the NLRB in Washington. It was joined by friends-of-the-court briefs from many of the major universities in the country including Boston University, Yale, Columbia, MIT, Johns Hopkins, Princeton, Washington University, as well as the Association of American Colleges and Universities and the American Council on Education. Because of the appeal, the votes would not be counted and instead were impounded and put in a storage room at the NLRB in New York.

Although we knew that a majority had voted in favor of the union, the fall 2000 semester started without a union at NYU. We came off another summer facing the same problems we had each fall: how to get lists of those working, reach out to new workers, get people fired up after the long, momentum-killing summer.

We were not the only labor business on the university's plate, but it seemed as if the administration was trying to clear the decks to deal with us exclusively. The previous spring, undergraduates launched a campaign to stop the university from purchasing sweatshop-made clothing—part of the No-Sweat organizing that was happening all over the country. The founding of the Worker's Rights Consortium (WRC), a monitoring agency for university apparel, was held on the NYU campus in spring 2000. By the fall, undergraduates working with the WRC pushed through, without a lot of resistance, an agreement that the university would not purchase sweatshop-made clothing. The administration also agreed to be part of the WRC.

In addition, the university had recently signed an agreement with the building trades that all projects, even those it was subcontracting, would be built with union labor. The previous spring, NYU had subcontracted to have a dorm built with nonunion labor. Soon rats arrived on campus. Giant inflatable rats. Inflatable rats have become a labor tradition in New York City, used to identify employers in labor disputes. The rats come in three sizes and are powered by generators, the average rat being about fifteen feet. Because the university was subcontracting, it felt no need to use union workers. The building trades disagreed and held a number of demonstrations at the dorm site and on campus, one with more than three thousand workers and three giant rats. We worked together with a couple of organizers from the laborers union, basically participating in each other's events and putting them in touch with the undergraduates who were doing labor support work on campus. During the summer, the AFL-CIO held an annual event called Seven Days in June, which highlights organizing campaigns and targets especially bad employers. The summer of 2000 theme was the "March of the Rats." Of the almost twenty inflatable rats installed in Union Square, the biggest rat, a thirty-footer, had the name "New York University" on it.

The university was also in negotiations with its support staff, Local 3882 of the American Federation of Teachers (AFT). Local 3882 represents about sixteen hundred clerical workers and had worked under an open-shop contract for more than twenty years. Under an open shop, union dues and membership are optional. The union was in negotiations over the summer and into the fall demanding an agency shop, in which all workers covered by the contract pay dues. This was also a key issue in a protracted strike of Local 2110 against the Museum of Modern Art in the summer of 2000. The museum had been an open shop for more than twenty years. The workers there started the strike in late April and ended it, victorious, in early September, with an agency shop.

That fall, we discussed a strike for the first time with the organizing committee. Although some on the committee were prepared to take that kind of action at some point, the majority felt it was premature. Although we had been campaigning for NYU to "drop the appeal—count the ballots," it seemed that a majority of the graduate students were willing to let the issue play out at the labor board. We settled for a series of actions and a petition to the trustees.

In early October, with the clerical workers' contract still not settled and the labor board sitting on our decision, we invited John Sweeney back to campus to participate in a joint rally with the UAW and Local 3882 in support of both of our campaigns. Hundreds gathered at what had become our second home, the Judson Memorial Church, for an indoor rally and then marched on the university. Shortly after the event, the university reached an agreement with the support staff in advance of the expiration of their contract. The contract contained an agency shop provision, and we heard from the union that the university had said that it wanted to avoid a situation like the one at the Museum of Modern Art.

The university, however, made no changes in its position on the graduate assistants. The petition to the trustees was not really getting off the ground, no one had much enthusiasm for another petition, which was considered weak, but people were still reticent about pushing forward on a strike. We held protests and rallies, but we really all knew that these actions would not move the university.

On October 31, the NLRB in Washington upheld the regional director's decision and ordered that our ballots be counted. The decision was unanimous. The ruling rejected the university's claims that the graduate students' work is primarily educational and that collective bargaining would impinge on academic freedom. The board ruled: "We will not deprive workers who are compensated by, and under the control of, a statutory employer of their fundamental statutory rights to organize and bargain collectively with their employer, simply because they are also students."

The ballots were counted on November 8 and the count was 597 for the union and 418 against. There remained 295 challenged ballots. Both sides agreed that a good number of these were ineligible and the remaining ones were not determinative of the outcome. We met with university officials, and they insisted that the ballots cast by the MBA students be counted. As they were not determinative, we agreed to have them counted even though we thought that they were ineligible. On November 15, the challenges were counted, and GSOC-UAW was certified as the official collective bargaining agent at NYU, winning the election 619–551.

The university announced that it was considering its options. Memos to the community talked about how close the election was, especially after the MBA votes were counted, and claimed the RAs in the sciences were wrongly "excluded" from the vote. Nevermind that its "options" were to either abide by the law or break it. Yale president Richard Levin publicly encouraged NYU to break the law by refusing to bargain with our union. In a memo on November 9, 2001, the provost of NYU stated "the only way the University could obtain a judicial review would be to refuse to bargain with the UAW, go through an unfair labor practice procedure, and then take an appeal to the federal courts." The university also criticized the ruling repeatedly, which prompted NLRB Chairman John Truesdale to respond, "The argument is made that we don't understand graduate education, but I'm wondering if it isn't really that they don't understand collective bargaining."

On our end, we worked to mount a pressure campaign on the university, aiming to bring to the fore the reality that NYU was ruining its community and its reputation by continuing this fight. Meanwhile, we prepared for a strike to bring the university to the bargaining table.

Shortly after we won the election, on November 25, the *New York Times* ran an editorial in support of graduate employee unionization (we had met with the *Times* editorial board prior to our election in the spring of 2000, but better late than never). It said in part: "But the country decided nearly 70 years ago that the right to bargain trumped the inconvenience and other costs. American graduate programs, the envy of the world, are not so fragile they cannot coexist with unions, or provide workers the rights they enjoy elsewhere in the economy." We were thrilled to get the endorsement from the paper of record and used it in letters we sent to all of our supporters.

Our message to supporters was simple: By continuing to fight the union, the university is breaking the law and violating the rights of its workers. Its failure to bargain will lead to more serious labor strife on campus and will even further harm the already damaged reputation of the university.

We asked elected officials, the labor movement, clergy, faculty, undergraduates, and eventually student government to call on NYU to obey the law and bargain with our union. Some of our own members took to calling Robert Berne, NYU vice president and the point man on the antiunion campaign, to demand that the university bargain. He would take the calls and call members back, arguing with them at length that the Auto Workers wanted to bargain over academic issues. Soon this accusation was making its way into the university's conversations with our supporters in office as well as in its public statements. We also filed charges at the labor board over conduct associated with the election, including the threats made to international students through the e-mail system the night before the election.

Meanwhile, the Doonesbury comic strip devoted a week to the recent ruling on graduate employee unionization and focused on an imminent TA strike at "Walden." We were gearing up for similar action and were working with faculty and undergraduates. The faculty was once again circulating a petition demanding that the university live up to its legal obligations and bargain, ultimately gathering 167 signatures. Members of this faculty group were also officers in the recently revived chapter of the American Association of University Professors (AAUP), which wrote a resolution in support of our campaign.

By the end of the semester, even the Faculty Council (a group created the previous spring, apparently in order to voice support for the university's appeal to the NLRB) had called on NYU to bargain. This group had conducted a survey of faculty, the overwhelming number of whom believed the university was wrong to ignore its legal obligation. In a letter to President Oliva at the end of the semester, the Council said: "The majority thought that the University should abide by the election results, certified by the NLRB, and should bargain in good faith. . . . Faculty members expressed concern that *a non-bargaining stance and future legal action would adversely affect the relationship between faculty and graduate students*" (emphasis added). The letter explained that those faculty who were opposed to the union also disagreed with the university's actions: "Even for faculty who did not support the union, worry about the expense, time and energy diverted from the more pressing tasks of teaching and learning. Some cited concern that a long legal battle could have a negative effect on the reputation and prestige of the university."

Our faculty support group put together a packet that included this survey and the widespread press the campaign had gotten, including Doonesbury and an article in the *Economist*. The campaign was getting widespread attention, and the packet was meant to illustrate that any negative actions on the part of the university would get the same kind of attention.

The student senate passed a resolution that the university bargain with GSOC. The senate—an arm of the administration, with many members appointed rather than elected—had passed a resolution against us in the past, as had the graduate student council of the School of Education, which it issued without input and retracted after surveying graduate students in the school. Early on, we felt the best strategy was to not concern ourselves with student government; as a labor union, we did not want to send the message that there was much relation between student government and labor unions. When the student senate sent us a long questionnaire with antagonistic questions demanding that we answer promptly in writing, we didn't. We did say we would be happy to talk with senate members, just as we would with any student at the university. The senate did not take us up on the offer, and so we did not see the resolution in support of the administration as carrying much weight; the senate almost invariably supported the adminstration's position, even supporting a tuition hike. It was significant to us, however, when the senate passed a resolution against the university.

We started working closely with the undergraduates in the fall. They had been working on the anti-sweatshop campaign, democratizing student government, supporting the clerical workers' contract campaign and GSOC. They called themselves "kids," but what these kids do for fun is go to civil disobedience summer camp and visit maquilladoras over their spring break. We started meeting with them on a weekly basis in order to plan for an intense spring campaign. The undergraduate paper, and some of the writers in particular, had been reporting on the issue for years. Although the very first article written about GSOC in that paper misspelled Karl Marx's name (with a C!), a few of the more experienced writers had developed a fairly sophisticated understanding of the issues. Their articles simplified and clarified issues that the university strived to complicate, such as the exclusion of the research assistants or its refusal to bargain. The paper's editorial page called on the administration to bargain.

NYU sent out a lot of memos that fall, and ended many with a standard refrain: "Whatever the outcome, we will remain one community of scholars." By the end of the fall term, the NYU community had spoken out in support of abiding by the law, bargaining with the union, and ending the fight. The administration now stood outside its own community.

Phase VI: WHAT'S OUTRAGEOUS? TEACHERS' WAGES! WHAT'S DISGUSTING? UNION BUSTING!

We held an organizing committee meeting in early January prior to the semester and developed an organizing plan for a strike. The strike would be for recognition of our union, an unfair labor practice strike, as we had already filed unfair labor practice charges against the university for its refusal to bargain. We decided to elect a strike committee and hold a strike vote on March 1, but to keep our options open for a strike date, including keeping a date quiet until a day or so before any strike action. The advantage of not announcing until a few days beforehand is that the administration cannot replace workers so easily.

Prior to the beginning of the semester, the university sent us a letter saying that it would recognize our union if we agreed to the following preconditions: to hold a new election, to waive our legal right to strike, to withdraw all allegations of unfair labor practices, and not to bargain over a list of issues the university considered academic, such as tenure and stipend levels. The labor board recognizes two categories of bargaining subjects: mandatory and nonmandatory. Mandatory subjects are terms and conditions of employment, and both parties have a legal obligation to bargain in good faith over them. Nonmandatory subjects can be raised by either party, but neither side is obliged to bargain over them. Both mandatory and nonmandatory subjects were on the university's list. We met with the organizing committee, as this was an offer, no matter how ludicrous. The committee quickly agreed that their offer was nothing but a delay tactic, and so we sent a letter to the administration rejecting it. With regard to academic issues, we told them that our intention was and always had been to abide by the rules of the NLRB.

The university's determination to deny us the right to strike was instrumental in the discussions we were about to have in departments across the campus about striking. "Use it so you don't lose it" was our basic message. The attempt to try to get graduate employees to waive legal rights before the university even agreed to acknowledge other rights moved many supporters.

We organized one-on-one for the strike and held departmental meetings. Typically, some students had reservations. Although striking would amount to an economic hardship for most, the biggest concern came out of a dedication to the undergraduates that they felt responsible for. For some assistants, striking would be a wash for them economically. The union's strike benefits of $175 a week were close to what they currently earned working twenty hours a week for the university.

We also wanted to get out there and embarrass NYU prior to the strike, including meeting visiting parents who were coming for tours of the university. There were tours each week, and we alerted parents to the strike planned for the spring. Our presence, really only a few for each shift, drove the university crazy, and administrators and the head of security checked out our activities.

In the meantime, we asked the community, religious, elected leaders, and graduate students to call the top administrators and urge them to avert the strike and bargain. In these calls, and in their public statements, university officials called our decision to strike premature, saying that because they had not yet decided whether or not the university was going to bargain with us, we should wait for its decision.

They reiterated that the university's processes of "consultation" required that they continue to discuss the issue, when in reality they seemed to be looking for some group to support their actions when so many groups had opposed it already. They also continued to claim that the union wanted to bargain over academic issues.

We were meeting with the undergrads to come up with an overall plan to maximize student, and eventually parent, support. The undergraduate group was incredibly organized in its work. We came up with a petition, very simple language that asked students to demand that the university bargain with the union. We also wanted to go back to the petition signers and ask them to contact their parents with a letter that we would write. For the time being, though, we focused on how to get signatures. The undergraduates came up with a plan to do tabling (i.e., set up tables with literature) and "class raps." A group of undergraduates would visit classrooms for the last five minutes of class and talk to other undergrads about why having a union for teaching assistants would be good for the students at NYU. They also raised the issue of the strike. We developed a message that would help empower students by making a connection between their tuition money and their right to demand that it be spent on their education.

In their class visits, the activists spoke about the typical graduate assistant's conditions and the prolonged antiunion campaign and how much money it had cost the university. There were only about eight undergrads assigned to do these visits, but over the course of three weeks they visited more than a hundred classes and gathered three thousand-plus signatures. These same undergraduates also attended departmental meetings that we set up for graduate assistants about the strike. They came to pitch the class visits and get graduate students to sign up for them to come into their sections. They also served as an example of undergrads who stood in support of assistants who would not be teaching or grading or holding office hours with undergrads, saying to teaching assistants that it was just as important to teach students to stand up to injustice as it was to follow a semester lesson plan. Eventually, the undergraduate paper came out with an editorial encouraging undergraduates to support the strike.

We also delved into other more direct action that undergrads could engage in to support a strike when the strike happened. This group, like many recent undergrad activist groups around the country, was prepared to engage in civil disobedience.

Although the trustee petition never got off the ground in the fall, we wanted to start targeting individuals as well. We thought about the trustees as well as key administrators. L. Jay Oliva, who as president of NYU had never spoken on the union issue, had become much more of a public presence with his cabaret acts and musical theater. Oliva had performed cabaret at the new $3 million faculty and alumni club and was now set to perform in a student production of *Guys and Dolls* in mid-February. We didn't want to begrudge anyone a hobby, but this was too much for our committee to stomach. We had to target him. We decided to hold a rally outside of the event, calling it NO MORE SONG AND DANCE.

It was pouring rain, and we had no permit for an amplifier. We screamed in the rain with soggy, streaked signs and buckets and soda cans for noisemakers and we got our message to Oliva and to the trustees, who turned around and went home, deciding not to attend. In the following weeks, we approached the Bottom Line, a music club in Manhattan at which Oliva was scheduled to sing. We asked the manager to cancel the event or expect a major demonstration the night of the performance. NYU is the landlord for the club, but the manager was sympathetic. He made a lot of calls and alerted the community affairs department of the university that he did not want to be in the middle of a labor dispute. We also started to try to come up with a plan whereby Oliva would be forced to deal with or think about our union every single day. We anticipated stepping up this campaign to target the university in nationwide events if necessary.

In February, there were a few conversations between the university and top UAW and AFL-CIO leaders, including meetings with President Oliva. On our end, AFL-CIO President John Sweeney and Brian McGlaughlin, the NYC Central Labor Council president, attended an initial meeting with UAW Vice President Elizabeth Bunn. Subsequent meetings involved just UAW and NYU officials. These discussions started the ball rolling, and ultimately ended with union recognition. But initially the university refused to back off from its preconditions to bargaining. It further laid out its concerns about the union bargaining over "academic issues." We never felt that the university truly believed that the union wanted to bargain over tenure decisions or a student's academic progress. Why would we concern ourselves with such issues when our members were living in poverty? We said this repeatedly in our public statements. The university was using this as a scare tactic to remove legitimate issues from the bargaining table.

In late February, with the strike vote just days away, the university made its annual lobbying trip to the state Capitol in Albany. It lobbied for state money for a variety of things, including unrestricted money and money earmarked for the dental school. When it got there, however, legislators would not talk to NYU representatives about the issues they had come to lobby on. Instead, they were wearing GSOC stickers and asking NYU to deal with the issue of bargaining with the union. The UAW had a lobbying conference there that was ending on the day that NYU's was beginning. We got there first and asked our legislators to prioritize this issue. NYU could not hide—even its mascot, the cougar (who could not see very well out of his mask) was covered in GSOC stickers by the time we left.

On March 1, we prepared to hold a strike vote at a membership meeting at Judson Memorial Church. Prior to the vote, the administration and the UAW had been in discussions and were set to schedule another meeting. It was clear the administration wanted to meet prior to the vote, but based on previous discussions, we did not hold out much hope. The meeting yielded fruit. The majority of the initial preconditions to bargaining were not NYU's biggest concerns, and they came off the table. The university wanted us to withdraw allegations of unfair labor practices. We agreed to withdraw the one saying the administration refused to bargain, as well as the ones on election conduct regarding a faculty member and the use of the university's e-mail system. We did not withdraw the others, which involved unilateral changes that NYU had made in the terms and conditions of graduate employment. Additionally, the university, as it turned out, did not care so much about inclusion of the research assistants, after three years of arguing to the contrary. In fact, it wanted us to agree to exclude even more of them. Moreover, it wanted the MBA students whose votes it had fought so hard to include removed from the unit. Regarding academic issues, the union maintained its rights: in a letter outlining the agreement, signed by both parties, the issue is addressed:

> Such issues include, for example, the merits, necessity, organization, or size of any academic activity, program or course established by the University, the amount of any tuition, fees, fellowship awards

or student benefits (*provided they are not terms and conditions of employment*), admission conditions and requirements for students, decisions on student academic progress (including removal for academic reasons), requirements for degrees and certificates, the content, teaching methods and supervision of courses, curricula and research programs and any issues related to faculty appointment, promotion or tenure. *By these understandings, the UAW does not relinquish any rights it has under the National Labor Relations Act* (emphasis added).

This agreement was signed just two hours before our scheduled strike authorization vote. That evening, hundreds of people filed into the Judson church, and instead of voting for a strike, we moved to nominate members to the bargaining committee.

By the time the university recognized our union, NYU knew we had a campaign, almost a year old, to organize the thousands of adjuncts there. It had to be obvious to the university that our union would not simply go away. And our campaign looked like just the crest of a larger wave of organizing: Columbia grads were close to reaching a majority on their petitions, and campaigns at Brown and other universities were taking off. Now, we have a collective bargaining agreement in effect at NYU, and elections have been held at Brown, Columbia, and Tufts. Our union has negotiated an agreement with NYU (and without the need for legal hearings!) to conduct an election among more than three thousand adjuncts at the university. Brown, Columbia, and Tufts, however, have fought against counting ballots, hoping a labor board under the Bush administration will undo what so many have fought to achieve. Nonetheless, these attempts to turn back the clock will ultimately amount to a waste of more university resources, as graduate employees and adjuncts are unlikely to settle for less than what NYU student employees and their state counterparts have achieved.

CHAPTER 10

Democracy Is an Endless Organizing Drive

Learning from the Failure and Future of Graduate Student Organizing at the University of Minnesota

Michael Brown, Ronda Copher, and Katy Gray Brown

"Graduate union voted down for third time," read the headline of the campus paper, the *Minnesota Daily*, on May 12, 1999. After three years of effort, the attempt to unionize graduate assistants at the University of Minnesota had ended in defeat again. The election result this time was much closer than the elections of 1974 and 1990, which both lost by two-to-one majorities. The Graduate Student Organizing Congress (GradSOC) ran a strong campaign. In the process, we faced the challenges of organizing a large, diverse bargaining unit while countering a virulent antiunion campaign. Throughout, we also struggled with the tension between building the democratic union that we envisioned and organizing around the hectic logistical imperatives of an election. Our account involves many voices from Grad-SOC, yet the perspective provided is our own. Ultimately, we hope that other academic labor organizers can benefit from GradSOC's experience.*

Beginnings

The movement to unionize graduate assistants followed on the heels of two other unionization attempts at the University of Minnesota. In February of 1997, faculty voted against unionization by a twenty-six-vote margin out of more than thirteen hundred votes cast. The union campaign for faculty was essentially conducted via e-mail, with little outreach, and many felt that had more traditional organizing occurred the outcome would have been different. Five months later, university professional workers voted against unionization 932 to 651. Despite these recent losses, the general attitude on campus continued to be favorable toward unionization. Thus for graduate assistants who were looking to have respect and recognition for their efforts on campus, as one graduate student expressed it, "unionization was sort of in the air at that time."

Organizing this third attempt, we were well aware of the tremendous work ahead. The unit was enormous: eight thousand students in advanced-degree programs, of whom about forty-three hundred were employed in graduate assistant positions. If successful, this would be the largest graduate student union in America. This size, though, introduced a major problem. We were not sure if we had the necessary skills to organize such a large campus. From the beginning, we considered outside help.

GradSOC began through a conversation between two graduate students who were frustrated with their lack of power in decision making at the university. There was a student government organization, the Council of Graduate Students (COGS), on campus, but like other such organizations, it was not effective at addressing the power differential with the university. Beyond this general sense of powerlessness, some graduate students faced changes that further highlighted their lack of a democratic voice. For instance, during the summer of 1996, the composition department was incorporated into the English department—a move opposed by most graduate instructors who taught the composition courses. Graduate instructors felt their autonomy and the pedagogical integrity of their teaching were threatened. Upset about the conditions in the composition department, the university's imposition of a cap on tuition benefits that left many grad assistants short of program requirements, and without leverage to affect decisions about their workplace, graduate instructors began to discuss their options.

We also faced the problems workers throughout the American economy faced during the 1990s—declining quality of health-care benefits. Our dental insurance was gradually phased out completely. And since graduate student health insurance is not guaranteed, almost every two years the university puts out Requests for Proposals (RFPs) to find lower cost providers, which results in insurance carriers with less coverage and higher prices ("copays"). Students who had dependents faced extraordinarily high costs, prohibiting many of them from affording any coverage whatsoever. Considering this problem, among all the others, the question arose: "Don't you just think we need a union?"

After these initial conversations, a few graduate instructors in composition organized a meeting so that other graduate assistants who might be interested could discuss the possibility of a union. Friends, colleagues, and acquaintances were contacted about unionizing. One graduate student who attended this first meeting explained, "we were going to the meeting because we were pro-union. We thought it would be a good idea, we thought it could work." Throughout the fall of 1996 graduate students met to discuss organizational elements, union actions, and ideological questions. GradSOC was born.

Despite our enthusiasm, we did not know how to organize a union. We were committed to an organization that was nonhierarchical, democratic, and participatory. In order to achieve this goal, the founders of GradSOC sought the expertise of established unions. The American Federation of Teachers (AFT) and the United Electrical Workers (UE) were the two unions contacted, both of whom have graduate assistant unions within their organizations. The union at the University of Michigan, one of the oldest graduate unions in the United States, is affiliated with the AFT, and the union at the University of Iowa, which won recognition in 1996, is affiliated with UE.

Union organizers from UE and the AFT met with a core group of union activists. A handful of GradSOC supporters from the University of Minnesota went to Iowa to talk with graduate student activists about UE and their successful union recognition campaign. The AFT sent experienced union organizers to Minnesota and provided training and preparation for our first visible campuswide action. In February 1997, with the AFT's help, GradSOC organized a National Day of Action, which involved canvassing the campus with billboards, distributing literature, and talking to other graduate assistants about what was important to them, such as wages and affordable health care. A few months later, expanding our efforts to raise our profile on campus, GradSOC held its first May Day rally.

As we gathered information to decide on affiliation, we not only asked the AFT and UE about the resources each would provide, but also whether the union would address concerns aside from better wages and health insurance. Many of us felt strongly that our union should have a vision that dealt not only with the university environment but with larger issues of social justice. We wanted representation by a union that would reflect our commitment to participatory democracy. In the months before the affiliation vote, people talked informally with other friends and colleagues about unionizing. As a result, the group of core union activists had grown from twenty people at that first meeting to more than fifty at the affiliation meeting. Also, during this time, the e-mail list maintained by GradSOC grew to more than 150 graduate students who supported unionization.

In May 1997, after careful consideration, GradSOC supporters decided to affiliate with the AFT. This union had made a strong impression by providing GradSOC guidance on visibility and some basic organizing information and was well positioned to advocate for our interests at the state level. Yet a sizable minority of GradSOC supporters had voted for UE, and some left the organization because of the decision to affiliate with AFT. During the decision process concerns were raised over UE's organizing model, which advocates for a short-term, one-year campaign. Many GradSOC members believed that AFT's approach, modeled on a two-year campaign, was more appropriate for a unit as large as ours.

After deciding our affiliation, the AFT and the National Education Association (NEA) in Minnesota combined under one umbrella organization, creating Education Minnesota (EM). While the AFT agreed to provide organizational support, including two full-time organizers to oversee three part-time graduate student organizers, our official affiliation would be EM/AFT/NEA/AFL-CIO. For some, this combined superunion organization potentially offered our campaign more resources and expertise. However, this long list of affiliates would eventually be used against us in discussions about dues and the unwieldy influence of outsiders, "big unions."

With the AFT came substantial changes in how GradSOC looked and operated. In the fall of 1997, full-time union staff began to push for changes in the organizational structure. The AFT advised us to establish a hierarchical organizational structure consisting of a steering committee and stewards' council. Additionally, a definition of membership requiring a commitment to help build the union was created and agreed upon, and we began collecting membership cards. Within months of affiliation, the structure changed from egalitarian to hierarchical.

In the year leading up to the card drive calling for a union vote, GradSOC worked hard to establish itself as a broad-based, representative organization that advocated for graduate students. Our core membership was deeply committed to unionization on principle: we believed that in non-democratic institutions such as the university, workers should have voice in the decisions that affect them. GradSOC's organizing approach reflected the conviction that we should be acting like a union, and through our actions we believed skeptics would be convinced of the benefits of having legal representation. Even before a vote, we intended our work to testify to the strength of a union. During this period, GradSOC organized effectively around isolated departmental issues, most notably in the English department and the German, Scandinavian, and Dutch departments. In this year of membership building, GradSOC held its largest and perhaps most engaging action—a rally to call for improved health-care benefits for graduate student workers. Faculty, other unions on campus, and minority graduate students came together in support of health-care improvements and the need for unionizing. The university was perceived as acting responsively to our concerns, and GradSOC was widely credited for motivating the administration to act. This was the type of action that many of us had imagined— engaging the university on critical issues to develop broad support and establish the need for collective action. Many would say later that they felt this was the time when GradSOC was strongest, before we became completely occupied with the mechanics of the election itself.

While our organizing and membership were small outside departments in the humanities and social sciences, steering committee members, stewards, and staff all shared the sense that momentum was building. We entered our drive to collect authorization cards calling for a union vote with confidence and enthusiasm. When classes started in the fall of 1998, we began collecting cards. We were determined to surpass the state requirement for filing for a union vote (30 percent of the unit must sign cards calling for an election) by filing cards from more than 60 percent of the unit. This is a typical numerical goal for such campaigns, which is intended to assure a winning vote while taking into account a likely erosion of support as time passes. More important, our enthusiasm and confidence in our support led us to believe we could collect the cards before Thanksgiving—in four months versus the six months allowed by law. Our energies were directed entirely to collecting cards, focusing on the hundred largest departments, and we curtailed most other activities, such as building diversity in our membership and creating coalitions with other organizations on campus. This was both a short- and long-term strategy. One organizer covering the departments of German, Scandinavian, and Dutch, explained, "I think we thought, we just need to get through the card-drive, and then we can make sure that our organization is running the way it should be. But then we didn't have the structures in place that we needed in order to be ready for the election."

After an initial rush of eight hundred, the cards accumulated slowly. Our most committed and experienced organizers went into departments without internal leadership to collect cards, with some success, but the emphasis on card numbers left little energy to foster deeper commitment to the union. Efforts to develop new leadership from those departments and strengthen support fell to the side. Organizers would return to departments and labs time after time simply to track down students who hadn't been contacted, sometimes commuting to a different campus to do so. As a result, conversations centered on getting grad students to sign a card rather than on finding out what issues were important to them and how unionizing could improve our situation. The efforts of this period are well described by an organizer from the English department:

> There was always to some extent a numbers-pressure, and I know that at some point, I was more focused on being able to hand in lots of yellow cards than really making sure each new member I signed up really understood and felt involved in GradSOC and the campaign. . . . It does seem, however, the effort to get cards overshadowed the effort to shape a union. . . . The membership cards were a way of trying to get a commitment to that, making the new member feel invested and involved, but clearly we had to succeed to a much greater level in involving (particularly) RAs [research assistant] from the sciences, and that had to be about more than having them sign authorization and/or membership cards; departmental structures had to be set up.

Since cards were accumulating slowly, the Thanksgiving deadline was extended to the end of December, and our target card number lowered to 55 percent of the unit. When we failed to reach this, the steering committee agreed to make a final extension to the middle of January.

Two weeks before our new deadline of January 13, 1999, the university announced a pay increase for graduate assistants that would bring our salaries in line with the average for Big 10 universities. This development made the task of "selling" the union to new members more difficult: a workforce that was generally quite content had just received an unexpected pay raise. Graduate assistants at Minnesota felt they were treated fairly well, particularly since they already had health benefits, something that only unionized campuses can normally boast. As union organizers, we recognized the pay raise as a classic tactic to undermine our campaign, and the result of our union-building success. However, we failed to make this connection for most graduate workers, as we were preoccupied with the final push of our card drive.

GradSOC filed with the state office that oversees labor union certifications, Bureau of the Mediation Services (BMS), for a union vote on February 1, 1999, with cards representing 58 percent of the bargaining unit, and a majority from each of the seven disciplinary areas on campus. We were exhausted but happy to see the drive end. All of our energies had been focused on jumping the hurdle of filing, while the more ideologically meaningful actions of community building had been set aside.

What sustained us through this period was the belief that filing with a majority of the unit would give us confidence in a victory. However, even as we filed, we recognized that among this group of card signers there were areas of thin support, such as chemistry, engineering, and computer science. In these departments many grads do work as RAs on projects that help them complete their dissertations, and earning better wages than TAs in such departments as English and history. As soon as the initial rush of completing the card drive had faded, GradSOC staff announced the next phase of our campaign: assessment of our support among card signers.

Assessment became GradSOC's basic function until the election loss. There are two basic reasons for this. First, our energies had been poured exclusively into the card drive, and the steering committee had not developed a plan of action for an extended (and unforeseen) delay between filing and the vote. In part, this shortcoming is a result of uncertainty; we did not know what shape the election would take (mail-in ballots, on-site voting, etc.) until a decision was released by the BMS. Our expectation was that the election would be scheduled shortly after we turned in the cards, an expectation that had been reasonable based on past decisions by the state in the election process. Yet, union organizing often takes longer and needs more nurturing than the state-set timetable for union recognition. Second, we drew upon the sense that assessment, in the form of office visits and telephone calls, was the next step in the organizing model that succeeded at other schools.

Paradoxically, the waiting period after filing was both unbearable and welcome. We were anxious about what sort of ruling would emerge, but convinced ourselves that we could do little until we heard from BMS. By this point, GradSOC had been pursuing the card drive for many months, with little plan of action ready once the cards were filed. Moreover, many of us were exhausted from having hundreds of conversations just to get cards signed. Once that had been accomplished, we had little direction to carry us through while we waited for the BMS ruling. We knew that we should be doing something, but we honestly didn't know what.

This delay in the process would have been a great opportunity for the faculty, other unions on campus and even the members from EM to help with building credibility. This didn't occur for two reasons. First, we didn't realize we needed help—we had, after all, filed cards with a majority and thought our election would occur shortly. Further, the university had offered little public resistance to our organizing, beyond the pay raise. Conversely, these other organizations hadn't presented themselves as having a burning desire to help. Some tenured faculty continued to speak in support of unionizing and signed a public letter to that effect, but the University of Minnesota administrators sent out notices to all the directors of graduate studies in each department warning them about legal restrictions on their ability to provide union support. This created difficulty for union supporters who did not wish any negative ramifications, but it was even more problematic in areas where faculty did not support unionizing. Specifically, in one department, chemistry, a graduate student spoke openly about her advisor's intention to fire anyone who supported the union. At our largest rallies, the other unions on campus came out to show their solidarity; however, getting substantial organized support from the other unions on campus proved difficult, as they had their own union issues to address. Though administrative staff from unions were extremely helpful in locating graduate students in many departments and EM played a significant role in this, we failed to involve the general membership of GradSOC in our drive.

Revisiting Democracy at a Crucial Moment

Well before the card drive, the caucus groups that existed early on as axes of interest and organization had been abandoned, replaced by a highly centralized and hierarchical leadership structure to allow for more efficient decision making and action. Caucuses included students of color, international students, women, family issues, issues of sexual orientation and identity (lesbian, gay, bisexual, and transgendered students), and students in the natural sciences (who were underrepresented), among others. As we struggled to prepare for an election after filing our cards, some of these issues and groups resurfaced as being conspicuously absent from our leadership and agenda. For some people on the steering committee, the lull in activity allowed dissatisfaction to rise. Dissatisfaction with the direction of the campaign, how the organization had changed, and our compliance as these organizational changes occurred became powerful incentives to remedy these shortcomings.

Though there was a clear need to focus on ensuring the support of international students and those in the sciences in order to win the election, we had chosen to organize primarily around material rather than ideological issues to gain the broadest support possible. This strategy to inform our campaign by the numbers created a gap in some of our minds, leaving the issues that had originally motivated many of our organizers to be taken up only after winning the election. And not everyone on the steering committee shared this need to address large, more ideological issues. For some, the best strategy for winning was simply to explain to graduate students that unionizing improves wages and working conditions. Nonetheless, in returning to departments during the early stages of assessment, it became clear that our support among some constituencies—such as the natural sciences, international students, and students of color—was shallow. These groups were hesitant in their support, and many of us struggled to come up with concrete examples of what GradSOC had done to listen to and address their particular concerns when questioned.

After some heated internal debate about priorities, we attempted to remedy part of this with the creation of the Diversity Working Group in February 1999. Growing slowly, the work of this group culminated in a reception at which almost thirty people, many previously uninvolved with GradSOC, drafted a set of issues relevant to their varied constituencies and proposals for how our union should address them. This was the type of meeting for which many of us had been longing, but we were too late to take advantage of its potential. Unfortunately, it came right at the most difficult moment in our campaign—the dawn of new scare tactics and misinformation promulgated by an antiunion student group and directed at international students.

On March 8, five weeks after GradSOC had filed, the Graduate Students Against Unionization (GSAU) posted a slick and easy-to-navigate website rife with misleading information and arguments against unionization. GradSOC was caught off guard. Up to this point, e-mails from the administration and an adversarial relationship with the *Minnesota Daily* had posed the most visible challenges to the unionization effort. GSAU, founded by two students in chemical engineering, effectively waged a campaign to disparage academic unions in general and GradSOC in particular. That GSAU arose from this department was not surprising. Unquestionably, graduate assistants in chemical engineering are among the best compensated at the University of Minnesota, and the vast majority hold research assistantships. Further, the job market in this field is such that many students could find profitable employment without completing a Ph.D., and unlike the humanities and social sciences, graduate assistantships are viewed as apprenticeship periods (for more on this, see Kevin Mattson's chapter in section 2). GSAU's numbers were miniscule in comparison with GradSOC; its active membership never numbered more than a dozen graduate students. Their aim, however, was not to recruit a broad base of support—they needed only to raise questions about the union campaign.

Whereas GradSOC had worked for three years with face-to-face organizing, departmental meetings, and office visits, GSAU used a broadcast tactic involving campus posters and the Internet, showing the effectiveness of the new media in shaping ideas. Though impersonal, the message was extremely potent in challenging the trust we had built through our face-to-face channels. GradSOC was unprepared for this attack from fellow graduate students, which immediately put us on the defensive. A GradSOC member from human resources and industrial relations recalled, "People from GSAU were slick bastards. They were savvy, witty and appeared to be sincere. In comparison, we appeared obtuse, reactionary, and defensive." In other words, we failed to position ourselves as negotiators with the university and were pulled into public debates in which GSAU graduate students provided the perfect mouthpiece for inciting fears and doubts about unionization.

Playing into a perceived need for "another side to the debate," GSAU seized first upon the issue of dues to discredit GradSOC and spread distrust of unions. We were indeed very vulnerable on this point as laws prevented us from making any promises about future contract terms. Our own ideals of participatory practices led us to emphasize that any definition of dues would be up to us as GradSOC members. That is, once recognized as a union, we would be able to determine our own dues scale. Our inability to quote an exact fee, per semester, was used against us. We recognized, albeit too late, that what *we* viewed as an opportunity to decide collaboratively on dues was viewed externally as organizational indecision, or worse as willfully misleading.

GSAU fanned other fears, from exaggerated possibilities of strikes to threats regarding the visa status of foreign students should the union be certified. RAs were told that the number of hours they worked in the lab would be policed by union reps, and that it would take them longer to finish a degree. International students represent a particularly vulnerable community in many respects (one reason they need a union!), and the mere suggestion of these possibilities, though completely unfounded, was enough to shake the support of a sizable number.

Initially, we trusted that such a quickly assembled broadcast campaign—reliant upon e-mail, website, and flyers—could not shake the work that GradSOC had done in face-to-face organizing over the course of three years. After a few organized debates between GradSOC and GSAU members, we knew that sense of security was mistaken. GSAU's existence and the vehemence with which its members maintained their position tended to validate the opposition of those undecided grad assistants who had doubts or were apathetic. One pro-union American studies student said of GSAU:

> The content of what they said wasn't even that important, or impressive. It was the relentlessness of their foci, the slickness of their website in presenting mis-information (making it look really cred-

ible), and the vindictiveness of their attack on GradSOC itself. What they accomplished was to galvanize the anti-union votes that were already out there, and scare enough fence-sitters and weak Yes votes (particularly International Students) to turn them into No votes or abstentions. While they often looked ridiculous, they were insistent enough in their message that they gave No votes a venue from which to claim legitimacy.

GSAU was the university's dream mouthpiece, and its members had access to information that is none too easy to find. Though we cannot prove that GSAU had direct support from the administration, many within the GradSOC leadership thought so. With GSAU able to take an aggressive role in discrediting the union, the university was able to publicly maintain a low-key, comparatively neutral stance. In our minds, there emerged a rather tidy division of labor (busting). A student group with no legal accountability, GSAU was able to use very sophisticated information to create suspicion of unions in general, and of GradSOC and our affiliates in particular. Admittedly, the coalition of AFT and NEA in Minnesota to form EM hurt our campaign. GSAU argued that a tremendous amount of money from our dues would be going elsewhere. The mere listing of our name on the ballot (GradSOC/EM/AFT/NEA/AFL-CIO) gave GSAU fodder for their criticisms of "big unions" whose primary constituency lay elsewhere, and whose real motive was to siphon dues money away from campus. We were successfully painted not as an organization of graduate student workers, but as an external organization that was not only unnecessary, but in fact damaging. Our organizing had to overcome a broad and national antiunion sentiment that had been brewing for some time.

Two other factors worked against us, neatly dovetailing with the efforts of GSAU. The *Minnesota Daily* immediately fixed upon GSAU as "the opposing voice" in the unionization debate, conferring some legitimacy to its claims and never failing to get a quote from one of its members in stories about the issue. Our efforts to respond with letters to the editor were frustrated by unbalanced coverage, and the editorial board ultimately declared itself against unionization. Meanwhile, we had largely ignored the Council of Graduate Students (COGS), the existing graduate-level student government, and its leadership also made public statements against unionization, perhaps because our implicit message was that it was an ineffective body to address our needs.

Two weeks after the emergence of GSAU, toward the end of March, the BMS released its decision on the election format. Almost seven weeks had passed since we filed, and our frustrations about the delay were aggravated by mixed messages and poor communication from the BMS. Further, the election process determined by the BMS ruling was a devastating blow to us. We had hoped for a two-day, on-site election as soon as possible. University administrators called for a mail ballot with a period of two weeks, a proposal we criticized because the university's address lists did a poor job of tracking its transient graduate workers. The BMS ruled for a mail ballot with a balloting period of three and a half weeks. It is still unclear why the BMS made this ruling (perhaps it needed time to recover from its recent efforts in the statewide affiliation election for Minnesota state employees). No matter what, though, it is hard to imagine a less favorable process for our efforts, as one supporter from American studies explains:

> Without a doubt, in my mind, this is the central reason we lost. . . . The lag time between our filing and receiving an election order, and then the length of the mail ballot was exactly the right amount of time for GSAU and the University to do a lot of damage, scare people, spread mis-information, and divert people from the local issues, and not enough time for us to effectively organize in the new atmosphere of conflict.

We couldn't sustain the energy required for this voting structure, and in desperation, assessment of our card signers' support became the sole focus of GradSOC.

The Revolution Delayed

Even now, it's difficult to revisit the impact that losing the election had on us. Many steering committee members said afterwards that we should have organized around an expectation for the worst, though we don't know how this would have prepared us for the experience of watching the ballots being counted and realizing that we had lost. Even the observers from the university and GSAU seemed to empathize as spirits in the room fell and the final tally was announced. Some of us had been actively working for nearly three years, delaying our own studies and lives for a series of immediate goals and actions, every one of which seemed critically important. Suddenly we were forced to question everything we had done, with little energy to imagine what we might do next.

As we had directed our energies and practically all of our attention to winning the certification election, we were at a loss afterwards as to what to do. We were not sure how to salvage some part of our goals, and the years put into realizing them during the building of an organization and work toward the vote. Nonetheless, our desire for improving the condition of graduate workers was not extinguished.

GradSOC's defeat at the polls didn't quell our ideals of democratic organizing. Our commitments required us to continue the work of conversation and reflection. Believing that our experience could help other student union organizers, we circulated a set of questions among the steering committee members and some of the active stewards. The responses paint a picture of a strong campaign, with a devoted leadership and active membership, which nevertheless failed in its primary goal. Several GradSOC organizers also attended a national Coalition of Graduate Employee Unions (CGEU) conference, at which folks from other unions and involved in other campaigns were keenly interested in what had happened at Minnesota, particularly in the shape that the antiunion campaign had taken. At one point, someone who had volunteered with us for a stint during the election said that we had done everything right. This was difficult to reckon with, even in hindsight.

Though we continued to have meetings of the core leadership through the spring, we struggled to redefine ourselves as an (unrecognized) student organization. Our goals were to continue to advocate for grad employee interests and maintain a membership base with a structure that would allow us to mount a drive at some point in the future. This latter goal seemed like a vague hope to many, and one best left to others to pursue. During our drive, one of the most frustrating experiences was to encounter someone who had worked on one of the past campaigns and was still enrolled in the university, yet was unwilling to be actively involved with GradSOC. Though this mystified us at the time, it's a feeling that many sympathize with now. In addition, after repeatedly making the case that TAs and RAs constituted one community of interests defined by our bargaining unit, many of us faced the painful fact that the vote was roughly split along this line, with TAs largely supporting the union. One of the arguments that GSAU touted—one that increasingly resonated with assistants—is that the positions of RAs and TAs are fundamentally different and cannot be represented by a single union. Although we still believe strongly that both groups need a union, without a single overriding issue to organize around, this case proved fragile.

Partially inspired by recognized but underfunded unions in so-called right-to-work states, our goal was to reconstitute ourselves as a student organization that could begin to function as a union and make clear the gains to be made by doing so. By maintaining our membership, we felt that a future card drive could be rapidly organized and undertaken after the state-mandated waiting period between elections, and that a more stable base of support could be formed. By becoming more involved in the existing student governance bodies and by focusing on select issues, we hoped to emphasize the need for collective bargaining through a more powerful body, even as we were dismantling our office and saying goodbye to staff members. We estimated that a very small dues contribution per semester, if made by all of those who had signed membership cards (close to five hundred), would allow us to maintain an office staffed by volunteers. During our card drive and the election, we had lost sight of the fact that in order to gain support for a union, we needed to be unified and make legitimate demands and let other grad students judge the university by its response. A leader from political science summed this up, saying,

> Lesson 1: Build an organization with power. Unions work without winning elections. The time to run an election campaign is when you have built an organization that is evidently powerful and will evidently be more powerful with collective bargaining rights. Organize around issues and win things. Make clear to people what you have won and how you have won it. Make clear every time the university prevents you from getting what you need. When you have strong support, make the case that the time is right to convert that support into an election victory. Be a union with a record of winning, and force the university into being an employer with a record of saying no to your reasonable demands.

Though there was some attempt to form a cooperative effort among GradSOC members, the leaders of COGS, and the university administration during the summer after our defeat, our organization evaporated, as we lacked a clear definition and the will to continue. However, work is still being done to maintain an institutional memory and to build an effective body to address our needs. The GradSOC files are kept as archives at a secure, undisclosed location (hidden in an organizer's basement). Former GradSOC organizers are now working through COGS as the financial situation of grad employees worsens in an extremely tight housing market and the university trims budgets. In such a climate, we represent an extremely vulnerable group that needs the kind of voice that a union could (still) offer.

Reflections (Yet Another Debriefing): Toward the Next Drive

> Organizing graduate students is hard. They are already working 50–80 hours per week, and are on the whole self-involved. Because

they are already over-worked, asking them to create a union is difficult. But it can be done—but people need to see that it is in their
interest to organize, so that they will be willing to work. . . . Make
people want to learn about a union. With individuals, it is important
to listen to grads and present an honest discussion about pros and
cons of unionization, and why you got involved.

—R., political science

The opportunity to participate in decisions about our lives as graduate students motivated us to unionize graduate assistants. Yet it seemed at times
that we were unable to participate in the decisions being made within our
own organization. As graduate students, our training was in our chosen disciplines, not as union organizers, and we turned to the expertise of the AFT
to help us unionize. Unfortunately, we let our inexperience take precedence
over our vision of power and participation. Often this occurred for good reason, as generating consensus among hundreds of people is labor and time
intensive. However, in doing so we also compromised our vision of Grad-
SOC by following the typical model of union organizing.

This typical model for union organizing prescribes generating broad-
base support around central issues and using a few key organizers to generate that support. Turning in 65 percent of the voting population on election
authorization cards ensures that more than half the voting unit will support
the union, and it allows for slippage in support. However, many of the former steering committee members felt this was problematic. We spent too
much energy trying to get support and keep it versus building an organization in which people felt they were heard and respected. We never developed the broad-based leadership that would have withstood the antiunion
campaign. We lost by emphasizing numbers rather than the nature of our
membership. Most important, we failed to sustain a spirit of purpose that
could inspire commitment to our union.

There are several moments that posed significant problems for the internal workings of GradSOC and contributed to external problems. The
initial group of union supporters at Minnesota espoused a level, egalitarian,
and participatory organization. This type of organization is not within the
purview of the AFT structure precisely because it can slow down an organization's movements. However, the movement of decision making to the
steering committee, a small and very dedicated group of activists, was difficult for many members to accept. Additionally, this resistance grew increasingly problematic between full-time staff and the steering committee.
Long drawn-out discussions were meant to build consensus, but when disagreement persisted, the staff's attempts at solution often resulted in further

alienating steering committee members. Though everyone shared the end goal of union recognition, many graduate students in key positions could not resolve their internal conflict at having assumed leadership in a hierarchical organization.

The inability of GradSOC activists to embrace fully the hierarchical form, and of the AFT to recognize the difficulty that activists were having, prohibited any opportunity to remedy the problem. The long-drawn-out period between filing and the election decision provided an opportunity for reflection, exacerbating the organizational division. Many steering committee members felt the organization they aspired to was not developing, and in fact was regressing. So although efforts were organized to assess support, some of us began reconstructing our ideal union through the Diversity Working Group, bringing international and minority students back in. Further, many organizers were just burned out. For those not exhausted, the responsibilities of graduate education beckoned. People needed to return to their professional pursuits and their lives. The lull before the storm was costly.

The antiunion storm approached in a radical new way, through sophisticated and technologically savvy graduate students. Typically, antiunion campaigns are waged by the employer and are based on three standard arguments: (1) there's nothing wrong with current employer/employee relations, (2) a union will significantly change employer/employee relations, and (3) unionization will result in dangerous strikes, which will ultimately cause job loss.[1] At Minnesota, the employer periodically hinted at these, but it was GSAU that emphatically touted these arguments. Using technology to spread the word in a highly advanced work environment, graduate students could easily peruse the GSAU website and read all about the flaws of unionization. Perhaps more important, the fact that this evidence was presented by fellow grads implied that they could only be looking out for the best interests of all graduate students. The presence of a savvy and constituent-based antiunion group poses a serious threat to organizers.

The lessons of GradSOC must include a careful evaluation of the damage a surprise antiunion campaign can do. The technological age has changed the manner, if not the nature, of union busting. In a few clicks of a mouse, the entire GSAU campaign could be sent to another institution to thwart the grass-roots work of union organizers—and it likely already has been. The concordance of GSAU's campaign with the voting structure determined by the BMS was disastrous for GradSOC. Countless hours of work over three years, graduate programs and personal lives put on hold as we devoted ourselves to the union drive—all this lost in a matter of weeks.

Looking back on this, one student from political science recollected:

I began with the assumption that the goal was to win an election. That assumption was false. The goal should have been to build a powerful union. Power is inextricably linked with action. At some point along the way, winning an election might be both possible and desirable. But it is not necessary, and it leads you to focus on the wrong things. It leads you to cater to those who are and will remain against you. Unions are powerful precisely because union members stand together. We didn't stand together. We ran around separately persuading people who weren't with us that maybe they should be.

After three attempts at unionizing graduate student workers, we are wiser at the University of Minnesota. So, too, it seems, are our adversaries. Democratic organizers of all stripes should be deeply troubled by the inability of GradSOC's face-to-face organizing to triumph over a blitzkrieg of misinformation. The work of hundreds of committed students over three years was undermined by a handful of busters with access to resources and a computer. What and how are we to lift from this experience?

"I have always believed (and still do, although more painfully) that the group with the most human bodies and minds behind it, doing the work together, and working towards an honorable goal will win," a student from American studies wrote. We still believe this. At the University of Minnesota, we needed to do it better. In order to inoculate against scare tactics and misinformation, we needed a solid, broad-based leadership that embraced the ideals behind unionization. Without that, we failed. The drive for democracy, however, continues. We now are participating in other venues to advocate for graduate student worker rights and interests. The most critical task is to foster community structures that will keep the spirit and memory of GradSOC alive. If we can do this, we will have laid the groundwork for our victory in the next union campaign.

CHAPTER 11

Moving River Barges
Labor Activism and Academic Organizations
Cary Nelson

In the fall of 2001 a multiyear effort by Professor Michael Bennett of Long Island University began to bear fruit. The Modern Language Association's Executive Council had before it for the first time two very different proposals. The most dramatic was a resolution to censor the Executive Council for failing to act on an earlier motion, which Bennett had written and which the Delegate Assembly had passed, to begin penalizing departments that were teaching too many of their courses with contingent labor, namely part-time faculty typically paid slave wages and denied basic job security and benefits. The second proposal came from an ad hoc committee, of which Bennett was a member, offering some practical suggestions for beginning to deal with the overreliance on contingent labor in many English and foreign-language departments.

As typically happens in the MLA, a well-intentioned proposal arrives from the Delegate Assembly having been overwhelmingly approved but in a form not yet ready for Executive Council action. It could hardly be otherwise. A Delegate Assembly motion is usually written by one or two people and reviewed by a few others. The constituencies with a stake in the matter—most of the large literature and language departments in the country—have no opportunity for input before the proposal is passed. The document is then considered by an Executive Council with no guaranteed expertise in the matter and little patience for hard work. Like the well-known fable about a group of blind men gathered around an elephant and characterizing it by way of the foot or tail or trunk within their reach, the members of the Executive Council self-importantly relate their opinions or their fragmentary

personal experiences one after another. After two or three rounds of this it is
clear no consensus exists and none can be reached.

Thus had Bennett's earlier motion been handled. A group of organizations then met to discuss the problem of staffing ratios, but they did little
more than make clear how knotty the issue was. I had cosponsored the original Bennett motion and was thus in what I regarded as the quite wonderful
paradox of having proposed action and now being censured for failing to take
it. I was more than ready to censure myself, for I felt the Executive Council
had failed its moral and professional responsibility to address the issue seriously and take some actions, whether those in the Delegate Assembly motion or others. The ad hoc committee gave us our needed alternative. Their
proposals were not going to solve the problem, but they would move us in
the direction of publicizing which departments had admirably high percent-
ages of full-time faculty teaching their courses and which had dismally high
dependence on part-timers. The range is considerable.

Meanwhile, in the course of considering the censure proposal, which
would have come up for a Delegate Assembly vote in December 2001, the
Executive Council for the only time in my four-year experience actually
worked collaboratively on a text and adopted it. Some of the most brilliant
members of the profession threw themselves into this task with a kind of
fervor I had never before seen in this group. The text in question: a letter
proudly asserting that their failure to do anything meaningful about staffing
ratios over two years of negotiations was a fine example of the human spirit
at its best.

No one acquainted with Michel Foucault's work will be surprised to
learn that organizational affiliation is always a double-edged sword: it creates opportunities for action at the same time that it installs powerful constraints defining what actions seem possible; it constructs and reinforces
certain identities while casting out other identities as implausible or ob-
scene. Like all forms of social regulation, as Foucault helped us see in other
contexts, affiliation often promotes organizational and institutional ends
less by punishing offenses than by rewarding compliance. Not that punish-
ments, including monstrous ones, are ever absent from a properly affiliated
imagination; they haunt both actual and hypothetical trespass. But affiliation also enriches subjectivity and positions identities in such a way as to
win willing assent without seeming to extract compliance violently. Affiliation limits what it is possible to imagine, identifies outcomes we can fear,
and naturalizes the status quo within institutions.

So it is with academia and with all the forms of affiliation promoted
in this most paradoxical set of vocations, so many of them combining ex-

treme self-consciousness and an unexamined life. In academia one often subjects everything but the social constitution of one's own identity to intense scrutiny. There is a gap, then, between the theoretical assent my opening paragraph might win and the willingness of many academics to interrogate the nature and consequences of their own affiliations. Affiliations may be constitutive and constraining, academics might argue, but they are often blind to their own constraining ideologies. For they have been, perhaps irrationally, persuaded they are themselves affiliated exclusively with freedom.

So long as the academic system worked efficiently, affiliation might proceed harmlessly on dual tracks of equally focused inquiry and ignorance. From time to time, of course, multiple affiliations were brought together—or collided—in such a way as to produce desperately needed change. We saw that during the 1960s and 1970s when antiwar activism propelled academics into institutional critique and radically different forms of affiliation. We saw it again when simultaneous affiliation with feminism and the academy forced universities to confront their multiple discriminatory practices. And multiple affiliations produced activist confrontations between black students and the institutions in which they were enrolled. Other marginalized groups have since followed their lead.

These multiple and conflicting affiliations have been both theoretical and organizational, though they have not necessarily operated on the same plane for every individual. Yet it is often only the friction between multiple affiliations that opens a space for reflective critique. Even in academia—the very institution supposedly most devoted to unfettered reasoned analysis—the horizon circumscribed by one set of seamless and mutually reinforcing affiliations can severely limit our insight. One belongs to a department, one belongs to a campus, one belongs to a discipline and perhaps to its national organization. It is but one step further to the nation-state. This is a hierarchy of interchangeable affiliations that obliterates difference and contradiction within a setting that is, ironically, rife with them.

Yet affiliation on the other hand can position one to effect much-needed change. To abandon affiliation because of its inherent limitations and constraints is perhaps to be even less empowered. Necessary change seems most likely to occur, however, when multiple affiliations are in tension with one another. Out of those tensions—erupting across subject positions in dialogue and in conflict with one another—can evolve alliances that link affiliated subjects in new ways. And the social space occupied by multiple persons taken up in different affiliations in turn promotes moments of recognition and self-critique ordinarily suppressed by affiliations that merely reinforce one another.

It is time and past time for such patterns to assume prominence throughout higher education. We have been through three decades of a disastrous job market for new Ph.D.s in which "apprenticeship" has been steadily emptied of its authenticity as a subject position. Affiliation has for many "apprentices" been a mode of enslavement.

This chapter, then, is about networking and acting for change in academia. It is about people occupying places in key organizations and using those affiliations to make a difference in higher education. It's about a movement of intellectual activists that has no structure and no overall organizational name. I have combined a general political analysis of affiliation with academic organizations with an on-the-ground account of actual efforts for change because I am convinced an abstract account alone will not suffice; people need to see how a commitment to activist affiliation plays out in daily life. I narrate this story in the first person, foregrounding my own role because it offers an instructive example, an example at the very least of how senior faculty members can make a difference if they choose. But I emphasize at the outset that everyone I interact with here is putting just as much time in these issues as I am. And this group includes graduate students, part-time faculty, and administrative staff, all of whom are successfully combining local and national activism in their multiple academic affiliations. The full story would comprise a three-dimensional map detailing all their activities in the context of their multiple and occasionally overlapping intersections. The "organization" here is the ongoing strategic conversation across multiple affiliations about what we are going to do. Our main aims are to reform the Modern Language Association and other disciplinary and transdisciplinary organizations, refocusing their efforts on the problems of academic labor, and/or to improve working conditions for graduate employees and part-time faculty and gradually increase the number of full-time faculty positions throughout the country. Underlying such reforms must be increased democracy for all the segments of the academic workforce.

Because I think this nearly accidental alliance has had some success, at least in part, let me say by way of a preface that I have seen a series of alternative national organizational models fail. I have in mind in particular a series of progressive organizations in academia that frittered away their time creating structures and affiliations unconnected to action. When Teachers for a Democratic Culture was founded, I thought to myself, "This isn't going to work; there are no actions for this group to take. It isn't going to radicalize anyone." I had the same series of premonitions when Scholars, Artists and Writers for Social Justice (SAWSJ) arrived on the scene. Organizing and building membership either turns people into radicals or it accomplishes nothing. For examples of campus organizing efforts that dramatically change people's views of themselves and the institutions in which they work, I would point to continuing graduate employee unionization drives, to the No Sweat movement initiated in the 1990s, and to the growing campus and citywide living-wage campaigns.

To illustrate one way of taking advantage of networking and rearticulating affiliations among existing organizations rather than building entirely new ones, which is characteristic of "what we did this year," I am going to focus on my own life, beginning with February 24, 1999. On that day I left Champaign-Urbana, where I teach, to give a talk the next day at Rutgers University titled "Beware the Corporate University." That same day I also had lunch with graduate student and part-time union activists at Rutgers, including Karen Thompson and Patrick Kavanagh. Thompson has been active on part-timer issues for years, both in her union local and in the national American Association of University Professors. We talked about their upcoming contract negotiations and about the long-term prospects for alliances between tenured faculty and the more exploited labor groups on campus. Rutgers is unique in having AAUP units representing full-time, part-time, and graduate student employees. It is also unique in being the only such union to be constantly raided by other unions seeking to replace the local AAUP as bargaining agent.

At lunch we also set about drafting some specific language about guaranteeing a living wage for graduate student employees. Kavanagh, a Rutgers doctoral candidate and AAUP local staff member, and I have served on a national AAUP subcommittee charged with writing a universal Bill of Rights for Graduate Students. I had called for a national document years earlier, was one of the people who helped get this AAUP project started, and I had notified other members of the committee that I felt we should include precise language about how to calculate and guarantee a living wage. The principle could be stated like this: "Graduate students who teach one course each semester or one course each quarter are entitled to a living wage for the full calendar year." The formula, which recognizes varying costs of living across the country, might be framed this way: "An individual minimum living wage can be set at 30% of the U.S. census figures for median family income, adjusted by the Consumer Price Index." This would put graduate employees at the border of government figures for "very low income" and "low income." Hardly excessive, but my own department would have to raise salaries about 25 percent to meet this standard. It would be entirely doable, certainly over two years.

After telephone consultations, the AAUP subcommittee met to review a draft I had written. The members all had multiple affiliations with disciplinary associations in the sciences and humanities and with the multidisciplinary AAUP, a mix that not only gave us diverse experience and practices to compare but also seemed to encourage a certain collective backbone. No one wanted *lower* national standards in any area than those of his or her own discipline. We condensed my draft substantially, in part because the group wanted the public symbolism of creating ten numbered rights, thus paralleling the historic amendments to the U.S. Constitution. The subcommittee, however, felt very strongly about guaranteeing graduate student academic freedom. In one area—access to records and placement dossiers—the subcommittee went further than my draft, granting students open access to their files.

As the draft Bill of Rights went through repeated reviews by the national AAUP staff and by the AAUP's famous Committee A on Academic Freedom and Tenure, the title "A Graduate Student Bill of Rights" became the less incendiary "Statement on Graduate Students," the provision for open access to records disappeared, and the specific demand for a "living wage" was replaced by less decisive language. Curiously enough, it was the hard-won consensus on these issues that radicalized my subcommittee's members and helped us bond as a group; now our most radical achievement was being whittled away. Hardly a unique story, this mixture of advance and retreat is a typical result of negotiating with multiple constituencies in large organizations. Nonetheless, a recommendation that graduate employees working twenty hours a week earn enough to survive without seeking significant additional employment would stay in the document. Though no longer tied to the "living wage" movement and to its supporting scholarship, this principle would still challenge many institutions and provide support for activists on many campuses.

There are in fact engineering and chemistry laboratories around the country that extract sixty to eighty or more hours a week from their graduate employees, who then have little time for their classes and no time for their families. These fields as a result have historically been "Single Male Only" enterprises. A woman with a family who manages to put only sixty hours a week into the lab may be marked as a "slacker" and suffer less favorable evaluations. In many humanities departments, on the other hand, workloads of thirty to forty hours a week are common, with a student's own research effectively added on as an overload. So the twenty-hour workload standard mounts a moral and professional challenge to higher education as a whole.

Equally contentious was the firm support for graduate student academic freedom in the statement. Many long-term AAUP stalwarts have had little recent contact with graduate education; others come from departments without graduate programs. Faculty union activists in the AAUP, as it happens, were often willing to support academic freedom for graduate students. But some otherwise distinguished AAUP members clung to the apprenticeship model and felt full academic freedom was necessary only for faculty. As I tried to point out, graduate employees are now often *in charge* of large lecture courses, talking to five hundred or a thousand students about race in American history, or about American imperialism. If these graduate employees do not need the protection of academic freedom, who does?

Meanwhile, the rhetoric of apprenticeship was simultaneously undermining commitment to fair wages and even to the document's workload provision. Here multiple affiliations helped once again. The MLA in 1998 had affirmed one course per semester, or roughly twenty hours of work for compensation, as the appropriate maximum workload for graduate students pursuing a degree. AAUP members with MLA affiliations used the workload recommendation in the final report from MLA's Committee on Professional Employment to shore up the AAUP's position. The Statement on Graduate Students, meanwhile, allows some limits on academic freedom for graduate students learning about the discipline but secures their academic freedom as teachers, a reasonable compromise given the dual nature of graduate education. The document was printed in the AAUP journal *Academe*, approved by the National Council in June 2000, and published in the AAUP's *Policy Documents and Reports* (popularly known as the Redbook) at the beginning of 2001. The MLA's Delegate Assembly endorsed it in December 2000, and it was printed in the summer 2001 issue of the *MLA Newsletter*.

Although the AAUP cannot enforce such recommendations, publishing them in our "Redbook" beside our definitions of tenure and academic freedom gives them significant weight. Getting organizations like the MLA to endorse the entire Statement on Graduate Students will help local groups agitate for good practices on their own campuses. It will also give individual campuses a set of goals and principles to discuss.

To help that agitation along, I had drafted a resolution for the AAUP's national council in 1998, recognizing that all campus employees have the right to engage in collective bargaining if they choose. I serve on the National Council, which passed the resolution unanimously in November. In the fall of 1999 I began to urge national disciplinary organizations to endorse it. The American Studies Association passed a similar resolution on behalf of graduate student unionization in October 1999. Greg Bezkorovainy and I put our own resolution on collective bargaining rights before the MLA's

Delegate Assembly in December 1999, which passed it overwhelmingly. The key to the resolution's language is that it does not urge collective bargaining but rather confirms the democratic right of each constituency *to choose for itself* whether to negotiate its working conditions together.

The following year MLA members ratified the collective bargaining resolution by mail ballot. In 2001 we decided to try to get the MLA's Executive Council to put this right into practice in the form of a letter urging the New York University administration to begin bargaining with the university's graduate students in good faith. NYU graduate employees had voted to unionize and the National Labor Relations Board in an historic decision confirmed the vote. While I cannot comment on the discussion that occurred in the council meeting, I can recount some of my conversations before the meeting. A number of the Executive Council members had no concept of a "right" in this context, feeling that we should seek more information from the NYU administration about why it wanted to reject the results of a democratic election. I could not get some council members to understand that no arguments were likely to warrant their overturning a right ratified by the membership. Nor could they understand that arguments for and against graduate employee unionization tend to be quite formulaic. Thus it was foolish to expect any given university administration to advance a new and persuasive position. In the end, an exhausting and sometimes brittle debate produced a letter, and shortly thereafter the NYU administration agreed to the NLRB ruling. That was during my third year on the council, but my story takes me back to my first year of service.

After completing my 1999 talk at Rutgers I went to the AMTRAK station in New Brunswick to catch a train for Manhattan. I was headed off to two days of meetings of the MLA Executive Council, having been elected after nomination by a Graduate Student Caucus petition drive. Despite thirty years of MLA membership, it would be my first visit to the organization's offices. Two days around a seminar table in a windowless room had the potential to move MLA's first real action agenda forward. For the first time the organization would be acting, not just talking. It was beginning to seem possible that it would be more than a structure to help affiliated people add lines to their vitae and instead devote itself to securing higher education's future.

Two vitally important motions were up for a vote. The one that was potentially most controversial—to do a survey of part-time faculty salaries—had been jointly sponsored by the GSC and the Delegate Assembly Organizing Committee. This joint resolution came out of negotiations over a longer resolution first submitted by the GSC and its faculty allies. The need for this kind of data was laid out by two graduate students, Mark Kelley of CUNY and Bill Pannapacker of Harvard, in a *Chronicle of Higher Education* article. Gregory Bezkorovainy and I then decided to implement it with a motion, which we coauthored; then I gathered a dozen faculty cosponsors from around the country. Approved overwhelmingly by the MLA's Delegate Assembly on December 29, 1998, it called for the MLA to conduct the first ever nationwide survey of part-timer salaries, benefits, and working conditions. As the GSC understood the motion, fifty-two hundred English and foreign-language departments would be queried about their practices and then identified by name when the department-by-department results were published. Such data were not available for any discipline.

I had received a call a few days earlier from one of my graduate student coconspirators warning me that the MLA was floating a suggestion to cut back on the size of the survey by contacting only a representative sample of departments, rather than the entire fifty-two hundred. This impulse partly represented a confusion over the statistical difference between reliability and replicability. Phyllis Franklin, the MLA's executive director, believed a small sample, chosen on the basis of sound principles and buttressed by follow-up phone calls, would be more reliable, which was likely not to be the case. We could get reliable national data from a broad survey, but we could not guarantee replicability. I too wanted follow-up phone calls, but wanted them focused primarily on metropolitan areas where there were large quantities of part-timers.

Before leaving New Brunswick I had called New York to see if I could head off this initiative. Unfortunately, the call revealed other impulses to weaken the plan, namely a misunderstanding about the motion's aims. All the devils, it seemed, were in the details. The MLA staff was inclined to publish the data by region and institutional type, not by name.

The combined effect of these two changes—and the GSC certainly saw them as changes—would be to leave us pretty much where we already were. We already knew that some schools paid part-timers as little as $800 a course, whereas others paid as much as $4,000. We knew the range, which repeats itself in most regions, and we knew the pay rates at a few specific schools. Steve Watt and I include some of this information in our *Academic Keywords: A Devil's Dictionary for Higher Education* (Routledge, 1999). As Rich Moser of the AAUP had confirmed for me repeatedly, what part-timers needed in order to organize for change was detailed data in each region with all departments listed by name alongside their salary and benefits data. Part-timers had told me repeatedly that it was impossible for them to gather this information. Central administrations claimed not to have it, and departments had little incentive to cooperate with part-timer requests for information. After the Delegate Assembly vote at the end of December, however, they were looking for the MLA to solve their problem. Phyllis's two changes would save face for individual departments—a strong motivation for long-term head of the Association of Departments of English, David Laurence—but give part-timers little leverage to improve their compensation (it should be noted that the Association of Departments of English is a division of the MLA). To achieve that, part-timers needed to be able to cite exact salaries and benefits and make specific comparisons.

When I got into New York (about 9 P.M.), I started calling friends around the country knowledgeable about survey methods for arguments to buttress my case. I needed to know, for example, whether we would significantly decrease the response rate by planning to publish the data institution-by-institution. Among the people I called at home were Ernst Benjamin and Iris Molotsky of the national AAUP. Ernie had been doing faculty salary surveys for years and had drafted the important multiorganizational statement of principles on part-time hiring practices issued a year earlier. He would later help write the questionnaire for the part-timer survey. Iris was in the midst of gathering sample statements on graduate student rights. Both were seasoned veterans of organizational politics. In any case, by midnight, $100 worth of hotel phone calls later, I had the information I needed, which included the judgment that we would not lose a major portion of data by doing the survey the way we wanted.

Friday morning I was at MLA headquarters at 10 Astor Place. The debate over the data-gathering motion was extensive and sometimes pointed, but the proposal passed. It was helped in part by a companion proposal—to survey individual graduate programs in the field, then gather together and publish all the data about their individual admission requirements, placement rates, and pay scales, workloads, and benefits for graduate student employees. The schools would all be named, which would put these comparative data in one place for the first time. The disparity in degree completion rates and wage scales alone is astonishing. Neither students applying to doctoral programs in English or foreign languages nor those already enrolled in them have a broad grasp of the differences in departments across the country. Faculty advisors are equally ill informed. On the other hand, philosophy had already embarked on a similar national survey of graduate programs, and math regularly issued one. There seemed little excuse for MLA cowardice when math and philosophy were already committed.

As with the part-timer survey, knowledge here is power. Moreover, it was clear to everyone that this information would be useless unless it was

linked precisely to individual departments. Thus the MLA with either proposal would have to cross the bridge of identifying department practices by
name for the first time. In the past the organization has preferred to describe
good practices without specifying who does and does not adhere to them.
That lets the Association of Departments of English serve as a friend of
every affiliated department, ethical departments and rogue departments
alike. But advocacy for exploited labor and advocacy for department over-
seers has come increasingly into conflict.

In any case, both proposals passed the Executive Council in February.
Assuming the staff felt committed to the projects—it has wide latitude in
deciding which projects are affordable—the data-gathering projects for
both part-time faculty and graduate student employees would be under way
the summer and fall of 1999. As it happened, the staff in May presented a
tentative budget for 1999–2000 to the Executive Council that included the
survey. And in the end, despite earlier efforts to weaken the project, the
MLA ended up carrying out the survey with impressive intelligence and
dedication. Moreover, Phyllis Franklin used her long-term contacts to help
build a coalition of disciplinary organizations that would each do smaller
versions of the survey. Such, it seems, are the paradoxes of organizational
affiliation, though it is hard to find anyone in the MLA hierarchy inclined
to remember the GSC's role in this effort.

On Saturday evening Kirsten Christensen and I, the two GSC candidates elected to the Executive Council, went to dinner with Mark Kelley
and Greg Bezkorovainy, then president and vice-president of GSC. We updated them on the status of our proposals and heard their detailed plans for
the coming year. Kelley had already dramatically increased the GSC's national and international visibility over the past year. On his own campus he
helped draft a thoughtful response to the MLA's report on the job crisis.
Bezkorovainy was our point person in extensive negotiations with the MLA
over GSC's 1998 and 1999 Delegate Assembly motions and would become
GSC president in January 2000. He would prove our best drafter of legislation and a wonderful negotiator, calmly and relentlessly promoting logic
and reason in negotiations with the MLA.

The next morning I was on my way to Denver, on route to the University of Nebraska at Kearney. One of my Ph.D.s, Kate Benzel, is now a full
professor there; she had invited me to give my corporate university talk,
teach two classes (on Edwin Rolfe and Adrienne Rich), and meet with campus groups. I urged leaders of the faculty union to make increasing graduate
student and part-timer wages an issue when they bargained for their next
contract. Graduate students in English at Kearney teach two courses each

semester and receive $1,125 per course, for a total annual wage of $4,500. Until recently, they had no health benefits, but Kate, who had learned well the lessons I seek to teach, had waged a successful seven-year campaign to get them health coverage. When I met with the grad students I urged them to organize and become a more effective force in campus negotiations. I also told them that Rutgers, where I had just been, pays graduate student teachers about $6,000 per course. I would soon quote the $1,125 per course rate to a *New York Times* reporter who would use it in a story shortly thereafter. Back in Nebraska the dean fired off a series of e-mails to faculty complaining about the misinformation printed in the *Times*. "Things are a lot better than that at Nebraska. Salaries are now up to $1,170 per course." The director of Graduate Studies had his own counterargument: "We offer graduate students travel money to conferences." I asked him whether they could afford to eat once they get there. Meanwhile I heard of still lower salaries in Mississippi.

Late Wednesday afternoon I was back home, but Friday morning I was on my way to New York to present a shorter version of this chapter, which I had drafted on the plane from Nebraska, to a March 5–6 New York University conference on "Intellectual Activism: Coalitional Politics and the Academy." The conference included a fine Saturday afternoon open discussion about the implications of the No Sweat campaign on campuses across the country, which has been built around protests against university contracts with athletic clothing companies that exploit workers in overseas factories. The practices themselves are carefully discussed in Andrew Ross's collection *No Sweat: Fashion, Free Trade, and the Rights of Garment Workers* (Verso, 1997). Many of the student activists, we discovered, had parents who were veterans of the antiwar movement of the 1960s and 1970s. Others were first-generation college students from union families. And others still, among the growing number of Latino students, understood sweatshops all too well. A number of the student leaders of the movement, notably, are graduates of the AFL-CIO union summer program. Multiple affiliations were at work again. We saw real potential to interest these students in labor exploitation on their own campuses. I suggested a poster reading "No Sweat There/No Sweat Here" above side-by-side photographs of athletic shoes and piles of composition papers. A campus living-wage campaign is also a solid possibility. Such a campaign was already under way at Harvard, and a community campaign has been started in Champaign-Urbana. The Harvard campaign, of course, produced the extended sit-in in the president's office in the spring of 2001, along with an historic series of administration wage concessions.

On Sunday I was on a plane to Syracuse, New York, first to attend a community meeting called to discuss a possible countywide living-wage campaign, a campaign embodying principles like those laid out in books such as Robert Pollin and Stephanie Luce's *The Living Wage: Building a Fair Economy* (Free Press, 1997). It would encompass not only Syracuse University but also other large employers in the area. There was heated discussion about the potential impact on small businesses, along with details about wages in a variety of area firms. I was welcome to participate, but I was really there to learn more about the issue and about how an academic institution would fit into a larger campaign about the workplace. One of the things I learned is that Syracuse University administrators have argued they should not have to pay a living wage in job categories for which the prevailing local wage is less. Of course they *could* argue that gives them an opportunity to raise the local rate by putting pressure on other employers with their own salary structure. But the main reason for my visit was to meet repeatedly with graduate students interested in starting a unionizing campaign on campus and to give a general lecture on academic labor. I hope that I succeeded in recruiting a number of people to become active in MLA's Graduate Student Caucus as well.

Although my travel schedule is not always this heavy—this late-twentieth-century version of the picaresque required taking fourteen planes over two weeks—this mixture of writing, lecturing, and activist organizing makes up a good deal of my life. I make no apologies for focusing my current efforts on the industry I know best—academia. For decades people have viewed activism on behalf of higher education as somehow illegitimate, declasse. Exploited workers in other industries are noble figures, but university employees deserve no defense. The barons of the academy are free to grind their bones into dust. Real activism takes place outside the academy, in that place too many of us idiotically still refer to as the real world.

Of course this ideology has not served world revolution. It has rather left academic affiliation unchallenged and hidden and underwritten campus privilege. We saw that most dramatically when progressive Yale faculty with vertical and interchangeable affiliations made clear they would feel whole again only when their striking graduate students were behind bars. At the NYU conference Stanley Aronowitz mentioned that a Yale scholar of the history of slavery turned his striking student in to the administration, but Aronowitz oddly declined to speak his name (I won't: David Brion Davis), despite its having repeatedly been cited in publications about the Yale strike. Yale postcolonialism theorist Sara Suleri turned in her student teaching assistant, then crisscrossed the country in a mink coat purchased with profits from the Goodyear company's Asian rubber plantations; one suspects she regretted the coat was not lined with the hides of her teaching assistants. At the NYU conference, a recent Columbia University Ph.D. rose to express his regret that three of his progressive teachers—Franco Moretti, D. A. Miller, and Gayatri Spivak—had crossed fall 1998 picket lines during the Local 2110 support staff strike. Again, unexamined affiliation rules their lives.

I am not demanding that any of these purportedly leftist academics become activists in the campus labor movement. For one thing academia is not the only site worthy of intervention. One of my colleagues does his activist work in Indonesia, taking on a good deal more risk than we do. But it is time to demand that academics on the left endorse efforts to transform their own industry. Their campus praxis must match the ideological investments of their scholarship. Affiliation must be reflexive and self-critical.

Nearly forty years ago, when I joined the fledgling antiwar movement, heading off with a dozen other college students to interrupt a speech by the U.S. president Lyndon Johnson—we delayed the speech until we were wrestled to the ground by Secret Service agents—it seemed corporations could be cast out of the academy. We could put our bodies between Dow Chemical and the campus and retain the campus as another place, a place of difference, a place of idealized affiliation. Its compromised integrity would at least be critical and self-reflective. Now American campuses are in the process of becoming Dow Chemical.

Thirty years of benighted, high-minded leftist contempt for their own workplace has helped leave academia vulnerable to all the ravages of corporatization. But it can be changed. Join us. Start small. Like all things, one action leads to another. Activist affiliation opens opportunities for yet more activism. Your colleagues, of course, may not approve. Michael Denning's colleagues at Yale thought he had lost his way when he stood with Graduate Students and Employees Organization (GESO) for the duration. Two articulate graduate student activists whose ideas may better the lives of thousands of people, Mark Kelley and Bill Pannapacker, have been urged to curtail their activism by some of their faculty colleagues, fearful that the profession may cast them out in recompense for their more selfless version of affiliation. Except for Michael Bérubé (at Illinois until 2001) and a few assistant professors, many of my department colleagues view my national activism and my multiple affiliations as some sort of inexplicable obsession. What about my scholarship? What about real research (read lit. crit.), not the hundreds of interviews conducted in the course of writing *Manifesto of a Tenured Radical* and *Academic Keywords*? Of course I continue to do research in both modern poetry and the Spanish Civil War, just as Denning does in 1930s culture, just as GSC activists continue to work on their dissertations, but the real world of the campus seems to require more.

Historically and in the present, writing has been and is a sufficient form of activism. But in today's academy activist writing is inevitably tested by workplace practice. If the two are in conflict, their inherent values in contradiction, then progressive scholarship and the core of a professorial affiliation becomes a sham. It is not simply that careerist affiliation is sometimes mistaken for intellectual devotion, or that the lines between the two have become increasingly blurred, though that is also true, but these impulses have been intertwined throughout history. What *is* new is the dynamic relationship with an audience dependent on imitatable models of careerist spirituality. We pledge love and devotion in exchange for discourses we can emulate to win jobs and tenure. Yet it is now time we stop honoring faux activists who refuse to condemn the exploitation of their lower-paid colleagues. There are now a series of movements and organizations with versions of affiliation that give all of us alternatives.

Yet work within such organizations, it must be emphasized, is neither easy nor guaranteed of good results. Nonprofit member-based organizations like the AAUP and the MLA purportedly exist to serve their members' interests. Yet the staffs tend largely to run the show. There is a tendency for a staff culture partly contemptuous of members to develop over time, and certainly members will often enough act foolishly and reinforce this bias. Affiliated members who seek to move such organizations in a particular direction are inherently at a disadvantage. The staff has a sense of organizational history and a detailed knowledge of the budget; members' new initiatives will often be declared financially impossible or legally dangerous. Short of embarking on full-scale research projects it is difficult to prove the staff wrong.

Nonetheless, there are differences of both degree and kind in how such organizations function. Both the AAUP and the MLA have executive directors and an Executive Council of elected members. At the MLA, lawyers' advice is always delivered to the council in a letter following negotiations with the executive director. MLA Council members never see or talk to a lawyer; there is no opportunity to dispute a lawyer's opinion and no way to prove what is often enough obviously the case, that the MLA's lawyers say what the executive director wants them to say. At the AAUP the lawyers meet with both the Executive Committee and the larger National Council. There is plenty of time for discussion and for differences of opinion to be aired. The result is more democratic decision making, whereas at the MLA the lawyers have too often simply been weapons for the executive director to use to impose her ideology on the organization as a whole.

That is not to say that the AAUP is by any means fully democratic or that it makes full use of its national officers. Most program initiatives still come from the staff, and some absolutely basic policy issues are debated and formulated with excessive secrecy. In order to get maximum feedback on my "Graduate Student Bill of Rights," I circulated it to hundreds of people around the country. My aim was not only to get the best text possible but also to give the relevant constituency a role in the drafting of the document, to empower graduate students especially to feel it was at least partly *their* document, not just the AAUP's. As a result I received several dozen informative and thoughtful letters that were a real help in refining the statement. But some members of Committee A and some members of the national staff were incensed that I had released a draft, a document not fully vetted and approved.

Over the past several years a major debate has raged in the national office and among members of Committee A over whether the organization should, for example, pursue academic freedom cases involving graduate students and part-time faculty. I am among those who think it is imperative that we do so, indeed that we should publicize our interest so that people know they can refer appropriate cases to the Washington office. This issue obviously implicates the AAUP's mission and reason for existence in fundamental ways. Yet the discussion has remained largely internal to Committee A and the national staff. Even at Executive Committee and National Council sessions, references to this debate—and its attendant power struggles—were uninformative and oblique until 2001. It is instead probably an issue the membership as a whole should discuss. Indeed they might feel more involved in and committed to the organization as a result.

Yet the MLA's Executive Council is consistently far more passive than the AAUP's, which is actively involved in initiating proposals. Kirsten Christensen and I mostly found we were the only MLA Executive Council members with any agenda at all, with any program to put forward. The others regularly complained about how many GSC proposals were on the table but had no suggestions to offer of their own. The GSC representatives were not, to be sure, the only council members well informed about the state of the profession, but those best characterized as simultaneously accomplished and clueless were always in the majority. We were in a long-running movie whose theme song might have been "Something is happening, but you don't know what it is, do you, Mr. Chips?" The only time they all became energized was at the annual opportunity to appoint friends and colleagues to committees.

These two organizations also have very different levels of consensus about their missions. Although the AAUP represents multiple constituencies with different views of higher education—from teaching-centered colleges organized for collective bargaining to decentered research-oriented universities—there is nonetheless a nearly universal commitment among its members to the organization's role in defining and defending the basic principles of academic life. No comparable consensus exists within the MLA. The MLA's elected Delegate Assembly for most of a decade has proven itself a progressive group committed to activist reform. The Executive Council and the executive director are mostly dead set against anything of the kind. So the Delegate Assembly pushes and the council resists. Yet now and again a council majority can be assembled and action taken, the part-timer salary survey being the best example.

The politics of the MLA as a whole remain uncertain. Certainly progressive resolutions are routinely approved in membership votes, but with fewer than 20 percent of the members voting one is never certain how representative their views are. Of course such votes are the only indication of members' wishes available, yet both the executive director and the council feel free to dismiss such views as those of a radical fringe. At a meeting of English department chairs a few years ago, the current MLA president urged them to run for the Delegate Assembly because radicals were taking it over. Another recent MLA president stormed out of a meeting at the headquarters declaring that a graduate student would serve on the council over her dead body. Well, it came to pass, as a result of a membership vote, but I have seen no funeral notice.

It is clear that an executive director who serves too long can become a tyrant and largely eliminate many meaningful forms of member affiliation. After I published an essay critical of the MLA in *Social Text* in 1995, Phyllis Franklin called up one of the editors to express reservations about the essay and left the other editor with the impression that she hoped the journal would not publish me again. It was a questionable maneuver for a supposedly neutral executive director, but from her perspective, presumably, any action was justified in defending the organization. Of course *Social Text* ignored the request, if that is what it was. I saw myself as trying to reform the organization, but she no doubt saw this as a left-wing counterpart of attacks from the right during the culture wars. More recently, council members privately expressed the opinion to me that Franklin had taken a dislike to a quite effective member of the MLA staff and had discriminated against him in salary decisions. The consensus was that nothing could be done about it until she retired. Too much power can come to reside in an administrator who holds office too long, and both member affiliation and democratic process can be eviscerated as a result.

Some long-term staff also tend to resist historical change, becoming wedded to a view of the organization's mission that no longer matches reality. Both the AAUP and the MLA have begun to reach out to graduate students and part-time faculty against the wishes of some staff members. Yet both organizations have risked becoming irrelevant by ignoring major changes in the higher education workforce. Teaching and research are increasingly being performed by graduate students, part-time or non-tenure-track faculty, or by academic professionals. The organizations need to protect these highly vulnerable members and to represent their interests.

The reform efforts of the MLA's Graduate Student Caucus have produced a series of initiatives designed to make the job market less rapacious and to improve employment conditions throughout the profession. The survey of part-time faculty salaries, widely participated in by all but a group of Ivy League schools brimful of contempt and privilege, produced dramatic results much more quickly than we anticipated. It was published in December 2000, and within four months department members from more than a score of institutions had called the MLA to report they had used the data to win substantial increases in part-timer salaries. Thus the GSC and its allies have by now increased the salaries of many hundreds of teachers across the country. Yet the MLA's executive director has been hostile toward all these efforts. For the most part the council followed her lead. It was a wrenchingly difficult experience for Christensen, the GSC's first representative to the council and a graduate student at the time of her election, to face the relentless hostility of well-paid faculty at meeting after meeting.

In time the MLA and the AAUP will be transformed by demographic facts, as longtime tenured faculty and staff retire and as graduate students from the union movement continue to move into faculty positions across the country. The nature of affiliation with these organizations—the partial identities and opportunities for action they offer their members—will change dramatically as a result. But we cannot simply wait for these changes. For higher education is steadily becoming a more exploitive workplace, and affiliation needs to be reconceived now if that trend is to be resisted.

CHAPTER 12

Social Movement Unionism and Adjunct Faculty Organizing in Boston

Barbara Gottfried and Gary Zabel

For the past three years, activists in Boston have been challenging the corporatization of higher education by developing innovative and successful approaches to organizing the most exploited layer of the higher education teaching workforce, the thousands of contingent, or adjunct, faculty members who work in the Greater Boston Area. The Boston Project of the Coalition of Contingent Academic Labor (COCAL) has developed a multicampus approach to organizing, an openness to solidarity with other campus workers, and a willingness to go beyond collective bargaining issues to address broad questions of equity and democratic power. Like living-wage campaigns and anti-sweatshop struggles, the Boston Project is an example of a bold new labor-based social movement emergent on America's campuses.

The development of a new labor-based social movement seems paradoxical, since the "new social movement" theory that arose in the 1970s and '80s emphatically rejected the primacy of labor struggles. In the view of such theorists as Alain Touraine, Chantal Mouffe, and Carl Boggs, young people, women, gays, oppressed ethnicities and nationalities, and other formerly silenced groups that began to agitate in the 1960s constituted unique social subjects whose transformative activity could not be understood from the perspective of Marxist theories of class struggle. These groups fought not so much over the distribution of the material surplus as over the symbolic systems and informal power relationships in which "forms of life" are embedded. They addressed the needs of their participants for social and cultural meaning, an orientation perhaps best expressed by the motto of the women's movement that "the personal is political." Moreover, according to theorists, just as these new social subjects moved largely outside the terrain of economic battle, so too did they reject the traditional organizational forms of the labor movement. Unlike unions and left-wing political parties, movement organizations are self-consciously fluid and transient, coalescing when needed and dissolving when the need is past. Movements, in short, are not reducible to organizations, and movement demands go far beyond bread-and-butter issues.

What is particularly ironic is that the distinction between labor and new social movements is breaking down precisely in the arena in which it was first theorized, namely, the academy. This breakdown is directly attributable to a transformation in the class character of higher education. First of all, the college and university experience is no longer reserved for an elite, but has become a mass phenomenon. Nearly 75 percent of all students are educated in comparatively low-cost public institutions, including a large number of community colleges. At the same time, the overwhelming majority of undergraduates work in low-paid, contingent jobs while attending classes. Many face prospects that are only marginally better after graduation. According to the National Center for Education Statistics, 25 percent of the holders of bachelor's degrees work in jobs that require only a high school education. Second, just as the class character of the student body has changed, so has that of the faculty. Nearly 50 percent of college and university teachers are classified as part-time—meaning they work for low pay and without benefits or job security no matter how many hours they put in—and 18 percent hold full-time but temporary, non-tenure-track appointments. No wonder that the home of a paradigmatic new social movement, the student rebellion of the 1960s, has become the site of labor struggles.

Current labor struggles have been deeply influenced by the organizational fluidity and desire to contest issues of culture and power that characterized earlier campus-based social movements. Anti-sweatshop efforts by students to force university stores to cease stocking items produced by sweatshop labor are marked by the informal, grass-roots organizational style and appeal to justice and community that marked previous student movements, as are living-wage campaigns to set decent standards of minimum compensation for the lowest paid campus workers. The Boston Project of the Coalition of Contingent Academic Labor applies a similar social movement orientation to the task of organizing adjunct faculty.

Origins of the New Organizing Model

Nowhere is the importance of contingent academic labor more evident than in the Greater Boston Area. With fifty-eight institutions of higher learning within a ten-mile radius of the urban center, Boston has the highest concentration of colleges and universities in proportion to population of any city in the world. Each year, graduate programs award thousands of master's and doctoral degrees to aspiring professionals. Many of the new degree holders remain in the Boston area, in large measure because of the city's stimulating cultural and intellectual environment. Of those who choose the academic profession, few manage to secure full-time employment, forming instead a labor pool from which most of the city's ten thousand part-time faculty members are drawn.

The colleges and universities of the Greater Boston Area are subsidized in part by the cheap credit hours produced by this most exploited stratum of the adjunct faculty. The tuition generated by a handful of students—two or three students in courses taught at private institutions, a few more in public ones—pays the wage for a part-time instructor. The employing institution then appropriates the remainder of the money brought in by the course as an unpaid premium, that is, as academic surplus value.

The economic function of the contingent faculty extends beyond its role in generating surplus tuition. It also plays an important part in the extensive networks that link higher education with private companies and public agencies. The university industry is not only one of Boston's biggest employers, it is connected with the city's other major industries—medicine, financial services, high tech, and state and local government—in a dense web of funding, training programs, research projects, policy institutes, and revolving personnel. The contingent faculty supplies the primary cadres for a crucial node in this web, the continuing education programs that retrain workers and managers. Moreover, in regular day programs, especially at state institutions, it educates Boston's future teachers, nurses, social workers, computer specialists, accountants, and so on. Finally, in the natural sciences, contingent faculty members conduct research, increasingly funded and used by private companies. In this fashion, the contingent faculty acts as a crucial productive force in Boston's larger political economy.

Because of its strategic location in the corporation-state-university complex, a dynamic effort by Boston's adjunct faculty to organize would send ripples throughout the city, affecting students, parents, politicians, public workers, and private corporations. Such a movement would demonstrate how the public's interest in education is damaged by the imperative to maximize profits, with its penchant for leasing education assets to narrow private interests, while driving teachers' salaries down. It would be poised to make a natural alliance with tens of thousands of students, most of whom are already temporary or part-time workers, and many of whom face the continued prospect, after graduation, of insecure, underpaid work without benefits. It might even develop imaginative new forms of community and solidarity as antidotes to the culture of careerist self-absorption and competitive isolation ordinarily offered in our halls of higher learning. To accomplish such tasks, however, the contingent faculty would have to achieve a high level of self-organization and overcome their isolation from one another.

In most cases, labor solidarity and militancy are nourished by the concrete face-to-face relations that bind workers together on the job. The Wobbly organizing campaigns of the 1910s and 1920s, the workplace occupations of the 1930s, as well as the P-9, Jay, Maine, and Pitstown strikes of more recent years were all conducted primarily by groups of workers who had learned to depend upon one another, on a daily basis, in the factories, the retail shops, and the mines. By contrast, contingent faculty members are atomized. With temporary jobs on a single campus or part-time positions on multiple ones, they have little chance of developing the workplace bonds that sustain concerted action. If collective bonds are to come into being, they must be forged, at least initially, not in the process of work, but in the course of struggle. In this regard, it is instructive to consider the campaign that gave birth to the Boston Project, the successful battle in 1997–98 of part-time faculty members at the University of Massachusetts Boston campus for full medical and pension benefits and prorated pay.

As a state institution, UMass Boston shares in the generally high level of union organization that characterizes public colleges and universities in the Northeast. The Faculty Staff Union, an affiliate of the National Education Association, won recognition in 1976 as the collective bargaining agent of the UMass faculty. Though union organizers argued for the inclusion of all part-time faculty members in the bargaining unit, an administrative threat to tie recognition up in the courts forced them to accept a hurdle to part-timer membership that has had a decisive impact on the character of the union. To be admitted into the union, part-timers must teach a total of five bargaining unit courses in the span of three consecutive semesters. In 1997, 115 people had done so, while 109 part-timers taught in the so-called regular university but without carrying enough courses for bargaining unit membership, and 116 taught only in the Continuing Education Division, which was not unionized at all. Had all part-timers been represented by the union, they would have numbered 340 members, roughly 40 percent of the entire bargaining unit. But because only a third of this number enjoyed union membership, part-timers were vastly outnumbered by their full-time colleagues. As a result of this imbalance, the FSU had given priority over the course of its history to defending the interests of full-time faculty.

The union did, however, provide a context in which part-time faculty members could organize to assert their interests. During contract negotiations in 1986, part-timers from several departments formed a Part-Time Faculty committee that functioned as a caucus within the FSU. The committee mounted a campaign on behalf of a set of demands, above all a substantial wage increase, that succeeded in winning the support of students, staff, and a good number of full-time faculty members. Just as important, committee activists were sophisticated enough to keep strategic pressure on union negotiators, making it difficult for them to abandon part-timers at the negotiating table. Although there were no part-time faculty members on the negotiating team, the Part-Time Faculty Committee sent an observer to each of the negotiating sessions. Moreover, at a crucial moment, the committee picketed a negotiating session, angering union negotiators but also forcing them onto the picket line. By means of such savvy tactics, the committee succeeded in winning an increase in base pay for part-time faculty union members of about $1,000 per course.

Though the committee continued to meet for a couple of years following the 1986 victory, external factors soon made it impossible to build on that achievement. A serious crisis in the state budget resulted in a reduction in force that ended by driving one third of the part-time faculty out of UMass Boston. Desperation to hang onto jobs replaced the elan of the '86 campaign. Yet the Part-Time Faculty Committee had demonstrated that it is possible for atomized adjuncts to build the collective bonds necessary to improve their conditions. This was a seed that would lie dormant for a while, but that would one day bear fruit.

By 1997, the seed took bloom as the fiscal crisis died down and the state wound up accumulating a billion-dollar budgetary surplus. Though much of the surplus was rebated to taxpayers, and little of what remained was used to satisfy social needs, the state's appropriation to UMass Boston ceased to shrink, and that made it feasible to make new part-timer demands. In the fall semester, activists mostly from the philosophy, English, and math departments reconstituted the Part-Time Faculty Committee. Early on, the committee determined the key element in its strategy. It would work to get the FSU to invert its traditional priorities by making part-time faculty issues the focus of contractual bargaining. It held several large meetings at which perhaps half the entire unionized part-time faculty chose a negotiating agenda. The agenda was intended to make an appeal to the university community so morally persuasive that the union leadership would not be able to ignore it.

Massachusetts law mandates full medical and retirement benefits for any state employee who works at least half-time. At UMass Boston, most unionized part-timers teach two courses per semester to the full-time faculty's three, yet each was classified by the university as two-fifths of a full-time worker. The point of the classification, of course, was to prevent part-timers from obtaining benefits under the law. In a number of cases, this exclusion had serious consequences. Some part-timers were unable to get medical treatment for chronic health problems, and others had to depend on welfare programs for assistance. In justifying part-timer exclusion from the provisions of the law, the university administration and the FSU Executive Committee were in initial agreement. In their view, part-timers had been hired to perform only one of the three functions of full-time faculty members, that is, to teach, but not to engage in research or service. Yet nearly all part-timers kept current in their fields, and a good number published articles and books or presented at conferences. All met with students outside of class during regular office hours as well as on an informal basis, and several worked on committees.

In a survey conducted by the Part-Time Faculty Committee, the vast majority of respondents indicated that they spent more than twenty hours per week on their UMass Boston jobs. Still, there was opposition on the FSU Executive Committee to recognizing that part-timers were already working half-time or better. Wouldn't such recognition threaten the traditional claims of full-timers to be engaged in additional and more prestigious sorts of work? In order to circumvent opposition, the Part-Time Faculty Committee appealed directly to the full-time faculty with a petition asserting that part-timers deserved benefits because of the amount of work they performed. The overwhelming number of full-timers who were asked to sign the petition did so, but without awareness of the reservations of influential members of the FSU Executive Committee. In the one department where an FSU officer made his objections known, not a single full-timer signed. Nonetheless, the petition had a crucial political effect. Published in the campus newspaper with 170 signatures, it demonstrated the ability of the Part-Time Faculty Committee to mobilize the union's own full-timer base. As a result, the Executive Committee was pressured to endorse the part-timers' negotiating agenda.

It took months to solidify union support through meetings, flyers, posters, buttons, a student petition that garnered two thousand signatures, and a picket by more than two hundred part-timers and supporters. The result, however, was extraordinary. Negotiations concluded in June '98 with reclassification of union part-timers teaching two courses per semester as salaried, half-time employees with full medical, dental, and retirement benefits, a prorated floor of $4,000 per course, a 16 percent salary increase over the three-year life of the contract, and an additional cumulative $200 wage increase every semester.

In the wake of this victory, the FSU worked to bring the part-time faculty closer to the fully enfranchised center of the union. The Executive Committee arranged for a course reduction for first one and then two of the members of the Part-Time Faculty Committee to allow them to continue organizing, supported an initiative to promote part-timers to full-time term contracts, and, after some tension, endorsed a successful attempt by part-timers in 2000–2001 to unionize UMass Boston's Continuing Education Division as an autonomous chapter of the FSU. The union has also changed its culture more subtly, according part-timer issues an important place at Executive Committee meetings, in the FSU's membership bulletin, and in its communications with outside groups. Finally, at the end of 2001, the Executive Committee selected a part-timer to serve as the union's vice president when the seat was vacated in midterm.

The contract victory at UMass Boston inspired the current attempt to organize adjunct faculty on a citywide basis. In April 1999, UMass Boston activists hosted the Third Annual Congress of the Coalition of Contingent Academic Labor (COCAL), a loose national network of contingent faculty activists with centers of strength in New York City, Chicago, and the San Franciso Bay Area. One of the congress workshops, a meeting on regional organizing, founded the Boston Project, subsequently chartered as a chapter of COCAL.

Fifty-four of the fifty-eight institutions of higher learning in the Greater Boston Area are private, and so they present obstacles to organizing that the UMass Boston activists never had to face. When Boston COCAL was formed in 1999, at all but two of the private institutions, part-time faculty members were not represented by unions. This was a legacy of the Supreme Court's 1980 decision in *Yeshiva University v. the National Labor Relations Board*. Yeshiva University had appealed an earlier decision by the NLRB granting union representation to its full-time faculty. The university argued that its full-time faculty members were not covered by the National Labor Relations Act because they exercised managerial authority by helping determine curriculum, hiring and evaluating new faculty members, and implementing administrative decisions. In a five-to-four ruling, the Court agreed with the university's position. The result of the *Yeshiva* decision was the widespread decertification of faculty unions on private campuses throughout the United States. *Yeshiva* clearly does not apply to part-time faculty members. By no conceivable stretch of the imagination do they exercise managerial authority. However, by deunionizing the vast majority of private campuses, *Yeshiva* has taken from part-timers the larger faculty unions in which they might organize caucuses, and so develop the collective bonds necessary to assert their interests.

In part, COCAL's Boston Project is an attempt to get beyond the quandary created by *Yeshiva*. Through citywide meetings, pickets and other demonstrations, local organizing committees, and a regular newsletter, COCAL activists hoped to create the sense of community and solidarity that is an indispensable precondition for combating the exploitation of adjuncts. In three citywide meetings during the year following the creation of Boston COCAL, fifty activists from twenty campuses drafted a common program for adjuncts that managed to be both radical and commonsensical. At its core are demands for equal pay for equal work, full medical and pension benefits, job security and free speech rights, participation in governance, promotion to full-time positions, and narrowing of salary disparities within the entire higher education faculty. Activists made this program the theme of an ambitious public educational campaign, discussing it at campus meetings of adjunct faculty members, bringing it to students through dramatic pickets at Northeastern University, Emerson College, and Massachusetts Bay Community College, and promoting it by means of radio and newspaper interviews.

In addition to this citywide educational effort, activists established grass-roots organizations at a number of institutions. Depending on local conditions, some function as informal advocacy groups, others as union organizing committees. As an example of the former, adjuncts at Suffolk University worked successfully with their Faculty Senate to pressure administrators into granting an 8 percent increase in part-timers' base pay. As a dramatic and pathbreaking example of the latter, Boston COCAL helped launch a campaign to unionize the part-time faculty at Emerson College, the first successful union drive at a private campus in Massachusetts since the 1980 *Yeshiva* decision.

Why Emerson out of the fifty-four private-sector institutions in Boston with adjuncts who were not unionized? From its beginning, Boston COCAL included activists from a variety of unions and professional organizations, but it had an especially close relationship with the American Association of University Professors (AAUP). At that time all three national faculty labor federations—the AAUP, the National Education Association, and the American Federation of Teachers—had given verbal recognition to the importance of the adjunct faculty's explosive growth, but the AAUP was the only one to go beyond lip service by hiring a national field representative to focus on the issue. Part of that focus consisted of strategic financial support to COCAL's Boston Project. In spring 2000, the AAUP, with input from COCAL activists and a few faculty members at Emerson, decided that there were several compelling reasons for targeting that institution in a first effort at unionizing part-time faculty in Boston's private sector. First of all, the full-time faculty at Emerson was already represented by an AAUP-affiliated union that had existed prior to the *Yeshiva* decision, and which the college administration had agreed to grandparent in. Second, the college was heavily dependent on part-timers, who constitute more than two-thirds of its total faculty. Finally, there was a strong base of student support. Because so many of their favorite teachers were part-timers, students were aware that their teachers' contingency curtailed both teachers' daily availability and the availability of courses necessary to complete their degrees, and so had a direct impact on their everyday learning environment. For this reason, they had a direct stake in supporting improved pay and working conditions for the part-time faculty.

The general difficulties involved in organizing part-time faculty—the fact they are scattered, they are at the workplace a limited number of hours per week, they don't know each other, and so on—are exacerbated by the incredibly precarious situation of part-timers at nonunionized private colleges. Because they are hired on a per-course, semester-by-semester basis, and lack union protection, they can fail to be rehired at any time without explanation. Considering their vulnerability, the first priority in beginning a union drive at Emerson was to protect the anonymity of part-time faculty activists. In its early stages, the drive was largely covert: the AAUP hired a cochair of Boston COCAL, who did not teach at Emerson, as organizer of the drive; Emerson part-timers were asked to talk quietly to other part-timers about unionization but not to expose themselves publicly; all union contact with part-time faculty members occurred off campus; and when flyers needed to be distributed or other visible work needed to be done on campus, members of COCAL not teaching at Emerson performed the required tasks.

In August of 2000, the drive began in earnest. The AAUP's paid organizer pulled together a committee of ten Emerson part-timers who made strategic decisions about the direction of the drive and talked with other part-time faculty about the benefits of unionization. In October, the committee launched a card-signing campaign to call for a union election. The biggest initial difficulty was figuring out who actually taught part-time at Emerson. Activists were able to acquire part-time faculty mailing lists from many of the divisions of Emerson, but because the lists had been compiled the previous spring, they were only about 75 percent accurate. That is to say, the attrition rate between spring and fall had been about 25 percent of the part-time faculty, or approximately fifty of the almost two hundred people listed as teaching in the spring. In addition, home phone numbers were not included on the lists, nor were home addresses available for many of the part-timers, which made it difficult to obtain correct phone numbers. Eventually, members of the organizing committee were able to obtain fall faculty lists, but the lists were incomplete. Ultimately, the organizing committee was unable to obtain the missing addresses until the National Labor Relations Board hearing at the end of February. At that point, the Emerson administration was required by law to provide an "Excelsior List" of the names and addresses (but not the phone numbers, which then had to be searched for online) of all those it considered eligible for bargaining-unit membership within a week. That left less than a month before the election to contact all those not yet reached.

Despite these logistical difficulties, signed cards began to trickle in, and, as more and more part-timers at Emerson began speaking to their colleagues, more cards were returned. At the same time, efforts were made to garner the support of the full-time faculty. Although there was some hesitation at the beginning, traceable to the full-timers' sense of the tenuousness of their own union in the face of *Yeshiva*, once the drive got under way in earnest full-timers supported it by displaying AAUP posters and speaking to part-timers they worked with, who were often more well acquainted with full-time faculty members than they were with fellow part-timers. Eventually the full-timers held a union meeting, but rather than endorse the union drive directly, they indicated by vote their preference for one union which would include both full- and part-timers, though they knew that the administration would resist this, hoping instead to have two unions to play off each other.

By January, the organizing committee needed only a few more cards to exceed the 30 percent of potential bargaining-unit members necessary to file for an election, and through intensified face-to-face contact, especially on the part of the paid organizer, more than the requisite number of cards were signed by the end of the month. The cards were duly filed with the National Labor Relations Board; an NLRB hearing was scheduled for the end of February; and negotiations proceeded with the Emerson administration as to how the bargaining unit should be constituted, though virtually all differences between the administration and the organizers were worked out before the hearing was actually held.

One of the key reasons there was not much to argue about at the NLRB hearing was that the Emerson administration had come up with an extremely lenient definition of who would be eligible to vote in the union election. Administrators proposed that anyone in the day school or the Continuing Education Division who had taught a three-credit course in the fall 2000 and/or spring 2001 semesters be eligible to vote. The initial card-signing drive had targeted only the day school. Thus the administration in effect gave the potential union an additional fifty members (Continuing Education faculty), which increased the size of bargaining unit by 25 percent. The downside was that though some of those who taught in Continuing Ed also taught in the day school and thus knew about the union drive, most had no idea anything was brewing. The administration seemed to have been counting on the notion that a majority of Continuing Ed faculty would not support a union drive because they were "true" adjuncts—hired to fill a particular teaching niche in their specialty, but gainfully employed full-time elsewhere—and therefore not in any particular need of a higher salary or benefits. But this turned out to be a miscalculation on the administration's part, as many Continuing Ed faculty were in fact graduate students at other colleges or in the day school at Emerson and quite interested in unionization. While some adjuncts had full-time jobs and did not support the union drive, many saw no reason to vote against the union and deprive their colleagues of a living wage and benefits, and therefore either voted for the union or abstained from voting at all, as a victory required only one more than 50 percent of those voting, not of those who were eligible to vote. During the last, frenzied weeks of outreach between the NLRB hearing and the due date for the mail-in election ballots, the administration launched a huge paper campaign, sending five or six mailings of ten pages or more replete with legalistic arguments against the union to all those eligible to vote. However, the arguments were so patently specious and, according to a number of adjuncts, so condescending, that many who had been ambivalent or uncommitted prior to the administration's efforts decided to vote for the union.

The NLRB hearing at the end of February determined that the vote would be by secret ballot, mailed on March 30, returned to the NLRB by April 13, and counted on April 16. It was unusual for an administration to argue for that method of election. Typically it is the workers who prefer a secret mail ballot to protect their privacy, while management prefers on-site elections, which can be monitored and which allow management to exercise subtle intimidation of voters. However, the administration seems to have felt that people would be more comfortable voting "no" in the privacy of their own homes, again a huge miscalculation. Despite the administration's best, if misguided, efforts to defeat the union, and following an intense telephone effort on the part of Emerson part-timers, the AAUP, and some COCAL activists in support of unionization, the result was a landslide: 117 to 37 in favor of unionizing.

Lessons Learned

The Emerson drive constitutes a paradox from the standpoint of conventional organizing strategy. Unions ordinarily do not file for an election until 70 percent or 80 percent of potential bargaining-unit members have signed cards. The reason for this is the expectation that a number of union voters will change their minds after management launches its antiunion election campaign. However, the Emerson organizing committee filed with just over 40 percent, yet won the election by a 3-to-1 majority. This points to the necessity of rethinking strategy when organizing contingent workers. The great problem the Emerson activists faced was getting cards signed. They had to track down their colleagues, most of whom they had never met because, as contingent workers, they lacked the workplace bonds ordinarily enjoyed by conventional workers. Once the 40 percent hurdle had been overcome, the organizing committee did not hesitate to file for an election because it correctly expected even the adjuncts it had failed to reach to vote against their undeniable exploitation.

Following the union victory, the Emerson administration contested the election results by arguing to the regional NLRB that the AAUP could not legitimately represent both part- and full-time faculty members at the same college as that would represent a conflict of interest, since full-timers exercise supervisory power over part-timers. The AAUP argued that it did not represent either group of faculty; rather, each of its affiliates represented itself. The regional board found in favor of the AAUP and the part-timer union. The administration then took its case to the national NLRB, which also found in favor of the union. After a five-month silence on the part of the administration during which it considered further legal action, the administration decided to abide by the election results. After meeting with their AAUP counterparts, Emerson's lawyers advised the president of the college to negotiate, and on November 1, 2001, the president sent a letter stating the administration's intention to "bargain in good faith." Negotiations began on February 4, 2002, and are currently in progress (even still as of this writing).

The victory at Emerson is a crucial one for the future of part-time faculty unionizing efforts in the private sector, both in the Boston area and beyond. It demonstrates the ability of adjunct faculty members to unionize successfully provided they are willing to exercise their imaginations as well as their courage. Boston COCAL has acquired a reputation not only for innovative organizing tactics but for a willingness to cross sectoral lines in making alliances with other campus workers. Along with the AAUP, Jobs With Justice, and the Campaign on Contingent Work, COCAL has initiated an organizing project that brings campus unions representing janitors, clerical workers, technical employees, food service workers, and faculty together with students and other activists in a broad-based solidarity network. In addition to sponsoring two conferences on the academic labor movement, those participating in the network have adopted a Campus Workers' Bill of Rights that demands decent working conditions, a living wage, and benefits, but also universalizes privileges historically enjoyed only by tenured faculty. The document, which is meant to guide negotiations as well as more informal grass-roots campaigns, affirms the right of all workers to participate democratically in shaping the work process as well as to be protected from dismissal without just cause or due process. In this way, tenure and governance rights would be extended not only to part-time faculty but to everyone who works in academia, an extension of labor demands well beyond bread-and-butter needs.

Two months after the Emerson vote, COCAL activists succeeded in unionizing UMass Boston's Continuing Education Division as an autonomous chapter of the existing Faculty Staff Union, a chapter controlled by the adjunct faculty members who constitute the overwhelming majority of the CE bargaining unit. The activists used the UMass Boston drive as a springboard for creating an adjunct faculty caucus within the FSU's statewide parent union, the powerful Massachusetts Teachers Association, itself an affiliate of the NEA. The initial caucus meeting, which took place at the MTA's annual Delegate Assembly, drew roughly forty participants from ten or so campuses who adopted a reform agenda intended to pressure the MTA's Higher Education Division into using its considerable resources on behalf of adjunct faculty interests. The central plank in that agenda was a demand that the MTA's largest higher education affiliate, the fifteen-campus Massachusetts Community College Council (MCCC), give each of its adjunct faculty members a full vote in the election of union officers. Of the fifty-seven hundred faculty members who teach in the Massachusetts community college system, seventeen hundred are full-timers and four thousand are part-timers. Though part-timers constitute the vast majority of the MCCC's membership, they are kept a minority voting bloc within the union through bylaws that give each part-timer one fourth of the vote of a full-time faculty member. Such a fractional vote is unjustified even on the spurious grounds of proportionality since a good number of community college "part-timers" actually carry heavier course loads than full-timers by teaching on multiple community college campuses. At the MTA's Delegate Assembly, the Adjunct Faculty Caucus planned a petition drive to be conducted among union members on the community college campuses, and designed to pressure the MCCC to amend its bylaws by giving all of its members an equal vote. Not only would this rectify an evident injustice, but it would also make the community college part-time faculty a formidable force in the MTA's largest higher education union, thereby increasing their weight in the parent organization as well.

It is not surprising that the petition drive, which is currently under way, has elicited a hostile reaction from the MTA's higher education staff as well as from much of the MCCC's elected leadership. The drive threatens to overturn the status quo within the MTA and its largest higher education affiliate by shifting a significant amount of power to the part-time faculty. It is also not surprising that the MTA and MCCC elites regard Boston COCAL as an intruder, even though its original core activists are members of an MTA-affiliated union (the Faculty Staff Union at UMass Boston). In a revealing slip of the tongue, MCCC leaders have labeled the COCAL members within the MTA Adjunct Faculty Caucus "carpetbaggers," since many of them do not teach in the community college system. But "carpetbagger," of course, was the name given by southern racists to northerners who came south in the aftermath of the Civil War to help dismantle the slave system.

Boston COCAL's battle is not only with college and university administrators and the private economic interests they serve, but also with the undemocratic union structures that replicate the second-class status that adjuncts suffer in the workplace. Only a revitalized academic labor movement is capable of rolling back corporate control of every nook and cranny of the education process. But innovative organizing tactics are not sufficient to create such a movement. Faculty unions must develop a culture that welcomes the participation of part-timers, their most exploited members, because part-time faculty, both those who are unionized and their nonunionized counterparts, constitute the majority of those teaching on America's college and university campuses. If COCAL's Boston Project is successful, its most important contribution will lie not in the unionizing of this or that institution, but in the creating of a new social movement, a radically democratic labor movement, in the academy.

CHAPTER 13

Renewing Academic Unions and Democracy at the Same Time
The Case of the California Faculty Association
Susan Meisenhelder (with Kevin Mattson)

On March 26, 2002, the California Faculty Association (CFA) approved a new agreement with the California State University (CSU) system. Just weeks before, our members had been prepared to strike, finding ourselves struggling against a hostile administration. Now we voted 95 percent for the new agreement. The agreement was *big* for a number of reasons. The numbers, for one: CSU is the largest public higher education system in the country. Our agreement affects not just CFA's own twenty-two thousand members, which include full-time *and* part-time faculty as well as librarians and coaches, but also the 350,000 students (the numbers keep climbing) who attend the twenty-three campuses of CSU schools throughout the state. It is a well-worn cliché to call college students the "future of America," but in this case, the cliché fits. CSU's students are predominantly people of color and young working adults. Many of our students are the first in their families to attend college. We feel pride in negotiating an agreement that will improve the quality of education they will receive. We also believe this agreement serves as the first step—and *first* is an important qualifier—in forging a different vision for the future of higher education in America. We have struggled to articulate a new vision for higher education based upon the democratic role that professors must play in assuring the highest quality of education for all of America's citizens.

I want to tell the story of CFA precisely because it offers important lessons for the academic labor movement now getting off the ground. We've

221

heard about graduate students organizing (in my home state, one of the biggest and most successful drives took place at the University of California-Berkeley). We've also heard about struggles among adjunct faculty at numerous institutions. Our struggle is distinct in that it attempts to create one big union that can address concerns faced by a broad range of employees. We have also tried to move beyond contract negotiations by bringing our message to California's citizens more broadly. We do this because we are convinced that we stand at an opportune moment in history—a time when a democratic vision of higher education must be articulated by academic labor activists.

The Origins and Limitations of CFA

Faculty members formed the CFA in 1974 to protect academic freedom and job security. This came on the heels of Governor Ronald Reagan's famous attacks on the state university system, as he accused schools of harboring left-wing lunatics (who can forget his famous statement in the face of campus unrest: "If it takes a bloodbath, then let's get it over with"?). Faculty knew they needed to defend their rights lest they suffer from the political backlash that followed the late 1960s. In 1978, just two years prior to the famous *National Labor Relations Board v. Yeshiva University* decision that made it impossible for faculty members at private universities to unionize, CFA got a lucky break when the state legislature passed the Higher Education Employer-Employee Relations Act (HEERA), which allowed faculty to pursue collective bargaining. Four years later, the faculty took up the state legislature's invitation, about 85 percent voting for collective bargaining. Faculty governance was central to the mission of the CFA from day one. Our bylaws call on our membership "to provide a democratic voice for academic professionals within the CSU." The ramifications of this principle have become highlighted by our recent struggles.

Unfortunately, union democracy—like any democracy—is a tiring initiative. It takes energy and commitment from citizens. In this case, it took the time and energy of a professoriate that was already working quite hard just to teach and do research. Gradually, the union slid into what the political theorist Jeffrey Lustig called "service unionism." CFA focused on bottom-line issues: salary, basic working conditions, and more state money for the education system. As Lustig points out, CFA, during the late 1980s and early 1990s, "had not been a presence in public-policy discussions addressing higher education nor in larger efforts to influence the direction of the university. It had also adopted a plan of operations by which members paid dues as something akin to grievance insurance and for benefits packages, both of which services were provided by organizational staff."[1] Most members saw the union as little more than a yearly fee—a service that demanded little of their own initiative. Though our membership rarely dropped in numbers, it certainly backed away from the kind of rigorous participation that ensures the health of an organization. This passivity, of course, was a problem facing the labor movement generally during the 1980s and 1990s— a time when passivity really hurt.

Broadly speaking, unions stopped organizing new sectors of the economy and were hemorrhaging members during the 1970s. Then came the attack— the smashing of the airline traffic controllers' strike by President Ronald Reagan. Industrial plants left the United States, what some critics gently called deindustrialization. Jobs in the service sector failed to make up the loss because they paid next to nothing and provided no security. And as unions had failed to organize and grown passive (the AFL-CIO's George Meany famously quipped that it didn't "make any difference" if the unionized sector of the population shrank), they could not respond to the new pressures of a global economy that degraded the working conditions of many Americans. The wake-up call for labor seemed to come sometime in the 1990s—with a heightening of globalization—as a new leadership at the AFL-CIO rose up and pledged itself to change. Things were about to change for CFA as well.

Meet the New Boss

Our wake-up call came in the form of the corporatization of higher education. That may sound abstract, but it wasn't for us. There was a face to it: namely the newly appointed chancellor of CSU, Charles (Charlie) Reed (all campus presidents answer to the chancellor under the CSU system). Reed, who was appointed with little or no faculty input, thinks of himself as a "chief executive officer"—an appellation that state lawmakers have given him—who shakes up what he thinks of as stodgy and bureaucratic systems. One of the reasons he came to the university was because of Cornerstones, a project that imports corporate practices into the state system by measuring student performance through an increasing number of tests—those that especially cater to what businesses want from employees. Reed likes to argue that higher education must be useful to the immediate demands of businesses. "We have to educate our students, but it has to be relevant," that is, job-related, as he himself explained it.[2] He even likes to draw direct analogies between the universities and factories. Calling for the widening of CSU's summer services, he complained to a public gathering of business executives that the university does not operate at full capacity during this season. Reed griped, "How many of your plants are down two or three months of the year?"[3] It's rare for a chancellor to be so blunt about how he sees the university.

Unfortunately, it's not just rhetoric. If anything, his talk matches the practices of CSU for the past ten or more years. For instance, as with American corporations, CSU has paid the top administrative branches quite well over the years. From 1997 to 2000, campus presidents—those who sit just below the chancellor—have received salary increases of 33 percent, much higher than full-time and part-time faculty (the latter had barely received any pay raises in recent years before our agreement). In addition, the the number of administrators has also grown over the years, increasing by 33 percent between 1994 and 2001. This move entailed draining money away from teaching. During the last twelve years, for example, the percentage of the university budget going to instruction has decreased from 54.8 percent to 48 percent. Had the percentage remained constant, there would be $190 million today going to instruction that could fund smaller classes and even more tenure-track professors who could teach such smaller classes. The pay structure at CSU looks a lot like the pay structure of most American corporations—generous at the top and miserly at the bottom.

The corporate vision also entered in the late 1990s with the California Education Technology Initiative (CETI). Essentially, a deal was cut—between the administration and a consortium of high-tech corporations (Microsoft, GTE, Hughes, and Fujitsu)—in order to ensure what would have become a monopoly over students and faculty (for more on these sorts of initiatives, see David Noble's chapter 2 in this book). As if this attempt to merge the public and private sectors wasn't questionable enough, there was talk of marketing "courseware," as it was glibly referred to, that would have threatened faculty's intellectual property rights by selling course material privately. We saw this as a blatant step toward privatizing the university. The secretiveness of the initiative alerted faculty that things were starting to change for the worse at CSU. With the help of student activists, we fought and defeated CETI. But we were just starting to uncover an overall attempt to make the university into a corporation.

The next problem generated by the university's attempt to turn itself into a corporation came in the form of merit pay (for more on this, see Tanguay's chapter 3 in this collection). Trustees and the new chancellor were friendly toward a new merit pay system that had been instituted and wanted to extend it; faculty hated the system for several reasons. Merit pay, as is often the case at other institutions, was being glommed onto an already existing peer review system. It seemed as if administrators were telling us that we weren't doing a good job at evaluating our peers and that they wanted to take control over the process. And when we investigated the implementation of merit pay, we discovered enormous problems. First, there was gender. In 1999, we found that 64 percent of male professors got merit increases of $900 or more, while only 36 percent of women did. Second—and this problem correlated with gender—were the poor rewards handed to "lecturers" (what the CSU labels adjuncts or part-timers), who happened to be, more often than not, women. The really insidious side of merit pay came out when we looked at how it applied to part-timers. At our San Marcos campus, we discovered that 85 percent of tenure-track professors got some raise versus 15 percent of the lecturers. This example highlights how the merit pay system helped prop up a two-tier faculty system at CSU. Though the merit pay rewards were themselves fairly insubstantial, their uneven disbursement made clear just how unjust the system was—especially how it cemented discriminatory practices.

We publicized these problems and felt that we had a strong case against a system that, at first appearance, seemed commonsensical and popular (who can complain about professors being rewarded for hard work?). In our last agreement with the university, we were able to abolish the merit system precisely on the grounds that we had discovered structural deficiencies. There were numerous lessons here. Our successful fight against merit pay showed that the CFA could talk about the quality of education while challenging the corporate-speak of Chancellor Reed. After all, though Reed always liked to sound as if he was on the side of quality education, what with his talk of "accountability" and "pleasing the consumer," he had done nothing to counteract a general decline in the number of faculty members in comparison to an increase in number of students—one of the clearest indicators of the quality of education. We were making clear that high-quality education relied upon a fair and equitable reward system for faculty members—that is, *all* faculty members. In the end, we learned by struggling against merit pay that we could go public—through demonstrations and talking to politicians and the press—without sounding as though we were simply self-interested. But we also learned that we had uncovered a whole host of other problems that we needed to confront.

Thinking Long-term, Acting *Now*: Toward A Vision of Academic Citizenship

We knew that the issue of part-timers had to move to the center of our struggles—for all of the reasons already outlined in this collection. Our research into merit pay had unearthed just how much the university exploited

part-timers. Temporary and part-time faculty face lower pay, fewer benefits, and greater insecurity than regular faculty as they often race from
campus to campus to cobble together a living salary. This hurts students because the very nature of temporary and part-time positions threatens the
continuity of academic programs and often the ability of faculty in those positions to provide time for students outside the classroom. And the effect on
the university itself is negative as more and more faculty find that the tenu-
ous nature of their appointments makes it difficult to exercise academic
freedom, to participate fully and independently in academic shared governance, and sometimes even to make academic decisions in the best interests
of their students' education.

The trends in the California State University are shocking: between
1994–95 and 1999–2000 the number of full-time-equivalent students increased by thirty-five thousand. The net increase in tenure-track positions
during that same period was *one* position. Had the ratio of tenure-track to
non-tenure track faculty of 1994–95 been maintained (and increased use of
temporary faculty was already well under way at that point), there would be
eleven hundred more tenure-track faculty in the system today. To add in-
sult to injury, the numbers in CSU management ranks during this same
period increased by 24 percent.

To confront this problem, CFA developed a twofold strategy: In the
short term, we needed to improve the quality of life for our part-time instructors; in the long term, we needed to push back against the administration's overuse of part-timers, that is, we needed to push for more full-time
appointments. This was a challenge, since it was all too easy for full-timers to
see part-timers as second-class citizens, their plights unrelated to their own
concerns. We all know that at places like Yale, full-time tenure-track faculty
can mistreat teaching assistants—seeing them as little more than slave labor
or apprentices—and not even recognize the existence of adjuncts. In order to
connect full- and part-timers together, we had to make clear that our interests were bound together. We drew upon a language of "academic citizenship"—the idea that as individual faculty members, we need to look out for
our common interests and common good and protect the conditions of fellow
workers precisely because our futures are tied together.

There were numerous ways to do this. One was of particular symbolic
significance: we elected a lecturer to the vice presidency of the union in
1999—the first time ever. Then we provided information that could help
part-timers in the short term; for example, we wrote and distributed thousands of lecturer handbooks filled with information that the administration
failed to provide. We made clear what rights lecturers had, in order to cut

against the confusing anomie of working part-time in a vast bureaucratic system. We let lecturers know their rights that are often not—intentionally or otherwise—mentioned in letters of appointment (often the only thing lecturers read before coming on board). We detailed what benefits they were entitled to and how to demand them. We encouraged lecturers to form networks among themselves—to alleviate some of their isolation—and to work with representatives who were on each campus. Finally, we set out "guidelines for good practices" that lecturers could use to make sure they were not being abused by administrators.

While providing this sort of helpful short-term information, we had to be crafty in our negotiations, making sure that we didn't undercut our long-term goals with short-term victories. We needed, for strategic and ethical reasons, to get some short-term benefits for our lecturers. But we also knew that making conditions better for part-timers could potentially threaten our overall desire—to cut back on the overuse of part-timers by the administration. Hence the attempt to focus on health benefits for part-timers: this allowed us to improve short-term standing of part-timers but at the same time made it more difficult—that is, less profitable—for the administration to use part-timers. While negotiating benefits for part-timers, we would also demand more full-time tenure-track positions. This strategy blended a short- and long-term strategy and showed that we were an inclusive union representing the interests of all employees.

As a public-sector union, we had a distinct advantage in improving the quality of all our faculty. We could use a political legislative strategy to confront the problems. But articulating this sort of political power wasn't as easy or obvious as it might first seem. First, we needed to overcome attitudes prevalent among many white-collar employees—the sort that make faculty uncomfortable with demonstrating and picketing for legislation. As Jeff Schmidt has documented, there are numerous characteristics of professionals that often inhibit their ability to affect the institutions within which they work. Schmidt's research focuses on an obvious question: Why on tests of political point of view do professionals who are often liberal seem so conservative and timid within their workplaces? Schmidt analyzes everything from SATs to graduate school and concludes that the socialization and self-definition of ourselves as "professionals" involves a feeling that "getting political" and "taking a stand" are somehow "unprofessional." He argues that white-collar employees are "paralyzed . . . by the individualism inherent in their outlook" and that "they retreat in fear at the mere suggestion of joining with others in struggle."[4] CFA tried to counteract this by articulating a different view of professionalism, one that requires people to care about their working conditions—precisely those things that allow them to focus their energy on professional duties. As Robert Birnbaum explains, there's a vision of professionalism as an honored tradition that "presumes a calling—a vocation—a dedication to service" and, I would add, an understanding of the importance of collective action on behalf of that calling.[5]

By acting on this sort of professionalism, we have been able to articulate a connection to the working lives of our students. Our standing as professionals did not entail a distancing from the realities of ordinary working Americans. In fact, it made clear the connection between our professional lives and our concern for the future of our students' work lives when they left the university. We needed to show our students that, as citizens, their professors would fight for political change to benefit their working conditions so that they might do the same. To make this connection explicit, we initiated a drive for legislation that included AB 2549, a bill that would allow CSU lecturers to obtain health and retirement benefits. We also sponsored SB 1661, which would provide family leave benefits for all members, allowing workers to find a sensible balance between family and civic responsibilities and their work lives. This bill, which holds to a broad definition of "family" that includes domestic partners, would provide up to twelve weeks of family leave payments for birth or adoption of a child. Finally, we have endorsed SB 277, which would require HMOs to *ensure* coverage—attacking one of the major issues facing all workers, namely, the degradation of our health-care system. We believe this sort of legislation makes clear that we want to defend not simply the standing of those professionals in our own unit but the interests of American workers more broadly construed.

Our recent victory and agreement with the administration reflect these struggles. We have won benefits for part-timers, making it harder for the university to continue exploiting them. We have expanded health-care coverage for all employees in our union. We have also made clear that the union will continue to negotiate for more full-time hires. These accomplishments illuminate why the CFA thinks of itself as "one big union" capable of addressing the concerns of its members and, in effect, raising attention to the problems facing American workers more broadly—even those within the white-collar ranks.

Changing the Terms of the Debate: The "Future of CSU"

Our biggest hope in this last victory is that we have made our case to a wider public. Too often, faculty unions—even those within the public sector—

have been cut off from public debate. During contract negotiations, the wider public hears talk-radio pundits attacking supposedly well-fed, over-paid faculty members—the "new class" or *privilegentsia*, as neoconservatives call them—looking for even fatter paychecks. Professors are characterized as just another selfish elite in this discourse, even if this flies in the face of real-ity—namely, the increasing number of underpaid lecturers who try to carve out living wages by traveling from campus to campus. Instead of seeing fac-ulty unions as being concerned with the future of education and asserting their right to democratic control over their work lives, we are characterized as self-motivated actors trying to leech off the public sector.

Recognizing this, CFA has tried to initiate a conversation that can chal-lenge this characterization while prompting a wider debate about the future of higher education. This project, initiated two years ago, is called the "Fu-ture of CSU". Recognizing the almost overwhelming power of the dis-course of the corporate university, with its powerful, restrictive notions of efficiency, accountability, and productivity, we decided that talking about a different vision for the university required a very different conversation. Thus, we decided to sponsor hearings on our campuses that would bring together students, faculty, alumni, scholars with expertise in higher educa-tion, as well as community and elected leaders to talk about their experi-ences, their concerns, as well as their hopes and dreams for our universities. Bringing these groups together was also politically important, we believed, for it would take alliances of these groups to change the direction of our state university. These conversations would provide space for democratic deliberation about the future of higher education—a space in which a civic alternative might be articulated against the dominant corporate vision of the university administration.

We have now had three hearings and have scheduled similar events on all of our campuses. The events have been heartening. Students, faculty, and elected leaders reacted with shock at research data generated by CFA detailing changes in the system over the last decade. Most striking perhaps, was the way people talked about the university and what it means to them. Remarkably, no one talked about it as a "profit center" or "engine of the economy," just as no one referred to students as "consumers" or faculty as "content providers." Describing universities as "treasures," "oases," and "sacred places" may sound foreign in today's business world, but such lan-guage used by students, faculty, staff, and alumni in describing their experi-ences with the California State University points to a very powerful public notion of the ideal university—what some refer to as the "People's Univer-sity"—quite different from that of the corporate vision.

Within these discussions, faculty members and students together have defined a vision of education that centers on the responsibility of democratic citizenship. They have agreed that education can certainly help prepare them to be better workers, but that it also must prepare them to be better citizens—that is, critical thinkers capable of reflecting upon the social conditions they live within and assessing what they like and what they want to change about their society. Education can open up new ways of perceiving our collective responsibilities, not just about how to be efficient workers. But it can do this only if students have full-time teachers who can work with them to engage in this project. It can do this only if faculty have a voice in shaping the future of their institutions.

Here's where we come full circle. The "Future of CSU" project has helped CFA move away from being purely defensive; we can now take the initiative back from those who want to turn universities into corporations. At a time when privatization and commercialization are affecting the university as never before, nothing is more important than guaranteeing faculty a voice in public policy debates, especially those surrounding the future of higher education. In so doing, we can widen the debate about the future of higher education: making it not just about the bottom line but about the ways in which education helps us see the world differently and helps us ask questions about what sort of society we want to live in.

The Future of Higher Education and Academic Labor

To those outside the academy, it may seem strange that there is so much discontent and turmoil within it. Politicians, media pundits, and business leaders share a remarkable consensus that education—and higher education in particular—is indispensable to the future of individuals and nations alike. If our gross national product grows too slowly, the solution is to use education to create a more productive workforce. If we want to live better than our parents did, then we must go to college. If there is to be something resembling racial equality in this country, then access to education must be equalized. If a backward region or country wants to reach new levels of prosperity, then it must educate its citizenry. If a politician wants to capitalize on discontent over stagnant living standards, then expanding access to higher education through tax credits or a similar mechanism will gain more support than the "class warfare" approach of taxing the rich or reversing the flight of American capital overseas. The United States even exports much of this philosophy abroad. We have truly liberated Afghanistan, we tell ourselves, because Afghani women and girls can again go to school.

Much of the American public seems to share this confidence. The United States boasts the highest rate of college attendance in the world, far outpacing even other industrialized and wealthy nations. A college education is expensive—the largest family investment after housing—but millions of Americans gladly save for it nonetheless. And our higher education system is not only large and comparatively accessible, but it is also perceived to be of high quality. Why else would hundreds of thousands of students from all over the world come to the United States to attend college and graduate school?

Even the best-known political battles over higher education draw much of their vigor and acrimony from the near-universal assumption of its importance. Affirmative action in university admissions stirs such controversy not only because it raises difficult questions about race and academic merit, but precisely because college admission has become a major sorting device in the American class system. Debates over the curriculum—the so-called "culture wars" between academic traditionalists and multiculturalists—are proxies for a larger cultural debate that both sides give such importance because universities are now our preeminent cultural institutions, molding millions of young minds every day. In these days of high-tech entertainment and the book industry's obsession with blockbuster books, college is one of the rare moments when people actually read literature and serious nonfiction. That's why *what* they read has become so very important.

Since virtually everybody agrees that higher education is critically important, then these should be boom times for educators, with politicians and millions of citizens singing their praises and lining up to give them the resources they need to run the best universities that they can. But they're not. More than half of college instructors lack secure, full-time employment. The rising expectations and shrinking respect of their employers join with the consumerist mentality of their students to make many wonder if their profession can still serve the values that drew them to it. These feelings are particularly acute in the younger generation of academics, those now in graduate school or who have just left it. Saddled with years of student loans, enveloped in long searches for decent jobs, many young academics feel bitterness toward the profession that, as Cary Nelson puts it, devours its young.

There is a good reason for this curious juxtaposition of the universally acclaimed importance of education and the increasing disenchantment of educators. The essays in this volume demonstrate that what lurks behind the rising discontent of university instructors is the corporatization of the academy. Contemporary colleges and universities have increasingly taken corporations—premised on the idea of profitable efficiency—as their model for internal organization. Administrators happily import the arsenal of corporate management techniques with little regard for the autonomy and power that faculty have traditionally enjoyed. Distance learning technology is a favorite here, both for its promise to make the "delivery" of education more effective and for the opportunities it provides for profitable cooperation with the private sector. Merit pay systems, designed to create incentives for maximum productivity, are implemented even when they create enormous amounts of unnecessary work and reams of uninspired publications. The aspiration and illusion is that enlightened managers can direct the work of their faculty much as their counterparts in the business world direct that of their employees.

The use of disposable faculty—often part-time, and certainly not tenure-track—is the best-known and perhaps most important practice of the corporate university. The last thirty years have seen the national business elite fully retreat from the old Fordist notion of relying on a large and permanent workforce that would trade its loyalty and decades of its members' lives in exchange for secure jobs, pensions, and retirement plans. With business executives wielding more and more power on university boards, and the corporation supplanting all other models for large organizations, it is little surprise that universities have followed suit, shifting enormous portions of their labor demands onto the shoulders of casual teachers, their own graduate students as often as not.

Although the teaching and research done at universities have been important parts of the national economy since the industrial revolution, the developments discussed here have reversed much of what once buffered universities from the market. The means and ends of higher education are traditionally very different from those of the economy as a whole. Traditional universities do not exist to generate a profit from capital investment, most research and teaching have little or no marketable use, and many full-time professors exercise enormous discretion over what, when, and how they work. Because the more recent corporate practices are so at odds with the traditional university, some have argued that universities must be entirely remade into for-profit corporations. One such vision is embodied in the University of Phoenix, where professional managers direct employees in the delivery of carefully researched and test-marketed modules, updated every several years just as GM or Ford puts its automobiles on a product cycle.

All of this is bad news for those whose work actually makes possible the daily functioning of universities. The most obvious burden they bear comes from the simple exploitation of their labor. Alexis Moore's interminable drive across southern California, from one bit-part job to another, is all too typical of instructors in the new university. Challenging working conditions and poor pay are just the tip of the iceberg. The isolation from other instructors and lack of any assurance of being hired back the next term mean that these jobs undermine not only the living circumstances of teachers but also the notion of a community of scholars that collaborates to ensure that students leave school as knowledgeable citizens. The working life of so many adjuncts today sharply contrasts with the larger aspirations and expectations of graduate school. Trained to lead the life of the mind after working up the ladder of apprenticeship, graduate students instead find themselves members of the educational proletariat. Whatever else they may be, they are surely workers.

There are still good jobs in academia, of course. Many tenure-track positions offer job security, good pay, and the autonomy necessary for productive scholarship and engaged teaching. Even these positions, however, bear the mark of the corporate university. A fully tenured faculty member has recently complained about how, when evaluated, he feels like a commodity being judged by a generation of cool consumers. The complaint may sound minimal (in comparison to the plight of adjuncts it is), but it shows just how much a corporate ethic affects those who would seem most sheltered.[1] As we go down the academic totem pole but still before we confront adjuncts, the pressures only increase. The vast reserve supply of dedicated and talented teachers has allowed many universities to ratchet up the teaching load and publication expectations of tenure-track faculty. Moving to a better job is difficult in this glutted market, and quitting will only place you among the desperate thousands seeking employment.

The shrinking percentage of the professoriate with excellent tenure-track jobs depends directly on the grad students and adjuncts whose teaching frees up senior faculty for leaves and light teaching loads. Elite faculty, however, are loath to acknowledge this reality. The course of the grade strike at Yale University makes it shockingly clear just how far established faculty will go to help thwart organizing efforts on the part of graduate students. That those organizing were their own students and that blacklisting them contradicted the principles and values of their own scholarship were no obstacles.

Those tenure-track faculty who do acknowledge their connection to the larger political economy of higher education can all too easily find themselves staring at the true face of the corporate university. Joel Westheimer's denial of tenure—after receiving numerous superlative evaluations, even from the administrators who later demeaned his scholarship as inadequate—reveals the lengths to which administrators will go to protect what they see as their managerial prerogatives. Although his case is extreme, it is also diagnostic. An increasing proportion of senior faculty, department chairs, and administrators depend on the goodwill of their managers and not on their scholarship or teaching for their positions, salaries, and future prospects.

Little wonder, then, that an increasing number of academics are turning to labor organizing and other forms of activism to seek redress for their grievances. In doing so, they seek both material benefits, such as better wages, and the return of some of the autonomy and power that faculty once boasted. One of our major aims in this volume is to explain why such a movement has taken off the ground.

It's little surprise that graduate students have taken something of a lead in this movement. After they all, they are facing the brunt of job restructuring as they find their teaching assistantships look increasingly like plain old work. This is why the successful union drive of New York University teaching assistants is so important. Theirs was a milestone victory, one that may well pave the way for the unionization of other private universities. NYU's contract is both a reminder of the concrete benefits that unionization can bring and a legal precedent that—for the time being, at least—has brought graduate teachers at private schools under the protections of the National Labor Relations Act (NLRA).

Adjuncts have also embraced labor organizing as a response to their exploitation. Our stories about Boston and California in the last section make this clear. Unlike grad students, adjuncts can't tell themselves that there is a pot of gold at the end of the rainbow, if only they publish some articles, write a great dissertation, and stay on their advisor's good side. And few suffer any illusions as to their status. They are hired and fired on the basis of student enrollments, and paid as little as possible. This is labor, pure and simple. So organizing seems less and less out of the realm of their imagination.

But there are significant obstacles to organizing by graduate students and adjuncts. Many graduate students, especially those outside of the humanities, expect to secure good jobs after graduation, and so view labor organizing as a distraction at best. As the failed drive at Minnesota suggests, grad students can fall prey to the familiar arsenal of antiunion tactics. Warnings that employees will lose control of their work, that relations with their advisors and peers will be strained, and that their dues money will be siphoned off to advance political causes with which they disagree can all fall on receptive ears. Adjuncts face a different and perhaps even more daunting set of challenges. They rarely know one another, have little investment in one particular employer, and even less time. Their full-time colleagues and existing unions often view their organizing as more of a threat than an opportunity. And the idea of what it means to be white collar—standing above the working class as educated and privileged—still poses an enormous cultural barrier (even if it's becoming more and more of a fiction).

Academics are turning to alternative forms of organizing to surmount these obstacles. Cary Nelson demonstrates how disciplinary associations such as the Modern Language Association might serve to unite the profession—including its most powerful senior members—behind measures to combat the academic employment crisis. The reinvigoration of these organizations would return the profession as a whole to the basic mission of protecting the interests and dignity of all of its practitioners. Other organizing projects raise their visions beyond merely changing the terms of work at one university. Boston's Coalition of Contingent Academic Labor (COCAL) understands that all academic employers in the metro area must be organized if working conditions for adjuncts are to improve. Similarly, the California Faculty Association has taken on the entire California State University system, while making it clear that its efforts are about quality education as well as the jobs of its members.

There can be no doubt about it now: a burgeoning labor movement has arisen to combat the corporatization of academy. Where the architects of the new university speak of flexibility and cost-saving, the movement speaks of benefits and steady work. Where some college presidents assume that universities are businesses, the movement sees them as self-governing, democratic communities committed to pursuing public—not private—goods. Where certain administrators consider students to be consumers of an expensive but economically essential product, the movement sees them as something more than just consumers—as citizens who must be offered opportunities at democratic self-governance themselves. In other words, the academic labor movement has initiated a debate about the future of higher education that must be entered into by anyone concerned with the future of democracy.

How successful this movement will be is difficult to say. But the essays assembled here do offer a clear sense of what academics have to do if they are to prevent the academy from being remade entirely in the image of the corporation. The building blocks of this effort will likely remain individual organizing drives on specific campuses, aimed at forcing schools to sign collective bargaining agreements with their instructors. These agreements can serve the interests of faculty and the wider democratic uses of education by delivering material benefits to instructors and maintaining or restoring their power over the curriculum and other institutional initiatives.

Employers—no matter in what sector of the economy—rarely greet union campaigns with open arms. And so like all others seeking unionization, academics must overcome the opposition of their employers to their organizing efforts. In order to draw supporters, they will have to make the case that unionization will help both faculty and the overall processes of education. Recent legal developments—the partial erosion of the *Yeshiva* decision that removed faculty at private universities from the provisions of the NLRA, and the NLRB decisions backing graduate unionization—will be helpful. But American labor law provides few effective protections for organizing, and these particular decisions could be easily reversed or gutted by conservative justices and board appointees. So the strength of the future academic labor movement must rest, like the labor movement as a whole, on organizing and broader political change.

As any academic organizer will attest, convincing faculty of the importance of joining a union is no easy task. While most adjuncts feel exploited, many graduate students and tenure-track faculty are so grateful to have their positions that to worry about the terms of employment seems beside the point. This is the biggest irony (some might say tragedy) of our current situation: just how bad it has become in the world of academia is what explains the rise of a movement, but just how bad it has become also explains the difficulty and fragility of the movement. Some instinctively reject any notion that they are "workers" as romanticized or self-indulgent. And the majority, trained and socialized into a particular discipline, assumes that improvement in the conditions of their own work will come only from individual scholarly and teaching achievement. These obstacles, however, are far from insurmountable. The academic employment crisis has gone on for long enough to make even the most careerist of young academics aware that larger structural forces are working against them.

That more than a few faculty are outright opposed to unionization—by themselves, adjuncts, or their graduate students—is perhaps a more pressing issue. This opposition is in part attributable to the fact that not all instructors have been directly harmed by the corporatization of higher education. The teaching loads of senior faculty at the most prestigious universities have actually declined over the past several decades, even as the workload of most teachers grew increasingly onerous. Institutions have been able to hire adjuncts or their own graduate students to teach large portions of their curricula, thereby freeing more research time for their high-profile faculty. These senior teachers thus have no direct incentive to reject the corporate refashioning of the university. Although their tenured status and generally closer relations to administrators endow them with much greater institutional power than any other category of faculty, these professors are the least likely to use it in wider interest of academics and higher education. If the academic labor movement is to secure the support of more than a small minority of them, it will have to appeal not to their self-interest but to the larger social goals of education that prompted so many to become academics in the first place. This will be a difficult case to make, as the accounts about Yale make brutally evident.

In part, this is because of the peculiar status of academic politics. Ask most people, and they will tell you that the academy is awash in politics, especially in the humanities and social sciences. Although it is not nearly as leftist as conservative critics charge, academic culture, at least at most elite universities, was perhaps more influenced by the cultural changes of the 1960s than any other major sphere of American life. Professors are more likely than most Americans to espouse liberal principles (though not necessarily about their own workplaces), use gender-neutral language, and talk about oppression.

On the surface, the left-leaning nature of academia's culture would seem to make it more amenable to organizing efforts. But it often cuts in a different direction. If anything, "radical scholarship"—the term itself is becoming an oxymoron—has replaced activism. Left-leaning academics tell themselves that they are progressives and that their work is socially important, even as they ignore problems closer to home or help to defeat efforts to solve them (as was the case at Yale). Too often, it leads academics to talk only to other academics, or worse yet, it allows people within certain disciplines (history, English, etc.) to talk only to others in their discipline (with the requisite jargon). If left-leaning academics want to push back against the corporate university—and they should—they must examine the limitations of scholarship. If for no other reason than that the architects of the new corporate university see scholarship not for its findings but for its quantifiable elements (the numbers of articles to be counted for the sake of merit pay), the so-called academic left needs to realize, once and for all, that scholarly inquiry and radical publications can never replace actual political action. This does not mean that scholarship should be thrown aside, but it needs to be seen for what it is and, more important, for what *it isn't*.

With this said, there's critical intellectual work to be done in organizing the academy. Those who wish to reverse the corporatization of higher education must articulate a clear and compelling vision of why higher education is important. It is no coincidence that the advocates of corporatization offer not only an arsenal of techniques—merit pay, a downsized permanent teaching faculty, the abolition of tenure, and so on—but a rationale for transforming the academy. The market is God, and they are going to make education kneel and pay homage to it. Universities will produce marketable research and students with skills valuable to their prospective employers. Academic organizers must offer their own countervision for the future of higher education based on education's role in a democratic society. Educators have a responsibility to concern themselves not just with private ends (doing well in the market when one exits school) but with public and civic goods as well. There is nothing terribly radical about this notion—it harks back to Thomas Jefferson's vision of higher education as the American republic was being founded. What makes this idea radical in our own day and age is the changed circumstances of higher education—the changed circumstances that this book has examined.

Such an emphasis on the purposes and importance of education will allow organizers to tap into some of the forces that have made past labor movements successful. The COCAL effort in Boston and the California Faculty Association's campaign are harbingers of future organizing efforts in their explicit engagement with the question of the purpose of education. The success of student anti-sweatshop and living-wage movements at Harvard and other universities fly in the face of claims that the current generation of college students is so obsessed with success that it is unwilling to consider and act upon pressing moral questions. At the same time, of course, academics and others appalled at what's been done to universities must understand that the fate of educators is bound up with that of all other labor. There is no reason for academics to expect to be treated with dignity and respect, and to have their right to organize honored, if all other workers are despised and oppressed.

Some might say there is a conservative tone to this book, that is, a defending of "old practices" (like full-time professors' spending time with students in classrooms) against the "new" (distance learning) or a harkening back to an era in which university teaching and research were not so enthralled to the corporate paradigm. Emphasizing the virtues of a "traditional" education as part of an organizing campaign risks pushing this tone to an uncritical acceptance of a mythic better past. It is true that the academy used to be a better place in terms of political economy and employment practices. But in other critical realms, such as racial segregation and institutional sexism, it was not. And the employment practices of a renewed academy don't have to look exactly like those before the corporate ascendancy. Union contracts and an engaged and proactive faculty, for example, may provide some of the security and freedoms that the tenure system was designed to protect.

In the end, though, perhaps conservatism, though not the sort that blindly celebrates every dimension of the past, is an appropriate tone. After all, what progress has come to mean here—the computerization of learning, the part-timing of the labor force (euphemistically referred to as the creation of "free agents"), the commodificiation of just about all realms of life—is not something we should rush to embrace. If the trends discussed here are left unchecked, universities may well be gutted of most of what makes them valuable. More and more faculty will have fewer and fewer job protections and security, and will be left with little choice but to meekly follow the commands of their supervisors. Bottom-line thinking will dominate the horizons of these bosses and of students, who will come to see their educations as just another consumer product. For-profit institutions like the University of Phoenix will thrive and perhaps become the norm. Liberal education may survive, but only as a window dressing at a few elite places encrusted with ivy, so that our rulers can have things to talk about other than the recalcitrance of their servants at their cocktail parties.

If something resembling this comes to happen, then the corporate world will have fully stolen higher education from teachers and its more noble purpose of educating citizens for the responsibility of self-government and democracy. This book has shown that all of this is happening today but that it doesn't have to be this way. Our mixed message—a warning plus a sense of hope based on the initiative of a movement starting to fight back—stands at the center of this project. What has animated this book is the idea and hope that we can steal the corporate university back for ourselves and for democracy.

Notes

Introduction

1. Daniel Pink, *Free Agent Nation: How America's New Independent Workers Are Transforming the Way We Live* (New York: Warner Books, 2001), p. 257.
2. See, for instance, the very important preface (still) to E. P. Thompson, *The Making of the English Working Class* (New York: Vintage, 1963).
3. Dorothy Sue Cobble, "Lost Ways of Unionism," in *Rekindling the Movement: Labor's Quest for Relevance in the Twenty-First Century* (Ithaca, N.Y.: Cornell University Press, 2001), p. 85.

Section One

1. Mario Savio, "An End to History," in *The New Left: A Documentary History*, ed. Massimo Teodori (New York: Bobbs-Merrill, 1969), pp. 159, 161.
2. Savio, "An End to History," p. 161.
3. Howard Brick, *Age of Contradiction: American Thought and Culture in the 1960s* (Ithaca, N.Y.: Cornell University Press, 2000), p. 24.
4. Charles Heckscher, "Living with Flexibility," in *Rekindling the Labor Movement: Labor's Quest for Relevance in the 21st Century*, ed. Lowell Turner, Harry Katz, and Richard Hurd (Ithaca, N.Y.: Cornell University Press, 2001). See Kevin Mattson's review of this collection in *Commonweal*, June 1, 2002, 22–23.
5. See Bruce Gottlieb, "Nintendo University," *New Republic*, August 30, 1999, p. 8.

Chapter 1

1. National Center for Education Statistics, Digest of Education Statistics, "Table 180. Fall enrollment and number of degree-granting institutions, by affiliation of institution: 1980 to 1998," http://nces.ed.gov/pubs2001/digest/dt180.html.
2. Richard S. Ruch, *Higher Ed, Inc.: The Rise of the For-Profit University* (Baltimore: Johns Hopkins University Press, 2001), p. 65.
3. Market forecast by Fredrick McRae and Paige Pritchard of Thomas Weisel Partners LLC in *Bright I.D.E.As (Intellectual capital, Digital information and E-learning analysis)*, 8 August 2001, http://www.tweisel.com:80/Show-

Document?DocId=17526. Michael Heise, director of Center for Education Law and Policy at Indiana University, in *Higher Ed, Inc.*, p. 65.

4. "At a Glance," University of Phoenix website, http://www.phoenix.edu/corporate/. University of Phoenix, Securities and Exchange Commission Form 10-K. 21 August 2001.

5. John Sperling quoted in "A Haven from Prejudice: With Academia Elsewhere Closed to Teaching for Profit, the Company's Boss Turned to Arizona," *Financial Times*, 21 May 1996, p. 5.

6. Peter Sperling quoted in Tim Cornwell, "Millionaire Rebel Takes Revenge on Ivy League; Tim Cornwell on the Man Whose Vision of 'McEducation' Terrifies US Academia," *Independent*, 9 November 1997, p. 15.

7. Ruch, *Higher Ed, Inc.*, p. 75.

8. Katherine Hutt Scott, "U.S. to University: Take Attendance: University of Phoenix Gets Order after Financial Aid Audit," 15 April 2000, *Chicago Sun-Times*, News, p. 25.

9. University of Phoenix, Annual Report to Security Holders, Form 10-Q or Quarterly Report, 28 November 2001.

10. Gregory Cappelli quoted in "The ABCs of Education Stocks," *BusinessWeek*, 24 September 2001, p. 128.

11. John Sperling, *Rebel with a Cause: The Entrepreneur Who Created the University of Phoenix and the For-Profit Revolution in Higher Education* (New York: John Wiley & Sons, 2000), p. 32.

12. Melanie Warner, "Aquafarms Cloning Aging Pot; Inside the Very Strange World of Billionaire John Sperling," *Fortune*, 29 April 2002, p. 98.

13. Thomas Frank, *One Market under God: Extreme Capitalism, Market Populism, and the End of Economic Democracy* (New York: Doubleday, 2000), p. 178.

14. Sperling, *Rebel with a Cause*, p. 2.

15. Sperling quoted in "A Haven from Prejudice," p. 5.

16. U.S. Department of Education, *Title IV/Pell Grant Program Year-End Report 1999–2000*, Submitted by NCS Pearson (Washington, D.C., 2001), p. 6.

17. U.S. Department of Education, Office of the Inspector General, "University of Phoenix's Management of Student Financial Assistance Programs, Final Audit Report" (Washington, D.C., 2000), pp. 4, 42.

18. Sperling, *Rebel with a Cause*, p. 183.

19. Ibid., p. 178.

20. Center for Responsive Politics, Education: Top Contributors http://www.opensecrets.org/industries/contrib.asp?Ind=W04&Cycle=2000. Education: PAC contributors to Federal Candidates, 2001–2002, http://www.opensecrets.org/pacs/industry.asp?txt=W04&cycle=2000.

21. Stephen Burd, "A Republican Aide Played a Key Role in Crafting a Bill with Bipartisan Support," *Chronicle of Higher Education*, 16 October 1998, p. A44. *Amendments to the Higher Education Act of 1965*, 105th Congress, 2nd session, H.R. 6.

22. Massachusetts Board of Higher Education, *Mindpower in Massachusetts: The Commonwealth's Natural Resource: A Report on Public Higher Education* (Boston, 1997), p. 5.

23. James F. Carlin, "Restoring Sanity to an Academic World Gone Mad," *Chronicle of Higher Education*, 9 November 1999, p. A76.

24. "University of Wisconsin System Licenses Lotus LearningSpace for Distance Learning," *M2 Presswire*, 24 September 1997.

25. Massachusetts Board of Higher Education, *Mindpower in Massachusetts*, p. 24.

26. Lee A. Daniels, "Kodak-Fuji Rivalry over Business Takes an Academic Turn," *New York Times*, 29 August 1987, Sec. 1, p. 1.

27. Elizabeth N. Smith, "Ohio State U. Academic Plan Seeks to Boost Competitiveness," *University Wire*, 5 July 2000.

28. Bill Scanlon, "Employer-Shaped Curriculum Backed, 'Cultural Change' Urged for Colleges," *Denver Rocky Mountain News*, 7 August 1999, p. 1B.

29. Scott S. Cowen quoted in Ruch, *Higher Ed, Inc.*, p. 14.

30. Linda J. Sax et al., *Findings from the 2001 Pilot Administration of Your First College Year (YFCY): National Norms* (Higher Education Research Institute at University of California at Los Angeles, 2002), p. 37.

31. Russell Jacoby, *Dogmatic Wisdom: How the Culture Wars Divert Education and Distract America* (New York: Doubleday, 1994), p. 10.

32. Sax et al., *Findings*, p. 27. Nellie Mae, Credit Card Usage Analysis, Summary Statistics, December 2000: http://www.nelliemae.com/library/cc_use.html.

33. Ruch, *Higher Ed., Inc.*, p. 80.

34. David Stamps, "The For-Profit Future of Higher Education," *Training* 35, no. 8 (August 1998): 22.

35. Ruch, *Higher Ed., Inc.*, p. 130.

36. SEC Form 10-K.

37. Lawrence Soley, "Higher Education . . . or Higher Profit: For-Profit Universities Sell Free Enterprise Education," *Institute for Public Affairs*, 20 September 1998, p. 14.

38. Ruch, *Higher Ed., Inc.*, p. 80.

39. Schools as diverse as the University of Texas (http://www.utexas.edu/law/depts/admissions/know.html), Miami University (http://www.miami.muohio.edu/president/opinion/20th_century.cfm), and Arizona State University (http://www.cob.asu.edu/exec/howard_norman_university_advantage.cfm) all distribute promotional material to this effect. *BusinessWeek* magazine helpfully offers a "B-Schools ROI Calculator" for especially market-savvy graduate students (http://bwnt.businessweek.com/roi/enter.asp).

40. Gordon C. Winston, "For-Profit Higher Education: Godzilla or Chicken Little?" *Change* 31, no. 1 (1 January 1999): 12.

41. Ibid.

42. "A Haven from Prejudice," p. 5.

43. Jeffery Selingo, "Aiming for a New Audience, U. of Phoenix Tries Again in New Jersey," *Chronicle of Higher Education*, 21 September 2001, p. 23.
44. Dawn Gilbertson, *Arizona Republic*, 14 October 1995, p. E1.
45. Stamps, "For-Profit Future," p. 22.
46. Ibid.
47. Scanlon, "Employer-Shaped Curriculum," p. 1B.
48. Soley, "Higher Education," p. 14.
49. Association of Research Libraries, "ARL Statistics, Interactive edition," http://fisher.lib.virginia.edu/arl/index.html.
50. Selingo, "Aiming for a New Audience," p. 23.
51. Jacqueline Raphel and Shelia Tobias, "Profit-making or Profiteering? Proprietaries Target Teacher Education," *Change* 29, no. 6 (21 November 1997): 44.
52. Jeffery Selingo, "For-Profit Colleges Aim to Take a Share of State Financial-Aid Funds," *Chronicle of Higher Education*, 24 September 1999, p. A41.
53. Sax et al., *Findings*, p. 5.

Chapter 2

This essay has been adapted from David Noble, *Digital Diploma Mills: The Automation of Higher Education* (New York: Monthly Review Press, 2002).

Chapter 3

1. CUPA-HR, *2000–2001 National Faculty Salary Survey* (Washington, D.C.: CUPA-HR Publications, 2001).
2. Karl E. Weick, "Educational Organizational as Loosely Coupled Systems," *Administrative Science Quarterly* 21 (1976): 1–19.
3. As quoted in A. Bartlett Giamatti, *A Free and Ordered Space: The Real World of the University* (New York: W.W. Norton, 1988), pp. 36–37.
4. R. L. Taylor, G. G. Hunnicutt, and M. J. Keefe, "Merit Pay in Academia: Historical Perspectives and Contemporary Perceptions," *Review of Public Personnel Administration* 11 (summer 1991): 51–64.
5. D. J. Campbell, K. M. Campbell, and H. Chia, "Merit Pay, Performance Appraisal, and Individual Motivation: An Analysis and Alternative," *Human Resource Management* (summer 1998): 131–146.
6. See Taylor, Hunnicutt, and Keefe, "Merit Pay in Academia."
7. Quoted in Debra Blum, "Concept of Merit Pay for Professors Spreads as Competition among Institutions Grows," *Chronicle of Higher Education* (October 18, 1989), p. A1.
8. CUPA-HR, *2000–2001 National Faculty Salary Survey.*
9. See Robert L. Heneman, *Merit Pay: Linking Pay Increases to Performance Ratings* (New York: Addison-Wesley, 1992).
10. Roger Bowen, "A College That No Longer Puts Teaching First Pays a High Price for Its Exalted Reputation," *Chronicle of Higher Education* (June 10, 1992).

11. Cordelia Ontiveros and Sam Strafaci, "Merit Compensation in Higher Education: Programs for Faculty and Staff Support," *CUPA-HR Journal* 48 (1997–98).

12. Personal communication with Kathryn Nantz, faculty member and leader at Fairfield University, February 2002.

Chapter 4

1. Piper Fogg, "Colleges Have Cut the Percentage of Full-Time Faculty Members, Study Finds," *Chronicle of Higher Education*, October 28, 2001; National Center for Education Statistics, *Digest of Educational Statistics*, 2001 (http://nces.gov).

2. Roger Kimball, "Bennington Lost," *Lingua Franca* (July/August 1994): 66–68; Paul Elie, "Et In Arcadia Bennington: A Professorial Fall from Grace," *Lingua Franca* (March/April 1993): 32–36; Denise K. Magner, "A Parlous Time for Tenure: Minnesota Professors Are Furious over Plans They Say Would Erode Job Security," *Chronicle of Higher Education*, May 17, 1996, p. A21.

3. Piper Fogg, "Colleges Have Cut the Percentage of Full-Time Faculty Members, Study Finds," *Chronicle of Higher Education*, October 28, 2001; Jill Carroll, *How to Survive as an Adjunct Lecturer* (Houston, Tex.: Adjunct Solutions, 2001), p. 7. For updated national statistics, see the National Center for Education Statistics website at http://nces.ed.gov/pubsearch/pubsinfo.asp?pubid=2002130.

4. John L. Pulley, "Brown U. T.A.'s Have Right to Form Union, NLRB Regional Director Rules," *Chronicle of Higher Education*, November 30, 2001; Fogg, "Colleges Have Cut the Percentage of Full-Time Faculty Members, Study Finds."

5. Yale University, *Report of the Ad Hoc Committee on Teaching in Yale College*, April 25, 1989, p. 4.

6. George Wilson Pierson, *A Yale Book of Numbers: Historical Statistics of the College and University, 1701–1976* (New Haven, Conn.: Yale University Press, 1983), p. 359.

7. Ibid., 362; *Report of the Ad Hoc Committee on Teaching in Yale College*, p. 6.

8. See "The Postdoc Crisis" (2002) at www.geso.org; their data are from the National Science Foundation, Division of Science Resources Studies, *Graduate Students and Postdoctorates in Science and Engineering: Fall 1999*, NSF 01-315 (Arlington, Va., 2001).

9. Joanne P. Cavanaugh, "The Postdoc's Plight," *Johns Hopkins Magazine* (February 1999), pp. 57, 59.

10. GESO, "Casual in Blue: Yale and the Academic Labor Market" (1999); Karen W. Arenson, "Staff on Tenure Track Is Teaching Less at Yale, a Study Says," *New York Times*, March 30, 1999; "UAW Analysis of Undergraduate Class Instruction in the College of Arts and Sciences for the Spring 1999 Term."

11. *Chronicle of Higher Education*, August 10, 1994, p. B1.

12. Jennifer S. Lee, "Postdoc Trail: Long and Filled with Pitfalls," *New York Times*, August 21, 2001. For a description of efforts to classify waiters, broadcast technicians, truck drivers, middle-level managers, and even farmworkers as independent contractors, see Steven Greenhouse, "Item in Tax Bill Poses Threat to Job Benefits," *New York Times*, July 20, 1997.

13. P. D. Lesko, "What Scholarly Associations Should Do to Stop the Exploitation of Adjuncts," *Chronicle of Higher Education*, December 15, 1995, p. B3; Scott Smallwood, "Jill Carroll, a Proud Part-Timer, Thinks Many Adjuncts Need a New Attitude," *Chronicle of Higher Education*, August 3, 2001; "Postdoc Crisis," p. 4.

14. Linda Ray Pratt, "Disposable Faculty: Part-time Exploitation as Management Strategy," in Cary Nelson, *Will Teach for Food: Academic Labor in Crisis* (Minneapolis: University of Minnesota Press, 1997), p. 267. Quote is from "Postdoc Crisis."

15. David Allen Harvey, "A Depressing Job Market?" *Perspectives* (January 2002): 33.

16. Carroll, *How to Survive*, p. 110.

17. Ibid., pp. 23, 27.

18. Ibid., pp. 94, 20; Courtney Leatherman, "Do Accreditors Look the Other Way When Colleges Rely on Part-Timers?" *Chronicle of Higher Education*, November 7, 1997; Cary Nelson and Stephen Watt, *Academic Keywords: A Devil's Dictionary for Higher Education* (New York: Routledge, 1999), p. 199.

19. "Debt," in Nelson and Watt, *Academic Keywords*, pp. 100–101.

20. Carroll, *How to Survive*, p. 18; Joyce Appleby, "Of Parcels and Part-Timers," *Perspectives* (October 1997): 9.

21. American Association of University Professors, *Policy Documents and Reports*, 9th Ed. (Baltimore: Johns Hopkins University Press, 2001), 73.

22. Nick Paumgarten, "Starting Over," *Lingua Franca* (September/October 1995): 46–52; on Minnesota, see Ernst Benjamin, "Some Implications of Tenure for the Profession and Society," *Perspectives* (April 1997): 16.

23. American Association of University Professors, *Policy Documents and Reports*, 73.

24. Carroll, *How to Survive*, pp. 60–61.

25. For the accounts of the conference and its conclusions, see *Academe* (January/February 1998).

26. *Report of the Ad Hoc Committee on Teaching in Yale College*, p. 6; Peter Applebome, "Down and Dirty in the Ivory Tower," *New York Times*, October 17, 1998, p. A19.

27. Lesko, "What Scholarly Associations Should Do."

28. Cited by Benjamin, "Some Implications of Tenure," p. 15.

Section Two

1. See Robin Wilson, "A Higher Bar for Earning Tenure," *Chronicle of Higher Education*, January 5, 2001, p. A1.

2. Mark Edmundson, "On the Uses of a Liberal Education: As Lite Entertainment for Bored College Students," *Harper's*, September 1997, p. 44.

Chapter 5

1. Randolph Bourne, "The Price of Radicalism," in *The Radical Will*, ed. Olaf Hansen (New York: Urizen Books, 1977), p. 299.
2. Norman Birnbaum, "Intellectuals and Unions," in *Audacious Democracy: Labor, Intellectuals, and the Social Reconstruction of America*, ed. Steven Fraser and Joshua Freeman (Boston: Houghton Mifflin, 1997), p. 242. This book is a compilation of essays that came out of Columbia's teach-in.

Chapter 7

Quotes in this essay come from materials found within the GESO Archives in New Haven, Connecticut, or interviews done by the author.

1. Unions first arrived at Yale in the 1940s with the organization of a small group of maintenance workers. Union leaders then organized Yale's entire service and maintenance staff and, in the early 1980s, its clerical and technical staff. When the TAs began to organize, they allied themselves with Locals 34 and 35 of the Hotel Employees and Restaurant Employees International Union, which represented these other campus workers. In the late 1990s, the unions also began to organize, along with Local 1199 of the Service Employees International Union, a major sector of workers at Yale–New Haven hospital. Like the TA union drive, that effort is still ongoing. Yale's leaders have bitterly fought each of these campaigns.
2. Of course, the grade strike and the university's response to it were in part responsible for these later developments. In what now appears to be a classic case of the law of unanticipated consequences, the Yale administration's effort to crush the strike focused national attention on the rise of casual academic labor and also launched a National Labor Relations Board investigation of Yale's anti-strike tactics, which subsequently led to a federal ruling that TAs at private universities are in fact employees with the right to organize. This ruling led, in turn, to the unprecedented wave of campus organizing at private universities that we are seeing today.
3. David Brion Davis, "Some Themes of Counter-Subversion: An Analysis of Anti-Masonic, Anti-Catholic, and Anti-Mormon Literature," *Mississippi Valley Historical Review* 47 (1960): 208.

Chapter 8

Acknowledgments: I am deeply grateful for the courageous and selfless support of colleagues too many to list here; I would, however, like to make special mention of Robby Cohen, Dean Hubbard, and Gordon Lafer as well as Bill Ayers,

Michael Berkowitz, Pamela Burdman, Larry Cuban, Todd Gitlin, Jeff Goodwin, Maxine Greene, Christine Harrington, Lisa Jessup, Ben Johnson, Joe Kahne, Kendall King, Rachel Kirtner, Julie Kushner, Barbara Leckie, Hank Levin, Gary Lichtenstein, Ann Lieberman, Anjana Malhotra, Kevin Mattson, Deborah Meier, Toby Miller, Nathan Newman, Nel Noddings, Carol Pittman, Maida Rosenstein, Andrew Ross, Carole Saltz, Ellen Shrecker, Diana Turk, David Tyack, Amy Stuart Wells, Ellen Willis, Sam Wineburg, Jon Zimmerman, and members of the AAUP NYU chapter, SAWSJ, Jobs With Justice, Teachers College Press, and GSOC-UAW.

1. More than 170 NYU faculty signed a petition urging the administration to remain neutral rather than engage in antiunion propagandizing (see also Hal Cohen, "Losing Their Faculties," *Village Voice*, September 12, 2001). For faculty resistance and its relationship to cultural studies, including an account of another faculty member's testimony before the labor board, see Toby Miller's (2001) "What It Is and What It Isn't: Cultural Studies Meets Graduate-Student Labor," *Yale Journal of Law and Humanities* 13, no. 1: 69–94.

2. *CALS News* (Cornell University) 4, no. 3 (November 1997).

3. *School of Education Alumni* 8, no. 6 (fall 1997).

4. Piper Fogg, "A Promising Professor Backs a T.A. Union Drive and Is Rejected for Tenure," *Chronicle of Higher Education*, August 10, 2001; Karen Arenson, "NYU Is Sued over Denial of Tenure," *New York Times*, October 3, 2001; Josh Rogers, "NYU Professor Who Backed Union Denied Tenure," *Villager*, June 21, 2001; Gordon Lafer, "Graduate Student Unions Fight the Corporate University," *Dissent Magazine*, summer 2001; "AAUP Chapter Protests Tenure Denial at NYU," *Academe*, September–October 2001; William Lucia and Lisa Fleischer, "Labor Watchdogs Criticize NYU over Tenure Case," *Washington Square News*, October 29, 2001. See www.eisnerassociates.com/Westheimer for full text of articles.

5. See Karen Arenson, "Labor Board Rules That NYU Denied Tenure to Union Backer," *New York Times*, February 28, 2002; and Piper Fogg, "NLRB Readies Complaint against New York U. for Firing Professor Who Backed Union," *Chronicle of Higher Education*, February 28, 2002.

6. A source high up in the administration of the School of Education at NYU reports that few faculty (and virtually no untenured faculty) ever fill out department chair evaluation forms for fear of the close relationship between the dean and the department chairs. Needless to say, there are no faculty evaluations of the dean or other senior administrators.

7. Roger Bowen, "The New Battle between Political and Academic Cultures," *Chronicle of Higher Education*, June 22, 2001, p. B14.

8. I do not imply here that faculty who are intellectually disengaged are the *only* faculty who may be antiunion. As Lawrence Glickman pointed out to me, lessons from the organizing drive at Yale University (see Lafer, "Graduate Student Unions Fight the Corporate University") teaches us that, sadly, some of

the most productive (and progressive) scholars may also resort to threats and retaliation against graduate students for their union activity when those activities run against individual faculty interests. Rather I argue that faculty dependent on administration for professional recognition are especially vulnerable and easily pressed into antiunion campaigns regardless of what they might think about, for example, graduate students' right to make a living wage.

9. Fogg, "NLRB Readies Complaint."

Section Three

Chapter 10

*All quotes from students in this essay come from written reports collected in the weeks following the election.

1. On these points, see Rick Fantasia, *Cultures of Solidarity: Consciousness, Action, and Contemporary American Workers* (Berkeley: University of California Press, 1988).

Chapter 13

1. Jeffrey Lustig, "Perils of the Knowledge Industry: Faculty Union Blocks Unfriendly Takeover," posted on CSU website: http://www.calfac.org.

2. Quoted in *CHE*, February 11, 2002.

3. Quoted in Jeffrey Selingo, "New Chancellor Shakes Up Cal. State with Ambitious Agenda and Blunt Style," *CHE*, June 11, 1999.

4. Jeff Schmidt, *Disciplined Minds: A Critical Look at Salaried Professionals and the Soul-Battering System That Shapes Their Lives* (Lanham, Md.: Rowman and Littlefield, 2000), pp. 208–209.

5. Robert Birnbaum, *Management Fads in Higher Education: Where They Came From, What They Do, Why They Fail* (San Francisco: Jossey-Bass, 2000), p. 225.

Conclusion

1. Mark Edmundson, "On the Uses of a Liberal Education: As Lite Entertainment for Bored College Students," *Harper's*, September 1997.

Notes on Contributors
and Editors

Michael Brown is a Ph.D. candidate in philosophy at the University of Minnesota specializing in political philosophy and ethics, and is also participating in the Program in Peace and Development Studies at the Universitat Juame I in Spain. His dissertation topic concerns the role nonviolence plays in struggles for justice within and across diverse societies. He is an active member of the Fellowship of Reconciliation, and belongs to the Industrial Workers of the World, Dept. of Public Service (Educational Workers).

Katy Gray Brown is an assistant professor in the General College of the University of Minnesota. She holds an M.A. in peace studies and a Ph.D. in philosophy, specializing in political philosophy. She is a member of the Fellowship of Reconciliation, and belongs to the Educational Workers unit of the IWW.

Ronda Copher is in the Ph.D. program in sociology at the University of Minnesota concentrating on the life course with particular attention to the intersections of work and family. Her dissertation examines the differential ways in which people construct life pathways through social institutions, the meanings derived from these constructions, and their implications for life chances in a number of realms. During the drive at Minnesota, Ronda's involvement within the union informed her ethnographic research on organizational legitimacy, and she continues to participate in grassroots efforts for social justice.

Ana Marie Cox became a journalist after unsuccessful attempts to negotiate, first, the lonely, echo-y halls of graduate school and then the shark-infested cubicles of New York book publishing. For three years, she was the editor of Suck.com, the web's longest-running daily column; she coedited, with Suck.com founder Joey Anuff, *Suck: Worst-Case Scenarios in*

Media, Culture, Advertising, and the Internet (1997). She has been an editor at the *Chronicle of Higher Education* and *Mother Jones* and has written for *Reason*, the *Columbia Journalism Review*, and the *Washington Post Book World*. She is presently the Washington columnist for *In These Times*.

Barbara Gottfried teaches women's studies at Boston University and is the cochair (with Gary Zabel) of the Boston Coalition of Contingent Academic Labor (COCAL). Under the auspices of the American Association of University Professors, she was the lead organizer for the part-time faculty union drive at Emerson College in Boston that resulted in a landslide victory in favor of unionization.

Lisa Jessup is an organizer with Local 2110, UAW, an amalgamated local union in New York City. She became involved with the union in 1993 when she took a job as an ESL teacher at a refugee resettlement agency during an organizing and first contract campaign there. She has organized and represented workers in book and newspaper publishing, not-for-profit agencies, and universities. She is currently working on campaigns for union recognition for teaching and research assistants at Columbia University and a union election for the adjunct faculty at New York University.

Benjamin Johnson is an assistant professor of history at Southern Methodist University. His articles on agrarian radicalism, environmental politics, and academic labor have appeared in *Environmental History*, *Thought and Action*, and *Social Policy*. His book *America's Unknown Rebellion: The Plan of San Diego and the Forging of Mexican American Identity* is forthcoming. He is a former organizer and director of research for Yale's graduate student union.

Patrick Kavanagh currently works for the Communications Workers of America (CWA) Local 1037 in Newark, New Jersey. Prior to joining the CWA staff, he worked with the Rutgers chapter of the American Association of University Professors (AAUP). His essays on academic labor have appeared in various publications.

Before entering academia, **Kevin Mattson** was an activist in the Washington, D.C., area. He now teaches American intellectual history at Ohio University (OU) where he's also an associate of the Contemporary History Institute. Before coming to OU, he was associate director of the Walt Whitman Center for the Culture and Politics of Democracy at Rutgers University. His writings have appeared in both scholarly and popular publications, and he has authored reports on higher education and young people's political engagement for the Carnegie Corporation of New York and the Century Foundation. He is also the author of *Intellectuals in Action: The Origins of the New Left and Radical Liberalism, 1945–1970* (2002) and coeditor of *Democracy's Moment: Reforming the American Political System for the Twenty-First Century* (2002).

Susan Meisenhelder has served as president of the California Faculty Association (CFA) since 1999. She has been involved in the faculty union movement at California State University (CSU) since her initial employment as a temporary, part-time faculty member twenty years ago. Her academic appointment is presently professor of English at CSU San Bernardino, where she teaches literature. She has published books of literary criticism on the works of William Wordsworth and Zora Neale Hurston and has held Fulbright professorships at the University of Botswana, the University of Zimbabwe, and the University of Mauritius.

Alexis Moore lives in Los Angeles, California. She is a practicing artist and has taught drawing and design at area community colleges and universities since 1984. She also writes grants and directs a nonprofit arts program for disadvantaged youth in metro Los Angeles. She has organized adjuncts to help them gain representation through collective bargaining, and helped to link them with other efforts by contingent faculty across California.

Cary Nelson is Jubilee Professor of Liberal Arts at the University of Illinois (Urbana-Champaign). He has been active in the academic labor movement for many years, taking a leading role in the Modern Language Association (MLA) and the American Association of University Professors (AAUP). In addition to his many books in cultural theory, he is coeditor of *Academic Keywords: A Devil's Dictionary for Higher Education* (1999) and *Higher Education Under Fire: Politics, Economics, and the Crisis of the Humanities* (1995). He is author of *Manifesto of a Tenured Radical* (1997) and *Revolutionary Memory: Recovering the Poetry of the American Left* (2001).

David Noble teaches in the Division of Social Sciences at York University (Canada). He has been a leading activist combating the dangers of distance learning at higher education institutions across the United States and Canada. He is also a leading historian in the history of technology. His many books include *America by Design: Science, Technology, and the Rise of Corporate Capitalism* (1977), *Forces of Production: A Social History of Industrial Automation* (1984), and *The Religion of Technology: The Divinity of Man and* *the Spirit of Invention* (1997). His selection in this anthology comes from his most recent book, *Digital Diploma Mills* (2002).

Corey Robin teaches political science at Brooklyn College, CUNY. His articles have appeared in the *New York Times Magazine*, the *Times Literary Supplement*, *Lingua Franca*, and *American Political Science Review*. His first book, *Fear: Biography of an Idea*, is forthcoming.

Denise Marie Tanguay is professor of management in the College of Business at Eastern Michigan University, where she has served as a special assistant to the provost for planning. Tanguay is a current member of the National AAUP Collective Bargaining Council's Executive Committee, a member of AAUP's Committee D on Accreditation, vice president of the EMU-AAUP local and a member of its negotiating team for the 2000–2004 contract, and a former member of the AAUP's Committee A on Academic Freedom. Tanguay's research activities include published research on merit pay in the unionized sector, a national report on the corporate hiring and use of retirees for the American Association of Retired Persons, a monograph on employee involvement programs for the U.S. Department of Labor, as well as publications in such journals as *Human Relations*, *Human Development Quarterly*, the *Gerontologist*, and the *Chronicle of Higher Education*.

Joel Westheimer is associate professor of education at the University of Ottawa. A former New York City public schools teacher and musician, he currently teaches and writes on democracy, social justice, youth activism, service learning, and community in education. He is author of *Among School Teachers: Community, Autonomy, and Ideology in Teachers' Work* (1998) and has published widely in journals and magazines such as *Phi Delta Kappan*, *Harvard Educational Review*, *Educational Administration Quarterly*, *Curriculum Inquiry*, *The School Field*, *Journal of Teacher Education*, and *Education Week*. His new book *Civic Intentions: What Schools and Colleges Must Do to Renew Democracy in America*, will be completed in fall 2003. (For up-to-date developments in his case and further documentation, see http://www.eisnerassociates.com/Westheimer.)

Gary Zabel holds a doctorate in philosophy from Boston University and teaches in the philosophy department at the University of Massachusetts Boston. He has organized grad TAs and RAs at Boston University (BU) in the late '70s and helped lead a faculty-clerical-librarian's strike at BU in 1979. He founded the Boston chapter of the Coalition of Contingent Academic Labor and is presently a member of the Board of Directors of Campaign on Contingent Work. His articles have appeared in *New Labor Forum*, *Dollars and Sense,* and *Labor Notes.* He has also been interviewed by newspapers, magazines, and TV on contingent faculty organizing throughout the United States, and in Canada, France, and Italy. During the last year, Zabel has participated in a leadership role in three successful unionization drives, two at University of Massachusetts Boston and one at Emerson College.

Index